Economy and Society

Professor Sidney Pollard

ECONOMY AND SOCIETY:
EUROPEAN INDUSTRIALISATION AND ITS SOCIAL CONSEQUENCES

ESSAYS PRESENTED TO SIDNEY POLLARD

Edited by Colin Holmes and Alan Booth

Leicester University Press
Leicester, London & New York

© Editor and contributors 1991
First published in Great Britain in 1991 by Leicester University Press
(a division of Pinter Publishers)

For enquiries in North America please contact PO Box 197, Irvington, NY 10533.

Editorial offices
Fielding Johnson Building, University of Leicester, University Road,
Leicester, LE1 7RH, England

Trade and other enquiries
25 Floral Street, London, WC2E 9DS, England

British Library cataloguing in publication data

A CIP catalogue record for this book is available from the British Library.

ISBN 0-7185-1337-1

Library of Congress Cataloguing in Publication Data
Economy and society: European industrialisation and its social
  consequences : essays presented to Sidney Pollard / edited by Colin
  Holmes and Alan Booth.
    p.   cm.
    Includes bibliographical references and index.
    ISBN 0-7185-1337-1
    1. Industry–Social aspects–Europe–History. 2. Europe-
-Industries–History.   I. Pollard, Sidney.   II. Holmes, Colin, 1938–
III. Booth, Alan, Ph. D.
    HD60.5.E85E26   1991   91-15971
    306.3–dc20   CIP

Typeset by Witwell Ltd, Southport
Printed and bound by Biddles Ltd, Guildford and Kings Lynn

Contents

Preface

The essays collected in this volume have been contributed by Sidney Pollard's former students, colleagues and past and current collaborators to mark his retirement after a celebrated career as teacher and researcher at the Universities of Sheffield and Bielefeld. This volume is dedicated to him for the help, encouragement and inspiration which he has provided for all students of European economic and social history over the past forty years.

Sidney Pollard: His life and work

Colin Holmes and Alan Booth
University of Sheffield and University of Exeter

The starting point is not in Sheffield where Sidney Pollard spent thirty years at the University, nor is it in Bielefeld where he taught from 1980. The beginnings lie in the *shtetlach* of Galicia, an area which has been described as a bastion of Orthodox Judaism. Pollard's father was born there at Stryj, a town near Lwow. His mother came from Radautz and then moved to Stryj.

Before the Great War, Moses Pollak, like many other Galician Jews, moved from the countryside to seek his fortune in Vienna, the capital of the Austro-Hungarian Empire, where he found work as a commercial traveller. The First World War brought more Galician Jews into the capital. As the Russians pushed into Austria's eastern provinces they unleashed a wave of anti-semitic pogroms and, in these circumstances, the Hapsburg Government helped to evacuate the local Jewish population. These developments provided the force behind the arrival in the capital of Pollard's mother, Leontine Katz. The early lives of Moses Pollak and Leontine Katz bear personal testimony to the importance of migration in Jewish history. They met and married in Vienna and Siegfried Pollak (later Sidney Pollard) was born in the Austrian capital on 21 April 1925, the second of two sons.

The presence of Jews in Vienna in the early twentieth century is one of the city's distinguishing social features. Indeed, by 1900 'the liberal bourgeois educated classes in Vienna were predominantly Jewish'.[1] However, it should not be assumed that this development occurred in the absence of tension. On the contrary, the significant social role assumed by Jews, particularly in the capital's cultural life, generated considerable anti-Semitism. In making this emphasis it needs to be recalled that the Jewish community in Vienna did not possess a monolithic social structure. The *Ostjuden*, the Eastern Jews, including those who came from Galicia, tended to reject the integrationist outlook of the longer-established Jews. This inter-group conflict had its parallel in other countries where Jewish migration and immigration occurred. But all sections of the Jewish community in Vienna had to contend with external hostility and the *Ostjuden*, whose religious Orthodoxy made them especially visible, encountered particular problems. The *Ostjuden* presence in Vienna terrified the young Hitler: a reader of *Mein Kampf* soon discovers evidence of his fear and loathing of this minority.

Pollard attended the Chajes Gymnasium in Vienna, a Jewish private school, named after Rabbi Chajes, a prominent Zionist who died suddenly in 1927. Jewish Social Democrats opposed the school for its fostering of Jewish consciousness. At the same time, a school which drew most of its students from the *Ostjuden*, attracted the attention of anti-Semites. Consequently the pupils were subject to frequent harassment. However, the school continued to function and an extant report reveals that Pollard excelled in virtually every subject except physical education. Apart from his competence in the core curriculum he developed a high reputation as a violinist. At this time his academic interests centred around science. Mathematics, in particular, exercised a strong appeal and some years later, in exile in Britain, he would have preferred to pursue these scientific interests had circumstances allowed. But this is to anticipate.

Political developments over which the Jews in Vienna could exert no control, acted as the first brake on Pollard's early expectations. After 1933, following the rise to power of the National Socialists, the Jewish community in Germany found itself facing increased persecution. Within the space of a few years, the Jews in Austria also witnessed a sudden and marked deterioration in their lives. The union of Germany and Austria in March 1938, the so-called *Anschluss*, marked the onset of this catastrophe. Indeed, 1938 is a decisive year in the history of Jews in Central Europe. In Germany the *Kristallnacht* pogrom of 9–10 November 1938 served notice to the Jewish community there that it faced a more savage hostility than many had previously recognised. In the shadow of such developments many Central European Jews, who had previously thought that anti-Semitism would be contained or blow itself out, began to make preparations to leave.

However, difficulties stood in the way of emigration. For their part, the National Socialists did not automatically block the process of departure. To their way of thinking, the emigration of Jews involved the export of a hated minority. Emigration, in the National Socialists' terms, would help to make Central Europe a 'Jew-free' area. As such, it remained one feature of Nazi policy down to 1941. But where could intending refugees find an exiled home? None of the possible receiving countries showed any great enthusiasm for admitting them. In the case of Britain, the 1919 Aliens Act placed strict controls over the entry, movement and deportation of aliens. Furthermore, in its wish to placate Arab sentiment in the Middle East, the British Government severely regulated entry into the mandated territory in Palestine. Some relaxation in official policy did occur as the pressure to leave Central Europe increased during the course of 1938. However, between 1933 and 1939 no more than 56,000 refugees were admitted to Britain, an estimated 50,000 of whom were Jewish. Anglo-Jewry's guarantee that these Jews would not become a charge on the public purse and that re-emigration would be encouraged helped to facilitate the arrival of such refugees, in generally unfavourable circumstances.

Against this background a number of child refugees landed in Britain. A relatively smooth arrangement developed between the Jewish community in Britain and Jewish officials in Berlin, but departures proved more erratic from

Vienna where, after the *Anschluss*, the capricious influence of the SS in the person of Adolf Eichmann complicated matters. In 1938, however, Pollard managed to leave Vienna in the company of 180 other children.

These child refugees could be brought to Britain as soon as sufficient money had been collected to keep each child for two years. The sum needed for this period was fixed at £100. In Pollard's case, a Jewish committee in Edinburgh raised the required amount of money. Pollard had a clutch of distant relatives living in Britain but it took some time to establish contact since the only relative whose name he knew kept his existence a secret, from her own children and others, because she feared that the young refugee would request financial support. To all intents and purposes, therefore, he stood alone in his exile.

After reception camps in East Anglia, Pollard moved in the spring of 1939 to Whittinghame Farm School, housed in A.J. Balfour's ancient family home in East Lothian. Along with the other children who came out with him, he worked on the estate farms of Lord Traprain, heir to the Balfours. The children were being prepared in this way for emigration to a Kibbutz as soon as they reached the age of seventeen. Although they were of school age, the child refugees did not receive any formal education. In Pollard's words 'We didn't learn anything except to speak English with a Scottish accent and Hebrew'. This negative impression runs counter to that of Norman Bentwich who described Whittinghame as 'the most romantic of the agricultural centres'.[2] However, this positive assessment is not supported by a recent study which, with due understatement, described Whittinghame as 'hardly a success story'.[3]

In 1941 the money for Whittinghame ran out and the school closed in 1942. Before the closure occurred, Pollard transferred in 1941 to another *aliyah* scheme at Bredon's Norton in Worcestershire. He stayed there for a brief period only and he was, in any case, losing the Zionism which had been part of the cultural baggage brought with him from Vienna. From Worcester he migrated to Cambridge, where he secured a place in a hostel through the efforts of Greta Burkill, a guardian angel to many refugees. Some time later he found lodgings and started work for Ridgeon's, a local firm of market gardeners. There he stayed until in 1943, at the age of eighteen, he volunteered for the British Army. This enlistment transformed Siegfried Pollak into Sidney Pollard.

Pollard's enlistment into the Reconnaissance Corps interrupted the studies he had pursued by correspondence course after his arrival in Britain. In Cambridge he had been successful in the London matriculation examinations. Then in 1943, through continued correspondence course, he had passed the Intermediate B.Sc. (Econ.). On the strength of this performance he was interviewed by an LSE Board and promised a place to continue his studies at the end of the war. The resumption of Pollard's academic career had to await his Army discharge and his release did not come in 1945. After the end of hostilities the Army employed him in Germany at regimental level as an interpreter in the British military zone of Germany. His discharge from these military duties, with the rank of corporal, came in 1947.

He went straightaway to resume his studies at the LSE, even though he had missed part of the 1946–47 academic session. His contemporaries in Houghton Street at that time included Donald Coleman, Eddy Cooney, Ralph Davis,

David Eversley, Walter Minchinton, Harold Pollins, Leslie Pressnell and Walter Stern. Pollard took his finals in 1948 and graduated with first class honours. However, his name does not appear on the School's list of 1948 graduates because, since he had not fulfilled the minimum prescribed period of study, his formal graduation occurred in 1949. By that time he had begun research as Leverhulme Scholar at the School. F.J. Fisher, then a Reader in Economic History, suggested an industrial history theme and Pollard chose to work on shipbuilding. His Ph.D. thesis on 'The Economic History of British Shipbuilding, 1870–1914', supervised by T.S. Ashton and H.L. Beales, was examined in 1950 by Beales with Edward Allen of Newcastle as the external. The formal award of the doctorate came in 1951.

Pollard's progression from postgraduate student to University lecturer did not come about easily. During his period at the LSE, Pollard had become – for six months – a student member of the Communist Party of Great Britain. This youthful political stance can hardly be regarded as exceptional. In the hopeful post-war years a number of students nailed their colours to the Communist mast, just as many young people of an earlier generation had in the 1930s. However, T.S. Ashton, who held the Chair of Economic History at the LSE, occupied a different end of the ideological spectrum. It was Ashton who claimed that, in his book *An Economic History of England: The 18th Century*, a reader would be unable to find the word capitalism.[4] An additional clear indication of Ashton's ideological position can be found in his contribution to F.A. von Hayek's collection of essays on *Capitalism and the Historians*.[5] In other words, the ideological tensions of the Cold War vibrated into the writing of economic and social history in Britain in the early post-war years. In these circumstances there is a view that Ashton, many of whose students secured posts in University departments and subsequently occupied chairs in Economic History, did not put his full and considerable weight behind Pollard's academic aspirations. On 28 June 1950, however, Sheffield University appointed Pollard as the first Douglas Knoop Research Fellow in Economic History. The University records make it clear that in these circumstances Pollard came to Sheffield 'highly recommended' by Ashton and that the University also received a strong reference from H.L. Beales. Even so, a distance persisted between Pollard and Ashton. The obituary notice of Ashton in the *Proceedings of the British Academy* which has Pollard beating a path, along with other young scholars, to Ashton in his retirement at Blockley smacks of wishful thinking.[6]

The University at Sheffield, to which Pollard came, had a long tradition of teaching and research in economic history. In 1910 Douglas Knoop, a Manchester graduate, applied for and was appointed to a Lectureship in charge of Economics at the University. Ten years later Sheffield made him Professor of Economics and Knoop stayed until his retirement in 1948. His interests lay in Economic History as well as Economics, a combination which is clearly reflected in a number of later appointments. It is one of the ironies of history that Pollard's referees for the Knoop Fellowship had both taught in Sheffield. Ashton served between 1912 and 1919 before moving on to Birmingham, and H.L. Beales worked in the University between 1919 and 1926 before transferring to the London School of Economics. The tradition of economic history at Sheffield continued with the arrival in 1926 of G.P. Jones, as Beales's replacement. This appointment marked the beginning of a fruitful collaborative venture between Knoop and Jones, an association which also reflected Knoop's growing, indeed obsessive, interest in Freemasonry. The vitality of economic history at Sheffield also benefited from the presence in the Department of Economics between 1938 and 1948 of A.G. Pool who, along with G.P. Jones, wrote *A Hundred Years of Economic Development* in 1940.[7]

On his death, shortly after his retirement in 1948, Knoop bequeathed to the University the sum of £39,343 and the Douglas Knoop Fellowship in Economic History, as well as its equivalent in Economics, relied on this legacy. With his acceptance of the Knoop Fellowship, Pollard began work on a study of labour in Sheffield. A number of influences dictated the choice of topic. Pollard did not trust the University Library to have sufficient holdings to allow him to pursue a national theme. In addition, labour conditions had already begun to interest him. Finally, he had formed the view that real labour history, what is nowadays sometimes called 'history from below', had not been tackled by historians. Out of this context came the well-known work on labour in Sheffield between 1850 and 1939.

The Knoop Fellowship provided an academic base, but only for a maximum of three years and Pollard had to reflect on his next step. His marriage in 1949 to Eileen Andrews and the birth of their first child in 1951 laid additional pressures on him. Once again his path was strewn initially with disappointment and contemporaries can still recall his developing anxiety about his future prospects. However, G.P. Jones, who had succeeded Knoop as Professor of Economics, became Dean of the Faculty of Arts in 1952 and the University created an assistant lectureship in Economic History in order to assist the Department of Economics with its teaching. Pollard found himself appointed to this post. This appointment did not carry with it a guarantee of permanence. However, in 1955 Pollard was put up to lecturer, and in 1960 he became senior lecturer in Economic History.

Before his appointment at Sheffield Pollard had engaged in some teaching for the London Services committee and also at Westminster College. Once in Sheffield his limited teaching role as Knoop Fellow and, more particularly, his period as lecturer, extended his experience considerably. In the course of these years he taught British Economic History and also offered a course on European and American economic history. He contributed also to the Business Studies programme organised by D.C. Hague, who then held the Newton Chambers Chair in Applied Economics. In addition, he conducted numerous courses for the Extramural Department and addressed audiences across the country on the history and economics of the Co-operative Movement, in which he had already developed a keen interest.

His flow of research in the 1950s and early 1960s reflected these various interests. Pollard's first monograph, now often overlooked, came in 1954 with the appearance of *Three Centuries of Sheffield Steel*,[8] a study of Marsh Brothers, a Sheffield steel firm. *A History of Labour in Sheffield 1850–1939*,[9] researched during his tenure of the Knoop Fellowship, appeared in 1959 and his interest in the labour movement led in 1960 to his being one of the founder members of the Society for the Study of Labour History. His personal commitment to the Co-operative Movement and his related interest in retailing issues resulted in a flow of articles on which he worked with J.D. Hughes, then in Sheffield's Extramural Department and later Principal of Ruskin College, Oxford. Finally, his interest in the historical development of the British economy led to the publication in 1962 of *The Development of the British Economy*.[10]

Against this background, Pollard's career moved into its next phase. The social science subjects at Sheffield came out of the Arts Faculty in 1959, when the University established a Faculty of Social Sciences. J.C. Gilbert, who had succeeded G.P. Jones in 1957 as Professor of Economics, became the first Dean of the new Faculty and exercised a scrupulous stewardship over its affairs. Following the creation of this new administrative structure, and as access to higher education expanded in the course of the 1960s, the University decided to build up the disciplines of Economic History and Politics which had functioned hitherto as satellites within the Department of Economics. In this expansionary climate, stimulated by the Robbins Report, the University created a Chair of Economic History.

Other Universities followed a similar pattern of development. As a result, Economic History enjoyed a boom period of rapid growth across the country. Pollard had expressed his interest in chairs in other institutions but nothing had materialised. However, on 10 July 1963 the appointing Committee at Sheffield unanimously recommended Pollard for the newly-created professorship. His application received support from J.D. Chambers of Nottingham, F.E. Hyde of Liverpool, H.J. Habakkuk of Oxford, and the redoubtable M.M. Postan of Cambridge, himself an earlier *émigré* from Russia. Two years later Sheffield appointed Bernard Crick to the newly-established Chair of Politics. The Faculty of Social Sciences seemed set fair, at an early stage, for a bright future.

Pollard delivered his inaugural lecture to the University in the Arts Tower, an architectural symbol of the 1960s, on 28 October 1964. He took as his theme, 'Economic History: A Science of Society?' In it he presented a powerful case for historical materialism as a method of analysis capable of understanding the complex inter-connectedness of society and of solving the riddle of the past. The lecture also laid great emphasis on the value of a study of the past as a means of achieving mastery over the present. Considered in the context of Sheffield and the early 1960s, the lecture amounted to a bold stroke and revealed that some youthful ideological influences remained with him:

> All of us owe an incalculable debt to the genius of Marx, and it has been a tragic loss for the study of history that his teaching has been so often banished or traduced because his latter-day followers have become closely associated, not merely with one political movement, but with a particular region of the globe . . .[11]

At this time the Department of Economic History counted as a small unit. Apart from Pollard, it consisted of one Knoop Fellow and two assistant lecturers. As such it had to rely on the University's Department of History making some papers available for those students who chose to study for the newly-established degree in Economic History. However, during the course of the 1960s and early 1970s the number of teachers increased. The result was that in 1980, when Pollard left Sheffield for Bielefeld, the Department, known since 1975–76 as the Department of Economic and Social History, contained ten members of staff. It had developed a successful undergraduate school based in the Faculty of Social Sciences. But Pollard's firm, indeed puritanical, commitment to the rigours of academic enquiry guaranteed a greater emphasis on staff research and postgraduate activity. One incontestable piece of evidence revealing the vitality and vigour of these years can be found in the large number of young researchers, supervised not only by Pollard but also by his colleagues, who took higher degrees in the Department and then proceeded to fill posts in higher education both in Britain and abroad. Pollard often 'fed' his research students with their initial topic and the questions they needed to ask of their material. However, they were encouraged to become independent researchers as soon as possible. Here we can detect the influence of Pollard's own experiences as a research student at the LSE and the hovering observation of T.S. Ashton, 'All historical study that is worthwhile must be individual'.[12]

In the midst of this research activity Pollard followed a consistent teaching schedule. He lectured to first year students on British economic history, concentrating on the period from the Industrial Revolution to the twentieth century. His examination papers on this course reflected his current research interests, and students often found his questions searching and difficult. In addition, he taught a third year special subject on the Industrial Revolution. In other words, part of the heavy teaching burden he had carried in the 1950s became transferred to his younger colleagues.

Some of those lecturers found him remote and he was conscious, at least initially, of the age gap which prevailed in the new Department. However, the departmental ritual of coffee at 11.00 and tea at 4.00, below the stairs in Sherwood Mount, and in the tearoom or secretary's office at later times, provided an opportunity for informal contact and offered a forum in which to exchange academic ideas and opinions. Furthermore, in spite of his busy schedule – everyone at Sheffield recalls his diligence – Pollard never gave the impression to those members of the Department who called in to discuss academic problems and issues that they were taking his time. On the contrary, he seemed to welcome being sought out in this way. Personal matters, however, were seldom raised and, for his part, Pollard revealed little. His work for the Holiday Fellowship during his period at the LSE, his involvement in rambling and walking which older colleagues at Sheffield recall from the 1950s, his interest in the cinema, as well as his proficiency with the violin and his knowledge of music, remained virtually off the agenda. In other words, he exercised his prerogative to remain a private person.

If for Pollard the great passion resided in research and the feeding of research into teaching, and hence his view that University teachers who did not travel along this route were selling their students short, how did he respond to the demands of administration, the third leg to University work? He tackled departmental business briskly and efficiently. In the morning, the crossword in *The Times* came first. Once the mail arrived, he dealt with it straightaway, usually dictating to the secretarial staff, who served him well over the years, rather than writing out draft replies in long hand. Faculty and University business, however, Pollard kept at arm's length. Nevertheless, he did serve as

Deputy Dean of the Faculty of Social Sciences between 1967 and 1969, but generally he revealed no taste or inclination for academic politics. His contribution to University life came in a different form.

Following his appointment in 1950, Pollard laboured in Sheffield for many years without venturing elsewhere on exchange visits or spending leaves of absence in other institutions. However, in the course of the 1960s and 1970s his growing academic reputation, assisted particularly by the appearance in 1965 of *The Genesis of Modern Management*,[13] which the American Newcomen Society voted as the best book on Business History for the years between 1964 and 1966, resulted in offers to visit and teach in other institutions. In 1969–70 he accepted a post as Visiting Professor in the Department of History at Berkeley; in 1973 he spent the Spring Term at Bar-Ilan in Israel; the following summer saw him in Bielefeld; in 1975 he passed the spring semester at Swarthmore; between August and September of 1977 he visited institutions in Australia; and in 1978–79 he returned to Bielefeld as Visiting Professor in the Centre for Interdisciplinary Research. In addition, in the 1960s he made two visits to the German Democratic Republic.

The period spent at Berkeley is especially significant. Pollard relished the academic atmosphere in California, and Berkeley's keenness to recruit scholars of international standing led to his receiving an offer in 1971 to take up a Chair. Notwithstanding understandable fears regarding his children's future – a temporary visit brought home the pervasiveness of the drug culture in California – Berkeley's interest provided a wonderful opportunity. But the past intruded to dash Pollard's hopes. His student membership of the CPGB told against him as, possibly, did his visits to the GDR where he developed an academic association with Jürgen Kuczynski, Professor of Economic History at the Academy of Sciences in Berlin (East) and a key figure in the establishment of the German Democratic Republic. The American authorities granted a temporary work permit but Pollard had no guarantee that he would secure a permanent visa when the time came for its renewal. Berkeley believed such fears were groundless. In the event, even though he had resigned from Sheffield on 14 May 1971 in the expectation of going to the United States, Pollard decided against taking the risk. The University of Sheffield, on the advice of senior academic staff, agreed eventually on 9 July 1971 to Pollard's reinstatement. 'Schwer und bitter is dos leben' runs the Yiddish lament.

Following this upset Pollard picked up the strands of his career in Sheffield but those close to him at the time, and colleagues who interceded on his behalf with the University authorities, can testify to his intense disappointment. One senses that the earth had shifted for him and his later years in Sheffield, punctured by the periods spent in other institutions, were characterised by an increasing degree of restlessness. Even so, when the time came, his departure to Bielefeld for a variety of complex academic and personal reasons, came as a shock to many of his colleagues.

The last years of Pollard's academic career have been spent in the Federal Republic. Bielefeld gained from his presence there alongside Jürgen Kocka and Hans-Ulrich Wehler. However, Pollard did not fasten himself to his new base. In 1983–84 he spent the winter semester at the Erasmus University in Rotterdam; in 1985 he visited the Rockefeller Study Center at Bellagio; and between 1985 and 1986 he held the post of Visiting Professor at the European University Institute in Florence. From his various bases in Europe, Pollard produced work on the wasting of the British economy,[14] his long-awaited work on capital formation,[15] and various pieces on European industrialisation.[16]

None of this activity meant a complete break with Britain. Whenever possible, vacations saw him in Sheffield. He did resign from his post as President of the Society for the Labour History Society but remained closely involved in the Society for Co-operative Studies and the Economic History Society. Pollard could also be regularly spotted at conferences. With his retirement from Bielefeld in 1990 he will return permanently to Britain, to Sheffield. Indeed, together with his second wife, the former Helen Trippett, whom he married in 1982, he has already bought a house in the steel city with which he is particularly associated.

One of the most distinctive features of social life in Britain has been the commercial, industrial and cultural influence exercised by immigrants and refugees. The contribution of Germans to the development of merchant banking and City affairs generally is well-known. The important role played by the Irish in the development of the Roman Catholic Church in England and Wales since the mid-nineteenth century, is also recognised. But in considering this theme of immigration and social development, an important role must be allotted to those refugees who arrived from the greater Germany in the 1930s. This impact is particularly noticeable in the academic world. Names such as Carsten, Gombrich, Peierls, Perutz and Pevsner feature among many more who have made their life's contribution in exile.[17] Sheffield benefited in a number of ways from this forced intellectual emigration. The work of Hans Krebs in the Department of Biochemistry led to the joint-award of the Nobel Prize for Medicine in 1953.[18] Erwin Stengel, an *émigré* from Vienna, came at a later date to the Chair of Psychiatry. But in Britain generally, and Sheffield specifically, we need also to recover the contributions of those who came to Britain as child refugees. Their attempts at adjustment often proved difficult; in general, they found it harder to carve out a new satisfying life in exile. The past intruded to wreck some lives and to diminish many others. Moreover, the experiences of exile often created new difficulties. However, some of these young people survived to succeed. Hans Eysenck is one: Sidney Pollard is another.[19]

In Pollard's case a full recognition of his contribution to the study of economic history has been long delayed. In the reference he wrote in 1963 in support of Pollard's Chair application at Sheffield, J.D. Chambers observed: 'He is, I should imagine, one of the best equipped economic historians writing at the present time, and when he has acquired greater confidence and willingness to put himself forward in public discussions, he will receive the general recognition which his published work so enormously merits'. In the event, other scholars with less talent and substantially fewer significant publications have followed an easier path towards academic recognition. However, some compensation came in 1988 when the British Academy elected him to a Corresponding Fellowship.

If we look more deeply at Sidney Pollard's academic development, it is essential to begin with the foundations which were laid at the LSE. As we have seen, his undergraduate career was brief, but its influence has been lasting. Pollard absorbed two approaches to the study of economic history. On the one hand, there was the Manchester tradition (the work of George Unwin, T.S. Ashton, G.W. Daniels and Arthur Redford) with its interest in the decay of proto-industrialisation; the emergence of the industrial revolution; the examination of businessmen in particular industries; the evolution of money and financial markets; and, through Unwin, in the work of the German historical school and the *methodenstreit* in economics at the end of the nineteenth century.[20] On the other, there was Cambridge economic history as exemplified in the work of Clapham, with its focus on British economic development in the post-railway age, on the broader questions of European economic growth and, above all, on quantities[21]. The Manchester tradition was absorbed at first hand from Ashton, but Clapham had to be studied from set texts.

The LSE degree also had a strong basis in economics but economic theory, especially as defined by Lionel Robbins, sat uneasily with Manchester empiricism and Clapham's scepticism about empty economic boxes. What Pollard built from these influences was a conviction that economic theory, by itself, could not supply the analytical basis with which to explain the processes of change in the economy.[22] Some of the economist's tools were indispensable for the economic historian, notably the perspectives offered by industrial economics as it was conceived in the late 1940s and Keynesian macro-analysis. As we have seen, Pollard has always drawn inspiration from radical as well as orthodox traditions, and his view of economic development has been profoundly influenced by the Marxist position that the accumulation of fixed capital is the driving force of market economies. But above all, there was a strong belief that to understand the processes of change the economic historian had to apply perspectives from the other social sciences.[23] Not only was the economic historian uniquely placed to deploy this multi-disciplinary analytical structure, Pollard believed that the economic historian should try to illuminate contemporary problems. As he gained his academic self-confidence, Pollard's major research projects were undertaken in the very strong conviction that the problems of the present could be clarified by historical analogy.

We have seen that there were a number of intellectual and logistical reasons for Pollard to begin work on the local labour movement on his arrival in Sheffield. But Sheffield's local economy had attractions to one trained in the Manchester tradition. From the 1870s Sheffield had had a dual-sector economy which combined proto-industrialisation (cutlery) and a much more modern sector (iron and steel). The difficult choices concerned the terminal dates of his study. His decision to bring the story up to date reflected a consistent preference for writing for a non-specialist, as well as an academic, audience. The richness of the source material and the attractiveness of the two-sector economy dictated that he could go no further back than 1850. The results can be seen in his *History of Labour in Sheffield*, where the wealth of example and detail is impeccably organised and ordered.[24] We know more about the Sheffield labour movement than that of any other major industrial centre, and the material is easily accessible and comprehensible to the lay reader. There was, however, a drawback to concentrating on the period since 1850; it threatened to divorce Pollard's work from the most controversial academic debate in British economic history – the arguments over the course of living standards from 1780 to 1850.

Ashton had lit a slow fuse under British economic history in 1949 by arguing that, though evidence was far from reliable, real incomes probably rose over the period of the industrial revolution largely as a result of the higher productivity levels of the factory system.[25] Gradually an alternative, radical picture began to be assembled.[26] Pollard's interest in labour conditions in Sheffield after 1850 cut him off from an empirically-based contribution, but he pointed out that the industrial revolution necessitated a massive investment programme, improvement in manufacturing methods implying development of transport and social capital, so that consumption would have to be constrained at a time of rising population growth.[27] But the further his research on the Sheffield labour movement progressed, the more heated the debate on living standards was becoming.[28] Pollard entered the lists with the argument that it was labour organisation, rather than rising marginal productivity, which induced capitalists to pay higher wages. This argument was firmly established in *A History of Labour*, in a number of articles, and in his most sustained contribution to the debate, *The Wealth of Britain*.[29]

A History of Labour in Sheffield was also the foundation of Pollard's contribution to social history. Whereas his economic history interests have been displayed over an ever-broadening canvas, the focus of his social and labour history has remained almost parochial, – Sheffield. However, his work on social history has been innovatory, despite the rather conventional 'econ-omist's social history' of his *History of Labour*. His work on the ethics of the 'Sheffield outrages' half justified the moral economy of the cutlers in a way which was extremely radical for its time, almost ten years before the publication of E.P. Thompson's *Making of the English Working Class*.[30] These themes have since been channelled into the work of research students, as can be seen from *Essays in the Economic and Social History of South Yorkshire*, to which a number of postgraduates made substantial contributions on local class formation.[31]

His concern for the development of social history is evident also in his organisational work. We have noted his early involvement in the Society for the Study of Labour History and his work for the co-operative movement, a body which provided self-help for ordinary people without help from the more powerful and which has sought to help all consumers. He has performed leading roles in both organisations. For the Labour History Society, he has served as joint-editor of the *Bulletin* and subsequently as chairman and president. He is also currently Vice-President of the Society for Co-operative Studies and has written extensively on Owenism and the philosophy of co-operation.

However, this is to jump over the most interesting and prolific stage in Sidney Pollard's career. He finished the *History of Labour in Sheffield* and its companion works in business and labour history[32] at a time when it was becoming clear that the British economy was growing comparatively slowly. The poor quality of British management was thought to be a major cause of economic failure. The Franks inquiry into business education was in progress. As we have seen, Pollard had been involved in courses run by Sheffield

University to broaden the education of managers. From this background, he saw an historical context for a contemporary question: of what did managerial expertise consist and how important was it in economic development? The obvious historical context was the British industrial revolution. Once again, it involved the shift from proto-industry to a modern sector. This was the period on which his supervisors had made their contributions and was also the ground upon which the standard of living battles had been fought. There was also immense historical interest in this period as a result of W.W. Rostow's speculations on the character of the 'take off into self-sustained growth' published in the early 1960s.[33] No-one had attempted a systematic survey of the contribution of managers to early industrialisation, probably because the primary sources were patchy, geographically dispersed and unreliable while the secondary literature on the firms during the period was voluminous and of varying quality. His conclusion, published in a number of articles and the full-length study, *The Genesis of Modern Management*,[34] was that managerial expertise had neither hindered nor accelerated the process of industrialisation, but that the stock of managerial personnel grew and gained in status. He did not, therefore, see managers as the driving force behind business dynamism, as did A.D. Chandler of a later stage of corporate capitalism.[35] As we have seen, there were excellent reasons for concentrating on management in the pre-railway era. He produced a classic study which remains, after a quarter of a century, the standard book on the topic.

The work on management revealed the rudimentary accounting principles adopted by early industrial enterprise and made it clear that fixed investment was much less important in the industrial take-off than circulating or working capital. These points were subsequently developed in various articles[36] and led to a major research project to produce reliable figures for capital formation in the period of the industrial revolution. The gestation period has been lengthy, almost twenty years, but the final volume, *Studies in Capital Formation in the United Kingdom, 1750–1920*,[37] will remain the standard work for a very long time. It combines estimates of capital formation in key sectors of the industrialising economy in the late eighteenth and early nineteenth centuries with Charles Feinstein's updated estimates of gross and net fixed capital formation in the period 1760–1920. This is a work of outstanding scholarship. Sidney Pollard's estimates of capital formation in coal mining, for example, involved the use of 622 colliery accounts to disentangle capital expenditure, a concept which contemporaries did not recognise – and certainly did not record separately.[38]

This corpus of work on the British industrial revolution appeared to suggest that the roots of the post–1945 economic *malaise*, a problem which was coming to weigh very heavily upon British social scientists as they strove to explain Britain's comparatively poor economic performance, could not be found before 1850. Pollard has come increasingly to the conclusion that systemic problems were not evident before 1914 either. His doctoral thesis had argued that British shipbuilders had been able to compete because they had a very flexible productive system, based on highly skilled labour which could produce ships of different types in a single yard.[39] Competitor nations, with more modern machinery and layout, ould not secure sufficient orders to cover their overhead costs. The *History of Labour* had also pointed to the vigour of the steel producers before 1914. Thus, his recent return to the performance of the British economy between 1870 and 1914, *Britain's Prime and Britain's Decline*,[40] reviews an enormous and highly controversial literature in terms which are far from pessimistic. His balance and scholarship are again of the highest possible order. Although he leans towards the hypothesis of continuing stable growth rather than economic failure, he identifies the emergence of 'short-termism', a 'wealth now rather than strength later' attitude, in investment behaviour. In some sectors, Britain was slow to innovate in those production methods which had become technologically sophisticated, but in others British producers retained their world leadership. Thus, there were competitive strengths and failures scattered patchily over both 'new' and 'staple' sectors of the economy. He found little real evidence of the currently fashionable *malaise* of 'institutional rigidity'. Indeed, the chapter dealing with the flexibility and vitality of the largely decentralised, market-oriented 'system' of scientific and technical education in Britain and its favourable comparison with the centralised, formal provision in Germany, is an object lesson in historical method and balanced judgement. It helps him to argue that British entrepreneurs, managers and industrial workers were responding successfully to the economic challenges of the early twentieth century. The book is a *tour de force*, the most persuasively argued and supported study of the British economy in the period 1870–1914 that is available.[41]

This corpus of work located the roots of the British disease neither in the period before 1914 nor in any inherent inability of British industry to respond to economic challenges. Pollard has identified mistakes in twentieth century British economic policy as the cause of the problem. Not surprisingly, this assessment is controversial. His solid textbook, *The Development of the British Economy*,[42] made the case in rather muted terms, but its purpose was to pioneer an advanced textbook on contemporary economic and social history. The best gauge of its success is that it has remained in print more or less continuously over a quarter of a century, and is still the work through which most undergraduates come across the name of Sidney Pollard. It is organised along the familiar LSE lines, on a sector-by-sector basis followed by a survey of labour organisation and living standards, and bears the distinctive trait of a huge range of sources logically synthesised and clearly mapped. It also set out his critique of twentieth century economic policy. At base, there is a view of the state as a servant of class interests. As will become more clear when we consider his work on European economic development, Pollard believes that early industrialisation proceeded against the background of liberalisation – the strong state and the free market fostered industrial development. From 1870, the state became more interventionist and, in the British context, policy has tended to burden rather than advantage industry. In *Britain's Prime and Britain's Decline*, the political establishment is criticised for rejection of policies for industry, in large part because manufacturing interests were excluded from the élite circles of policy-making.

These arguments are intensified and underwritten by a variety of rhetorical and polemical devices in two pieces on the twentieth century. In his editorial introduction to *The Gold Standard and Employment Policies Between the*

Wars,[43] the Treasury is blamed for listening uncritically to City advisers at the time of the return to gold, thus selecting an exchange rate which was in the interests of commerce and finance but which handicapped industry for much of the decade. In *The Wasting of the British Economy*[44] he argues that Britain's relative decline dates essentially from the period since 1950 and has resulted principally from the decision of policy-makers to look after the interests of the City and nurture the position of sterling as an international currency, rather than to foster the conditions which would have encouraged investment in British industry. The causes of Britain's relative decline have been an overvalued exchange rate, high interest rates to defend that exchange rate and the unwillingness of governments to provide the sort of discretionary assistance to investment and export that Britain's competitors have adopted without reluctance. Again, investment is the key to growth. However, the picture of the growth process as being uniquely dependent upon the rate of investment is somewhat over-simplified, as is the view that economic policy-making has disregarded the claims of industry because industrialists lack political power. It is significant that both these books were produced at times when British industry was being squeezed by policies to protect sterling and when policy priorities were seriously out of balance (the post-1967 stringency 'to make devaluation work' and in the aftermath of the devastation of British industry by the absurd monetary policies of 1980–1). Both might, therefore, be seen as the reactions of an angry man who was rightly convinced that a strong manufacturing sector had to be the foundation of British economic development and who was aiming his shafts at public rather than academic opinion, especially in *The Wasting of the British Economy*.

   This corpus of work on British economic and social development would have been enough to guarantee a place as one of the most respected social science historians of his generation, but Sidney Pollard has also changed the way we think about the process of European economic development – the primary focus of his activities since the early 1980s. His interest in European industrialisation is apparent in earlier work. European comparisons were pursued in *The Genesis of Modern Management*. He was the senior editor of *Documents of European Economic History*.[45] Visiting appointments in Europe and North America fostered links with scholars with a pan-European perspective. But there was also a contemporary angle. He began to think about European economic development at the time when the European Community had moved from its original limited conception, to an organisation which sought to bring the national economies of Europe into a huge integrated economic unit. How might we begin to understand the potential effects? Characteristically, Sidney Pollard's answer was to look for historical precedents, and in so doing he has posed a whole range of new questions for students of European economic development.

   In essence, his picture of European industrialisation is of a process which is, in its first stages, best understood as regional rather than national. Regionalism is a firmly established part of the Manchester tradition[46] but the more immediate stimuli were E.A. Wrigley and the growth pole analysis of François Perroux.[47] It is not simply that many of the early industrial centres crossed national boundaries but also that, in the manner of the Perroux growth poles, these early centres of industrialism transformed the economies of the much broader (again multi-national) regions in which they were located. Again, the focus is the transformation of proto-industrial organisation by a modern sector. Thus, early European industrial development should be seen as a process by which the advanced regions, invariably those which were on cheaply-worked coal deposits, began to 'colonise' the economic space between them by re-shaping long-established regional specialisms. Economic development in Europe from 1800 to 1870 was, therefore, a regional rather than national process, and the European economy became a more closely 'integrated' system of growth poles with their respective hinterlands. Of course, the region had long been a recognised economic unit for the study of industrialisation, but this notion of industrialisation spreading out from nodal points favoured by raw material endowments is new – not least for Pollard's own method of organising economic history. The sectoral approach has been dropped and the focus is no longer on the primacy of investment. It is true that this new approach tends to focus exclusively on the supply side, and that demand tends to be neglected, but the gains are considerable, especially when compared to be more orthodox approaches which concentrate on the nation state. This theme has been developed in a number of places, but its most persuasive exposition forms the kernel of *Peaceful Conquest*.[48]

However, *Peaceful Conquest* is rather more than a study of the European economy to 1870. The aim is to follow the ripples of industrialisation out from the early growth poles as peripheral areas began to respond to economic growth in Europe's early industrial centres. This theme is pursued in tandem with another which has deeply coloured Sidney Pollard's thinking on European economic development; that the rise of the nation state has been inimical to the process of development established between 1800 and 1870 and led to the 'disintegration' of the European economy between 1870 and 1939. Thus, the rise of the nation state has produced policies in response to internal political pressures which have attempted to rupture this emerging pattern of growth nodes and broad dependent hinterlands by seeking to protect inefficient agriculturalists or manufacturers. Most reviewers have compared these sections unfavourably with the treatment of the period up to 1870, but a number appear to have been looking for a more orthodox treatment of European economic growth rather than one which tries to follow the spark of industrialism across the continent. It is certainly true that shortage of space does not permit the sort of sophisticated assessment of the interaction of nation, region, 'disintegrating' forces and integrating forces (which resume the upper hand after 1945) which is possible for the earlier period.

Pollard's current interest is pro-industrialisation. Current debates on the problem were explored in both *Peaceful Conquest* and *Region und Industrialisierung*,[49] which were prepared for publication simultaneously. A key essay by Franklin Mendels pointed out that this form of production tended to be found on those soils which were insufficiently fertile for subsidiary crops. Industrial production had greater scope for expansion, so establishing the paradox of highest population densities on marginal agricultural land with incomes sustained by the intensive development of manufacturing under the putting out system. The comments on these ideas in *Peaceful Conquest* were challenging, but the prospect of the full 'Pollard treatment' of extensive reading and balanced synthesis is enticing – especially on this theme which has been so central to his best academic work.

To sum up Sidney Pollard's contribution to the study of economic and social development is an unenviable task. More than anything else he has epitomised the virtues of the most exacting standards of scholarship combined with a compelling soundness of judgement. All his work is notable for its wealth of detail and illustration. But he has always been far more than a mere compiler of 'facts'. The clarity of organisation in his work has been a persistent strength. He has used analytical tools from the social sciences, particularly but not exclusively from economics to order the wealth of material he has collected. However, he has always resisted the siren voices of 'new economic history' to view the unfolding of events solely through the filters of economic (and particularly neo-classical) theory. The reasons are admirably set out in his inaugural lecture: the development of economic theory over the past century has taken a direction which has permitted economists to ignore completely the broader social and historical framework which forms so much of the stuff of 'economic' problems of the real world. Sidney Pollard has been telling us for many years that we can improve our mastery of the present by understanding how society has changed in the past if we make that journey adequately equipped with theoretical tools and are prepared to acquire the breadth of information which permits real knowledge of the past.

It is to celebrate this unique corpus of work stretching back over the previous forty years that *Economy and Society* has been conceived and created. Its essays are also intended to mark his official retirement from academic life, even if it is fully recognised that he will never retire in the sense of putting down his pen and watching the fly die in the inkwell.

Acknowledgement

In compiling this biographical sketch and assessment we have received valuable assistance from the following sources: Sir Ken Alexander, Roger Allum, Bill Carr, Kate Carr, George Clayton, Catherine Finch, J.C. Gilbert, Peter Linacre, Brian McCormick, David Martin, David Pollard, Sidney Pollard, John Saville, Linda Shaw, Barry Turner, Harry Townsend and numerous colleagues at Sheffield and Exeter.

Notes

1 Beller, S., 1989, *Vienna and its Jews*, Cambridge University Press, Cambridge: 238.
2 Bentwich, N., 1956, *They found refuge*, Cresset Press, London: 95.
3 Turner, B., 1990, *And the policeman smiled*, Bloomsbury Publishing, London.
4 Ashton, T.S., 1955, *An economic history of England: the 18th century*, Methuen, London: preface.
5 Ashton, T.S., 1954, 'The treatment of capitalism by historians', in Hayek, F.A. (ed.), *Capitalism and the historians*, Routledge and Kegan Paul, London: 31–61.

6 Sayers, R.S., 1970, Thomas Southcliffe Ashton, *Proceedings of the British Academy*, LVI: 280.
7 Jones, G.P. and Pool, A.G., 1940, *A hundred years of economic development (1840-1940)*, Duckworth, London.
8 Pollard, S., 1954a, *Three centuries of Sheffield steel*, Marsh Brothers, Sheffield.
9 Pollard, S., 1959, *A history of labour in Sheffield*, Liverpool University Press, Liverpool.
10 Pollard, S., 1962, *The development of the British economy, 1914-1950*, Arnold, London.
11 Pollard, S., 1964a, *Economic history - a science of society?*, Sheffield University, Sheffield: 17.
12 Ashton, 1955, preface.
13 Pollard, S., 1965a, *The genesis of modern management: a study of the industrial revolution in Great Britain*, Arnold, London. Pollard continues to derive satisfaction from this book.
14 Pollard, S., 1982, *The wasting of the British economy*, Croom Helm, London.
15 Pollard, S., and Feinstein, C.H., 1988, *Studies in capital formation in the United Kingdom 1750-1920*, Clarendon Press, Oxford.
16 The most recent example is: Pollard, S., and Mathias, P. (eds), 1989, *The Cambridge economic history of Europe*, VIII *The industrial economies: The Development of economic and social policies*, Cambridge University Press, Cambridge.
17 Holmes, C., 1988, *John Bull's Island. Immigration and British society 1871-1971*, Macmillan, London: Chapter III.
18 Krebs, H., 1981, *Reminiscences and reflections*, Clarendon Press, Oxford.
19 Gershon, K., 1966, *We came as children*, Victor Gollancz, London.
20 On the decay of proto-industry, see Unwin G., 1904, *Industrial organisation in the sixteenth and seventeenth centuries*, Clarendon Press, Oxford. The Manchester approach to the industrial revolution can be seen in Ashton, T.S., 1948, *The industrial revolution, 1760-1830*, OUP, Oxford; Redford, A., 1931, *The economic history of England, 1760-1860*, Longman, London; idem 1926, *Labour migration in England, 1800-1850*, Manchester University Press, Manchester. The entrepreneur in business was studied by Unwin, G., 1924, *Oldknow and the Arkwrights: the industrial revolution in Stockport and Marple*, Manchester University Press, Manchester; Ashton, T.S., 1939, *An eighteenth century industrialist: Peter Stubs of Warrington, 1756-1806*, Manchester University Press, Manchester; Ashton, T.S., and Sykes, J., 1929, *The coal industry of the eighteenth century*, Manchester University Press, Manchester; Daniels, G.W., 1920, *The early English cotton industry*, Manchester University Press, Manchester; Redford, A., 1934 and 1956, *Manchester merchants and foreign trade*, Manchester University Press, Manchester. On finance, see Ashton, T.S., and Sayers, R.S., 1953, *Papers in English monetary history* OUP, Oxford. Ashton had lectured on monetary economics at Manchester. See also Unwin, G., 1927, *Studies in economic history: the collected papers of George Unwin*, edited with an introductory memoir by R.H. Tawney, Royal Economic Society, London and Ashton, T.S., 1955.
21 Clapham, J.H., 1926, 1932, 1933, *An economic history of modern Britain* (3 vols), vol. I: *the early railway age, 1820-1849*; vol. II: *free trade and steel, 1850-1886*; vol. III: *machines and national rivalries, 1887-1914*, CUP, Cambridge; idem, 1921. *The economic development of France and Germany*, CUP, Cambridge.
22 Pollard, 1964a, pp. 2-7.
23 Ibid, pp. 9-10.
24 Pollard, 1959.

25 Ashton, T.S., 1949, 'The standard of life of the workers in England, 1790–1830', *Journal of Economic History*, Supplement IX.

26 The debate is unravelled, at a surface academic level, in Taylor, A.J., (ed.), 1975, *The standard of living in Britain in the industrial revolution*, Methuen, London. Later contributions of note have been made by Crafts, N.F.R., 1985, *British economic growth during the industrial revolution*, Clarendon Press, Oxford; Lindert, P. and Williamson, J.G., 1983, 'English workers' living standards during the industrial revolution: a new look', *Economic History Review*, 2nd ser. XXXVI/1, 1–25.

27 Pollard, S., 1958a, 'Investment, consumption and the industrial revolution', *Economic History Review*, 2nd ser. XI/2, 215–26.

28 Most notably in the publication of Hayek, 1954.

29 Pollard, 1959; idem, 1954b, 'Wages and earnings in the Sheffield trades, 1851–1914', *Yorkshire Bulletin*, VI/1, 49–64; idem, 1965b, 'Trade unions and the labour market, 1870–1914', *Yorkshire Bulletin*, 17/2, 98–112; Pollard, S., and Crossley, D.W., 1968, *The wealth of Britain, 1085–1966*, Batsford, London.

30 Pollard, S., 1954c, 'The ethics of the Sheffield outrages', *Hunter Archeological Society Transactions*, VII/3, 118–139. Thompson, E.P., 1963, *The making of the English working class*, Gollancz, London.

31 Pollard, S., and Holmes, C., (eds), 1977, *Essays in the economic and social history of South Yorkshire*, South Yorkshire County Council, Barnsley.

32 Pollard, 1954a; idem, 1958b, *Sheffield trades council, 1858–1958*, STC, Sheffield; Idem, 1958c, *Shirley Aldred and Co. Ltd, 1796–1958*, Shirley Aldred, Worksop; idem (ed.), 1971, *The Sheffield outrages*, Adams and Dart, Bath.

33 Rostow, W.W., 1960, *The stages of economic growth*, CUP, Cambridge.

34 Pollard, 1965a. See also, idem, 1963, 'Capital accounting in the industrial revolution', *Yorkshire Bulletin*, XV/2, 254–271; idem, 1964a, 'Factory discipline in the industrial revolution', *Economic History Review*, 2nd ser. XVI/2, 254–271; idem, 1964b, 'The factory village in the industrial revolution', *English Historical Review*, LXXIX, 312, 513–531.

35 Chandler, A.D., 1962, *Strategy and structure: chapters in the history of industrial enterprise*, Harvard UP, Cambridge, Mass.; idem, 1977, *The visible hand: the managerial revolution in American business*, Harvard UP, Cambridge, Mass.

36 Pollard, 1963; idem, 1964c, 'Fixed capital in the industrial revolution in Britain', *Journal of Economic History*, XXIV, 299–314.

37 Higgins, J.P.P. and Pollard, S., 1971, *Aspects of capital investment in Great Britain, 1750–1850*, Methuen, London; Feinstein and Pollard, 1988.

38 See the chapter on coal in Feinstein and Pollard, 1988; Pollard, S., 1980a, 'A new estimate of British coal production, 1750–1850', *Economic History Review*, 2nd ser. XXXIII/2, 212–235; idem, 1983, 'Capitalism and rationality: a study of measurements in British coal mining, c.1750–1850', *Explorations in Economic History*, 20, 110–129.

39 Pollard, S., 1951, 'The economic history of British shipbuilding, 1870–1914', University of London, PhD. The thesis was frequently consulted, but when the Americans became interested in shipbuilding in the late Victorian period as an example of successful British entrepreneurship, it was published jointly with Paul Robertson who contributed chapters on management: Pollard, S., and Robertson, P., 1979, *The British shipbuilding industry, 1870–1914*, Harvard UP; Cambridge, Mass.

40 Pollard, S., 1988, *Britain's prime and Britain's decline: the British economy, 1870–1914*, Arnold, London.

41 W. Ashworth, 1989, in *Economic History Review*, 2nd ser. XLII/4, 613.

42 Pollard, S., 1962, *The development of the British economy*, Arnold, London. The second edition appeared in 1969 and the third in 1983.

43 Pollard, S., ed., 1970, *The gold standard and employment policies between the wars*, Methuen, London.

44 Pollard, S., 1982, *The wasting of the British economy*, Croom Helm, London. A second, enlarged edition appeared in 1985. The difficulties of viewing capital formation as an unambiguously independent variable in the growth process have been discussed by Alford, B.W.E., 1988, *British economic performance, 1945-1975*, Macmillan, London, pp. 37-40.

45 Pollard, S. and Holmes, C. (eds), 1968, 1972, 1973, *Documents of European economic history*, vol. I: *the process of industrialisation, 1750-1870;* vol. II: *industrial power and national rivalry, 1870-1914;* vol. III: *the end of the old Europe, 1914-1939*, Arnold, London.

46 See Unwin, 1924; Redford, 1926; idem, 1931; Ashton, 1939. The tradition can also be seen in the work of W.H. Chaloner, whose interests closely parallel those of Pollard but with a very different ideological slant: see Farnie, D.A. and Henderson, W.O. (eds), 1990, *Industry and innovation: selected essays by W.H. Chaloner*, Frank Cass, London, p.132.

47 Wrigley, E.A., 1962, 'The supply of raw materials in the industrial revolution, *Economic History Review*, 2nd ser. XV/1, 1-16; Perroux, F., 1950, 'Economic spaces: theory and applications, *Quarterly Journal of Economics*, 64, 89-104.

48 Pollard, S., 1973, 'Industrialisation and the European economy', *Economic History Review*, 2nd ser. XXVI/4, 636-648; idem, 1981a, *Peaceful conquest: the industrialisation of Europe 1760-1970*, OUP, Oxford; idem, 1981b. *The integration of the European economy since 1815*, Allen and Unwin, London.

49 Pollard. S., (ed.), 1980b, *Region und Industrialisierung*, Vandenhoeck und Ruprecht, Göttingen.

Part I: Economy

1 Does it pay to be late?*

David S. Landes,
Harvard University

It was more than a third of a century ago that Alexander Gerschenkron, then newly appointed to teach economic history at Harvard, wrote his essay on 'Economic Backwardness in Historical Perspective'. The essay posed the question, what does it take for a follower country to undertake industrialization and emulate its predecessors? Or to put it differently, does it make any difference to come along later?

What does it take? Gerschenkron answered metaphorically: an ability to leap the gap of knowledge and practice separating the backward economy from the advanced. Gerschenkron made no effort to ask why anyone should want to leap the gap. The advantages were obvious. Rather he saw the gap as in itself an incentive, an invitation to effort – like a gap in electric potential that, when sufficiently great, is crossed by energy in the form of a spark. (That's my metaphor, but it is not unjustified. Gerschenkron speaks explicitly of 'tension' between 'potential' and actual.) The greater the gap, the greater the potential for gain.[1]

1.1 Gerschenkron's model

In Gerschenkron's model, then, it pays to be late. Not before, but after. (He makes no effort to estimate the cost of relative poverty before industrialisation, but he doesn't have to. It's high.) The greater the gap, the greater the gain for those who leap it. Why? Because there's so much more to learn. As a result, follower countries grow faster than their predecessors. Their growth is characterized by what Gerschenkron calls a spurt (or spurts), a period (or periods) of exceptional rates of increase.[2]

Late growth, says Gerschenkron, also tends to be based on 'the most modern and efficient techniques', because they pay the most and nothing less can

* This paper was presented in June 1989 to a colloquium on early and abortive experiments in industrial development sponsored by the Centre d'Histoire Economique Internationale of the University of Geneva.

compete with more advanced nations. These techniques are typically capital-intensive, which would seem to be irrational in countries that abound in cheap labour.[3] Gerschenkron recognizes the paradox, but explains it by the quality of the work force. Good, well-disciplined labour is in fact scarce, he says, scarcer than in richer, more advanced countries. So it pays to substitute capital for labour.

That, for Gerschenkron, is half the story. The second half concerns the how: how did backward countries, poor in capital and good labour, manage to create modern, capital-intensive branches of industry? One knows how the 'First Industrial Nation' did it: Slow and easy – doin' what comes naturally. Britain built a labour force and accumulated capital as it went. In those early days, machines were typically small and cheap, scale was small, older buildings could be converted to industrial use; in short, threshold requirements were modest. But with the passing years, all of this changed – machines got bigger, were built heavier, and required buildings to their measure. Scale economies grew as transport facilities improved. By the time the first follower countries got into the contest, Britain had known two human generations of growth and industrial development. That's a long time.

What could the emulators do? Gerschenkron focuses on capital require-ments and, to a lesser degree, on enterprise – where did the initiatives come from?

British enterprise could grow like Topsy: by ploughing back earnings, by pooling personal resources, by borrowing from relatives or on the security of land, by renting facilities. Financial intermediaries, except for such loan brokers as solicitors, played a very small role. Banks confined themselves to supplying commercial capital – short-term credit, nominally to facilitate real transactions. Some of this took the form of lines of credit, renewed as reimbursed. In good times, such demand loans, repeatedly rolled over, were the equivalent of medium or even long-term credit. In bad, they would be called in; or maturities could be shortened.

The follower countries did not have the means or the time to grow that way. They needed more capital and they needed it quickly – to mount an industrial enterprise from scratch, to build a railway, a canal or a bridge. If the country was rich enough, Gerschenkron argues, if it had already accumulated wealth and commercial experience, it could create the private financial institutions that would mobilize the capital required. His best examples here are the *crédits mobiliers*, industrial or investment banks active in the France of the Second Empire, and the German universal banks (the four largest were the so-called D-Banken), which combined the seemingly incompatible functions and risks of investment and commercial banking. These, he argues, made a momentous difference in 'large portions of the Continent'.

But what if the country was too poor to finance the banks needed to finance industry? Well, then the state had to step in, either by creating or promoting the financial intermediaries, more often by using state agencies to finance, and if necessary operate, directly. Here his best example is Russia, although he adverts in passing to Hungary, which he contrasts in this regard with Austria, which is richer and more advanced.

For Gerschenkron, Russia is the paradigm of state-driven development. The push is to parity with the West by the adoption and assimilation of Western ways. The push is fitful and intermittent – partly because it is motivated from above and not every Tsar is inclined in this direction and partly because the effort, when it comes, is so exhausting that a period of respite is indispensable. Who pays the bill? The serf. Gerschenkron tells us it was Peter (alias 'the Great'), a passionate Westernizer, who 'perhaps more than anyone else . . . succeed[ed] in making [serfdom] effective' (p. 18). And in the long run, paradoxically, it was this policy of social immobilization and oppression that created the biggest obstacle to Russian development.

Just as the big banks in Germany preferred to put their money into the capital-intensive branches of heavy industry, so in Russia the state gave its support above all to mining and metallurgy, encouraging the formation of large enterprises operating on a large scale. Russian blast furnaces, he tells us, were bigger than the German (some were), illustrating a kind of law of backwardness: the later, the bigger and better.[4] Additionally, once the state-driven process of industrialization had made enough progress, the accumulation of capital made possible the establishment of investment and even universal banks, comparable in function and strategy to their German predecessors.

Gerschenkron concludes with a section on the 'ideological climate' of delayed industrialization. Here he does not argue explicitly that ideology, like special banking institutions, is a condition of overcoming backwardness. But he implies as much. *Laissez-faire*, he tells us, was not enough to propel the French economy; it took the doctrines of Saint-Simon to serve as a 'spiritual vehicle of an industrialization program' (p. 24). Similarly, he finds in Germany that Friedrich List's theories were an attempt to translate the Saint-Simonian message into a nationalist ideology of industrialization. The equivalent for Russia, ironically enough, was Marxism: the ideology of revolution in the service of nascent capitalism. (But of course!)

At the time Gerschenkron wrote this essay, concern with real lateness, the development of what we now call the Third World, was in its infancy. This was the age of very simple Harrod-Domar models, when decolonization had barely begun and the difficulties inherent in transition from pre-industrial to industrial were hardly suspected. Gerschenkron gives some attention to this matter in his 'Conclusions' and cites two possible impediments to twentieth century candidates: overpopulation ('industrial progress is arduous and expensive; medical progress is cheaper and easier of accomplishment' [p. 27]) and 'social tensions' of 'sinister proportions' due to 'great delays in industrialization' (p. 28). He does not specify the nature of these tensions, but he illustrates the point by the experience of the Soviet Union, where the tasks and promise of economic development have served to justify the 'ruthless exercise of dictatorial power' (p. 29).

He then finishes with an exhortation to the rich to concern themselves with the poor. The problems of backward nations, he tells us, 'are not exclusively their own. They are just as much problems of the advanced countries.' But, he hints, good intentions are not enough. Development projects will not work 'if they ignore the basic peculiarities of economic backwardness. Only by frankly recognizing their existence and strength, and by attempting to develop fully rather than to stifle what Keynes once called the "possibilities of things", can the experience of the nineteenth century be used to avert the threat presented by its successor' (p. 30). This last would seem to be a sibylline allusion to the possibilities of natural as against forced growth.

1.2 Criticisms

It is easy to find fault with the Gerschenkronian model if one measures it against the facts – that is, the hard facts and not the stylized facts. His analysis of the role of the Pereires and their *Crédit Mobilier* in French development is wrong; and his emphasis on, and discussion of, the Saint-Simonian contribution reflects a literature that was already outmoded at the time he was writing. His fascination with heavy industry derives from the particulars of two countries, Germany and Russia – he would have laid more stress on comparative advantage had he widened his array of examples. Even in the case of Russia, I think he underestimates the role of light industry, except when he wants to point to it to diminish the significance of enterpreneurship.[5] (If Russian serfs could learn to found and run cotton mills, presumably anyone could according to his argument.)

He does little with human capital. (As the enterpreneurship argument shows, Gerschenkron thinks of people as putty to be moulded, or perhaps as rational *homines economici* in the Smithian sense.) And that perhaps is why he does so little with knowledge as a factor of production. Except for a passing reference to 'the inability of a backward country to extend [a policy of continued modernization] to lines of output where very special skills are required' (p. 10), there is no attention to the effect of changing knowledge on the burdens, tasks, and opportunities of backwardness. But then, no economist at that time had any awareness of the significance of knowledge and its expression as technology for the larger process of growth. The use of national accounts to test the relative contribution of factor variables to aggregate product, and the discovery of the 'residual', still lay in the future. For Gerschenkron the pool of knowledge was there for all to fish in, and indeed it was the accessibility that created the tension (his word) between actual and possible.

I could continue, and indeed numerous scholars have already engaged in this kind of critique. Yet none of this, it seems to me, diminished the seminal importance of this article and its continuing interest. This lies not so much in the details as in the *Problemstellung*, in the definition of a *topos*. Is late development different? (Answer: yes.) How? (Answer: it requires special effort and institutional arrangements to mobilize factors and catch up.) To what end? (Answer: if things work out, you grow faster and better – in other words, you catch up with and maybe pass the front runners – if things work out).

1.3 Gerschenkron's model in perspective

So much for 1951. Suppose one looked at this problem again now, in the same large perspective. We have, after all, almost forty years of additional exper-

ience and knowledge. We know the story of European (or western) development a lot better than we did back then. We have also seen a large number of
non-western countries attempt development. The results are mixed: a few
spectacular success stories; a lot of uneven results that give grounds for hope,
depending on when one looks; a few examples of growth followed by serious
stagnation or retrogression; and a great many discouraging instances of
unacceptably modest gains or even hard incapacity. In the light of these data,
which may be quickly grasped by a look at the basic indicators table of the
World Bank's annual reports, what would a plausible model of late development look like? More particularly, how would it differ from the Gerschenkron
schema? Let me take up a number of these differences – I trust, the most
important – in no obvious order:

1.3.1 Politcal aspects and implications

Gerschenkron, as we have seen, made much of the links between industrialization and politics. But he dealt almost exclusively with the internal political
aspects – with the reciprocal relationship between hard economic driving and
political oppression. He says nothing about the implications of industrialization for the international balance of power, perhaps taking such considerations
for granted. Yet the matter is worth careful attention. We know, for example,
that the Industrial Revolution of the late eighteenth century drastically altered
the balance of power in a Europe that had made that balance the foundation of
international co-existence. No great nation could pretend to a significant,
autonomous role in the concert of Europe unless it learned those techniques
that had raised Britain to *primus inter pares* and enabled it to play the role of
banker and armourer to the Continent.

In this regard, the French revolutionary and imperial wars (1792–1815) were
probably the last in which the number of conscriptables counted for more than
industrial potential. Even so, the consumption of *matériel* was on an
unprecedented scale, and the French made strenuous efforts to augment
production by means of new labour-saving technologies. Some of these, such
as the plans for production of muskets using interchangeable parts, were
largely original. Most of them did not work out. The ideas were there, but the
resources – including time – were lacking.[6]

These considerations of relative power shed a new light on the ideological
underpinnings of industrialization. Gerschenkron, as we have seen, emphasizes
in this connection the role of what we may call doctrinal ideologies – explicit
schools of thought such as Saint-Simonism (France), List's national economics
(Germany), and Marxism (Russia). But these ideas, however eloquently
phrased and passionately espoused, touched directly and indirectly only a
fraction of the human actors involved in these industrialization efforts. To
understand the role of ideas in breaking the 'cake of custom', in mobilizing
effort and in generating commitment, one needs sentiments of wider resonance.

Of these, the most powerful was nationalism, which received an enormous
impetus from the French revolution, not only in France but elsewhere –

especially in those countries that fought against French occupation and rule with the ideological weapons of the enemy. Certainly, no history of German or Japanese industrialization can ignore the contribution of a collective commitment to nationhood and then power in the case of the former, independence and then power in that of the latter. The commitment showed in tacit compromises between older political élites and newer economic pretenders that staved off costly struggles for power while allowing the industrial interests a free and much favoured hand. Similarly, this commitment was displayed by a labour force that eschewed its own class interest at critical moments, while accepting those values of disciplined, collective labour that Gerschenkron thought so hard to inculcate in agrarian societies.

Now to be sure, we know from the historical record that this kind of nationalist commitment is not enough, indeed is not even a necessary condition of industrialization. Yet in conjunction with other favourable circumstances, it can make the difference between moderate development on the one hand and feverish on the other – as the contrast between multi-ethnic empires like Russia and Austria-Hungary, and nation-states like Germany and Japan shows. Conversely, the power that comes with super-rapid growth, when combined with overheated nationalism, can and did push such countries as Germany and Japan in the direction of expansion, the reopening of international accounts, and eventual military adventurism.[7]

1.3.2 Factors of production

The most important difference in my opinion would be the need to accord greater significance to the role of knowledge. The success of the European follower countries makes this clear. For one thing, these countries were effectively on the same intellectual and scientific level as Britain, and this from the very beginning. Even a country so socially and politically backward as Russia, with a cripplingly high rate of illiteracy, possessed at the top a small élite of savants of exceptional quality and power. To be sure, foreign immigrants and guests held an important place in this élite; but the relevant fact is that they did come and found, in the academies of St. Petersburg and Moscow, good company and opportunities for research and publication.

For another, this population of trained and gifted savants made all the difference when the decision was taken to promote secondary and higher education in science and technology: Gerschenkron could have made many of the same arguments here as he did for the mobilization of capital. The schools created by the French revolution had no precedent or equivalent in England. Like the later joint-stock investment banks, they represented a creative response to the problem of developing and mobilizing the resources of the nation. The most revolutionary of these institutions in its long-run consequences was the *École Polytechnique*, originally founded to train officers for the knowledge-intensive branches of the army, in particular, the artillery and the engineers. Yet the school turned out from the start to be much more than that. Its first faculty was an all-star cast of French savants so that it came, almost inevitably, to offer first-class programmes of instruction in mathematics and fundamental science, and became a training ground for France's technological élite.

The *Polytechnique* in turn became a model for similar schools throughout Europe, but here as in other spheres lateness paid off by allowing emulators to take the best and adapt it as needed. The German and Swiss systems, for example, were both more extensive than the French and more carefully adjusted to different levels of content and application. The Russians had farther to go and, more than the others, they drew on foreign talent. The one country that did not follow this example was Britain which for a long time did not have to, because it was first. This proved to be a major weakness when new kinds of industry called for new kinds of training.

This brings me to what we sometimes call the Second Industrial Revolution (electricity, internal combustion engine, liquid and gaseous fuels, organic chemicals and artificial materials), which depended far more than the First on formal training in science. The new techniques were experientially and sensorily opaque, and their principles were best learned in the classroom and laboratory. Here the follower countries had all the advantage, whereas Britain, though not without some leading figures (many of them immigrants), lost ground for want of a steady flow of qualified personnel and an unawareness of, or indifference to, their technological possibilities within the enterprise.

By comparison with this knowledge factor, the provision of capital for development now seems far less important. Not that it was not needed to finance investment, or that special institutions were not created for the purpose. But this task now seems to us to have been less difficult and less problematical, at least in the aggregate. (Shortage of capital may have seemed a mountainous obstacle to individual projectors.) Over the course of the nineteenth century, the follower countries of continental Europe and the United States – that is, the places of successful industrial emulation – had little trouble obtaining funds in the form of both loans and direct investment from earlier industrializers. The explanation is simple: capital was looking for higher returns than could be had in economies that had already exhausted what Schumpeter called the entrepreneurial profits of innovation.

Aside from the relative importance of the factors of production, there is the question of their mix. Gerschenkron places great stress on the preference for capital-intensive lines of activity, which he relates to the character of the financing of industry. Investment banks and the state, he tells us, prefer these. He does not specify why, perhaps because he finds the reasons obvious. Capital-intensive activities need capital, and that's what the lenders and purveyors of capital are for. Also capital-intensive activities tend to be bigger (to offer greater economies of scale), and bigness means more need for capital. In short, the banks and governments were following their comparative advantage.

Yet, it is clear, that is not the only way for an economy to go. Gerschenkron adverts in passing to the Danish experience. No spurts, he tells us, and no 'peculiar emphasis' on heavy industry. The reasons: the lack of natural resources (presumably ores and coal) and the opportunity for Danish agriculture to sell to the (rich, free-trade) British market. Again, this is a matter of comparative advantage, and Gerschenkron might have done a lot more with that aspect of economic choice. It is, after all, an important determinant of the character and success of the industrialization process.

It is no accident, for example, that France built its development more on light industry than Germany – it suffered, to use a formula of Rondo Cameron's, from a want of minerals in the diet. When it did open up important new deposits of iron ore in Lorraine in the 1890s (though the question must be asked, why so late?), it responded with record rates of growth in metallurgy. In general, it devoted more of its resources to such branches as textiles and to a wide range of small craft shops specializing in labour-intensive, often high-skill, non-standardized articles. Without going so far as to say with O'Brien and Keyder that France grew as fast as or even faster than Britain in the nineteenth century, or to hold it up in Piore-Sabel-Zeitlin fashion as a paradigm of 'small-is-beautiful', there is no doubt that it grew at a moderate and respectable pace, kept up well with advancing technology (even if it did not always introduce it or capitalize on it), and laid the basis for rapid, catch-up development after World War II.[8]

The same emphasis on light industry characterized Japan, which also began with textiles and achieved its first export successes in silk and cotton. Japan, like Denmark, was poor in the materials of heavy industry and did what it paid to do. Yet Japan is not Denmark. The latter has largely remained content to build on agriculture, food processing, and wood products and buy its heavy consumer durables from outside – and it has attained a very high standard of living doing so. Japan, in contrast, has developed the full range of manufactures, heavy as well as light, and has even succeeded in establishing itself as a dangerous competitor in branches such as steel making, where nature gave it little to work with.

The reason for moving into what would appear to be areas of comparative disadvantage was above all political – the government wanted Japan to be self-sufficient in all domains pertinent to national power. The reasons for economic success initially were government support and the acquisition of territories rich in raw materials (Korea, Manchuria). But this pursuit of empire turned to catastrophe in World War II and no one in 1950, least of all perspicacious economists, would have given the Japanese, now shorn of colonies, the slightest chance of building steel and consumer durables industries (especially automobiles) that would outstrip those of much more richly endowed nations.

We all know what happened. Subsequent success was built on technological emulation and innovation. Raw materials? They could be bought on the world market and shipped economically to waterside mills and factories. The cheap, easy shipping was also the result of technolgical innovation. It now pays for Korea to buy coal in western Pennsylvania, move it as slurry to a water transport terminal and then send it halfway across the world via the Panama Canal. Raw materials just aren't what they used to be.

1.3.3 The international context

Gerschenkron did almost nothing with this, and indeed, no one else did at that time. The general assumption of economists was that growth was largely a question of market responses and that the backward country of today was the industrial nation of tomorrow. If anything, observers were naïvely sanguine, the more so as the end of imperialism promised unimpeded development for erstwhile colonies. Part of the problem was that Marxist and socialist commentators in general believed their own doctrines of the gains and burdens of empire, both in regard to strong and weak, rich and poor. The colonial powers, they were convinced, deprived of their milk cows, would suffer a grievous – perhaps fatal – loss. Wasn't imperialism the 'highest', the last, stage of capitalism? And the colonies, now free, would flourish as the proverbial bay tree. Those who want to get a sense of this innocent view of the world turned upside down should read an article published in 1962 by Surendra Patel, in which the author demonstrates arithmetically, hence irrefutably, that the inexorable power of compound interest will very quickly allow developing countries like India to catch up with and pass their western predecessors.[9]

But this optimisim was not confined to the political left. Mainstream and neo-classical economists saw no reason why the classical Smithian mechanisms of comparative advantage and division of labour should not enable developing countries to follow the example of their industrialized precursors. The preferred model was staples theory. This body of doctrine had been developed initially to explain Canada's path to high product and high income. The theory postulates that the gains from a succession of export staples (furs in the seventeenth and eighteenth centuries, timber in the late eighteenth and nineteenth centuries, then grain and minerals in the nineteenth and twentieth) had drawn both people and capital, and generated the earnings to make possible balanced growth along a wide front of activity. It was subsequently applied to Australia (wool, meat, wheat, minerals), the United States (tobacco, cotton, wheat, minerals), and Sweden (timber, iron ore and semi-finished bar iron, copper) – all of which had done very well. The staples theory would also, with equal weight, be made to account for the transition of medieval England from a dependent primary producer (minerals and wool) to Europe's leading industrial nation.

Those, however, were the easy cases. The historical record shows more ambiguous experiences of what we may call failed or half-failed staples economies – countries richly endowed with natural resources and yet prevented, some would say by these very staples, from industrialization. Russia comes to mind. Already in the early modern period (the sixteenth and seventeenth centuries) its great source of wealth was its agricultural produce – grain, furs, hides, tallow – to which was added in the eighteenth century a mineral resource, crude pig iron from the Urals. All of these were eagerly sought after by the richer societies of western Europe and made possible a consistently favourable balance of trade – the makings, one would say, of industrialization. Yet Gerschenkron tells us that the great obstacle to industrialization in Russia was the institution of serfdom, and nothing was so conducive to the imposition and hardening of serfdom as the economic interests of export agriculture. These staples revenues also enriched a landowning class that had all the wrong values: a contempt for labour; no use for money, except to spend it; an indifference to waste; a crapulous, hedonistic self-indulgence.[10] The source of wealth, in other words, was the source of backwardness.[11]

Other examples of staples failure would be such Latin American countries as Argentina and, to a lesser degree, Brazil. Seventy-five years ago, Argentina, rich with the earnings from hides, wheat, and frozen meat, looked like a prime candidate for one of the front positions in the world economic competition. Today it is, if not a basket case (nature has been too generous for that), a prime example of development gone wrong. Brazil looks better, is growing faster, has built, largely thanks to coffee, one of the Americas' leading industrial conurbations in the São Paulo–Santos area. But Brazil also has yet to realize its potential. Mexico, Chile, Columbia, Venezuela, and other Latin American primary producers have done no better – and this after more than 150 years of independence.

The relative failure of Latin America to industrialize has spawned the biggest export industry in the area – the production and marketing of explanations for economic backwardness. The big export staple here has been so-called dependency theory, which is less a theory than a way of looking at the world – a stance or a perspective. The gravamen of this position is that a country whose prosperity is dependent on the decisions (to buy, to lend, to give, to share) and events (the ups and downs of the business cycle) of another, is incapacitated for growth. This is particularly true when the role assigned to the dependent economy is that of exchanging primary products of low value-added for manufactures of high value-added (victimization by the international division of labour), for built into such a relationship, we are told, are unequal exchange (the rich milk the poor), wide swings in income (excessive dependence on one or a very few export staples subject to wide price fluctuations), and generally deteriorating terms of trade.

This is not the place to attempt a general analysis and verification of this position. Suffice it to say that it represents the reversal of the traditional staples theory, in that it argues that export staples are not good for you. And that poses an interesting problem: if staples were good for a number of earlier industrializers, why shouldn't they work for all? In particular, were they more helpful in the past than they are now? Or to put it differently, is this one respect in which lateness hurts?

The questions become even more difficult if one accepts, as most do, that it is better to have saleable staples than not to have them, and better to trade than to huddle under the carapace of autarky. The law of comparative advantage has not been abolished, contrary to premature reports of its demise. Of course, cash-crop farming had its risks and there are those who deplore the loss of subsistence farming (though crop failures and famine have hardly disappeared) – after all, you can't live on coffee or palm oil or even bananas. Even so, the farmer who has to choose between growing his own food and earning money to buy food (and other things) in the market will ordinarily choose the latter, because it gives him a larger and more varied consumption basket. By doing so, of course, he throws himself on the mercy of outside forces – not only fluctuations in world prices but, even more, the arbitrary and often confiscatory prices set by his own rulers. These forces yield in no wise to the greed of colonial oppressors and multinational corporations for, as history abundantly demonstrates, it takes one to take one. This is no small matter, but is part of a much larger problem – that of the distribution of income and appropriation of surplus in poor and typically undemocratic societies. The fact remains that, from a macroeconomic perspective and *ceteris paribus* (keep your eye on the 'equality'!), the surplus to the economy as a whole is the larger for the rational pursuit of comparative advantage.[12]

Even if one accepts the advantages of trade, however, the record of staples failures remains to be explained. Two thoughts occur to me here. The first is that staples are not what they used to be in that they are far more substitutable. Their value is obviously enhanced by monopoly or its cartelized equivalent, where the only consumer riposte is to use less, whether by self-restraint or substitution – for example, drink less coffee, stop drinking coffee, or try tea, ginger ale or plain water. Similarly, with fuel, turn out the lights, wear a sweater or burn less fuel.

Technology here has significantly altered the options. Sometimes it favours the seller, by givi.ıg value to his product. Rubber, for instance, came into its own with the rise of the bicycle and then the automobile industries with their almost insatiable demand for inflatable tyres. Similarly, copper was a great beneficiary of electricity; tin, of food preservation; and oil, of the generalization of the internal combustion engine. It was the industrial nations who, in this way, created much of the wealth of the primary producers.

But what techonology gives with one hand, it takes away with another. When natural rubber becomes scarce because of trade wars and blockades, artificial rubber fills the breach. Copper wire has been increasingly displaced by glass fibres; tinplate, by glass and plastics; and even oil must reckon with conservation measures and alternative fuels. From this viewpoint, although the twentieth century has seen its staples booms (of which the greatest were the oil shocks of the 1970s), the gains to producers have been, on balance, less than they once were.

But one can find staples failure in the nineteenth century as well, and this suggests some further reflections on the tribulations of followship. In particular, it directs attention to another aspect of lateness neglected in the Gerschenkron model – one to which we turn our attention now.

1.3.4 Social and cultural determinants

Gerschenkron was never impressed by those explanations of rate and character of growth that accorded importance to the human factor. Entrepreneurial theses were anathema (as I can testify), on the assumption that there is plenty of that kind of talent lying around, ready to learn what has to be learned and respond to the tension of unassuaged backwardness. Besides, he felt, entrepreneurship was the same everywhere. This article of faith was slightly shaken by his work on the history of the Italian economy – but only slightly. He never studied Japan. The one concession he made in this area was recognition that it is not a simple matter to create an industrial labour force; but then the difficult only takes a little longer.

Yet the comparative experience of development, much richer now than in

1951, suggests that the human factors matter a great deal. (Let us leave aside the prominent, well-known instance of Japan, which has done more than anything to shake the confidence of economists in their conventional analyses and predictions.) It is not enough for societies, or more exactly their rulers, to want to industrialize. It is not enough to pour in supplies of the traditional factors – land, labour, and capital. What counts even more is the spirit underlying the effort, the way the pieces are put together, the aggregate result of an infinity of actions and initiatives. If I may take a simile from biology, the frontal lobes of the brain have no special function; these are located elsewhere. But it is the frontal lobes apparently that pull the messages together and make the system work.

1.4 The special case of very early late developers

It is instructive in that regard to consider instances of premature and hence abortive industrialization, typically motivated by extra-economic consider-ations and generated from above. Eighteenth century Prussia would be a good example, but for the purpose of this discussion, I would cite the experience of Egypt under Mohammed Ali, an Albanian adventurer who came in the train of the British (who had come to drive out the French). He rid Egypt of centuries of Mameluke rule by inviting these parasites to a dinner, closing the gates, and shooting them down like mad dogs in a cage. Mohammed Ali then decided to modernize (westernize) his country, the better to conquer everyone around. The story of his unachieved industrial revolution is one of the neglected chapters of economic history. Briefly, he laid the foundation by moving Egypt over to cash-crop agriculture, with special emphasis on the cultivation of a new, high-quality variety of cotton, Jumel (named after the Frenchman who developed it). The earnings from these crops, marketed through state monopolies, were then invested in, among other things, a massive educational and industrial effort – schools to train technicians as well as military personnel and a wide variety of mills and shops for the production of textiles, metals and metal products, chemicals, and the like. Mohammed Ali even moved to gain autonomy from European suppliers by purchasing models of machines and producing copies in Egypt. Mohammed Ali's vision, in other words, was very much like the reaction of continental European countries to the tidings of discomfort from across the Channel – once Britain industrialized, they felt compelled to do the same. Instant industrialization.

In Egypt, though, one critical factor was lacking: people. Native entrepre-neurs were non-existent, and no one who had anything to say about it was willing to work in one of these factories. Mohammed Ali brought in foreigners to run his plants and appointed Egyptians to watch over them (for supervision read interference). As for workers, he began with slaves from the south, but they died so fast (which says something about working conditions) that he soon had recourse to corvée labour. Some peasants mutilated themselves to avoid conscription but, as most people found that repugnant as well as uncomfortable, they mutilated the machines instead. Arson was an abiding threat. Maintenance was negligible. Before long, there were more machines idle than in use, and the standard repair took the form of cannibalization.

The whole scheme was in a state of galloping entropy by the time the Europeans, the British at their head, put an end to Mohammed Ali's monopolies and other constraints on international trade (exports as well as imports) and limited Egypts's ability to protect its infant industries by tariff walls. Egyptian scholars and some western historians prefer to see that as the reason for Egypt's industrial failure, but no one who reads the contemporary records can reasonably believe that. The most one can say is that Europe administered the *coup de grâce* to a project that was doomed from the start and already in its death throes. It was, in fact, another hundred years before Egypt could move once again in this direction – and then a lot more slowly and with only partial suscess.

Not everybody would agree with this analysis. Nikki Keddie, in an excellent essay on development in the Middle East, suggests that the British may not have killed the industrial experiment of Mohammed Ali, which was already 'failing', but that their one-sided policy of free trade (equality in inequality) may have prevented Egyptian industrialization in the latter part of the century, when the conditions of an indigenous effort might have been more favourable.

That is the kind of counterfactual that is particularly difficult to test, but there are good reasons to be sceptical. For one thing, even when Egypt did achieve effective economic independence, it did not make rapid progress toward industrialization. The country was still not ready. For another, as Keddie herself points out, tariff constraints, whether voluntary or imposed, are not in themselves a barrier to manufacture in countries with cheap labour – witness Germany in the mid-nineteenth century, and India and Japan in the latter half of the century. Nor does freedom of tariff policy assure the protection that is supposed to bring industrialization – as in Latin America, where strong local interests preferred trade to industry and were opposed to high duties, as were, for that matter, French wine producers and East-Elbian landlords. The difference between India and Japan on the one hand, Egypt and Ottoman Turkey on the other, lay primarily in the availability of domestic enterprise. In general, those who lay stress on the ability of governments to protect home industry assume that industry can be had for the asking – on order as it were. Would that it were so simple.

A word about British commercial policy. Keddie speaks of the British 'forcing much of the rest of the world to mold their economies in ways suited to British interests'. But the facts belie this assumption of quasi-omnipotence. It is true that all European traders were opposed to state monopolies of export commodities. They preferred market to command prices, even though the latter could only prevail in the short run. True also that British statesmen and economists believed in a pattern of international specialization that would give Britain the industry and the others the agriculture, mining, and other tasks of the primary sector. But preference and desires were one thing; enforcement, another. When John Bowring, indefatigable reporter to Parliament on the economies of other countries, wrote in 1840 of the *Zollverein*, he deplored the German effort to develop and protect manufactures in the face of comparative advantage. An international division of labour, after all, made such good sense for all concerned. The only trouble was, the Germans and others like them were not listening – and that was that. I cannot think of a single instance of the British making commercial policy for a country on the path to industrialization.

But, you may say, these were the follower countries, the success stories of what is now the First World. What were later to be called Third World countries were not always in a position to ignore British and other imperialist pressures, especially after engaging in stupid and costly imperialist ventures of their own. That was one of the built-in problems of Third World economic emulation – it was not so much doing what comes naturally as an artificial expression of overweening ambition or pride. The decree came down from on high: let there be industry. This is hubris, and the Egyptian example is perhaps the best. Had Mohammed Ali been content to build industry for its own sake, he would have done much better than he did. To be sure, Jean Batou argues that this was Mohammed Ali's original intent, to build industry for its own sake as part of a larger effort of national regeneration. Batou would trace this intention back to 1816, before the imposition of agricultural monopolies and the creation of a national army.

Perhaps this is possible, although it is clear very early on that industry was closely linked to, and shaped by, military aspirations. To which Batou responds that Mohammed Ali's imperial ambitions were part of the same vision; that Mohammed Ali saw military victory and territorial aggrandizement as a way of building a sense of Egyptian, even pan-Arab, nationhood and of laying the foundations of a new, industrial economy.

It should be said that Mohammed Ali's policies and acts were not always consistent with such a larger plan – but then, isn't that in the nature of politics, which is of nature and necessity heavily improvisational? Is it not also true that the same military effort that justified a programme of forced industrialization, necessarily limited and distorted its scope? His biggest mistake, in other words, lay in pursuing power, and in trying to exercise it before he could sustain it. Power is like happiness – a by-product. One doesn't achieve it by chasing after it, it comes to and stays with those who earn it by living and working well.

Even if Batou's thesis were right, it would only show Mohammed Ali to be so far out ahead of his subjects as to be ineffectually visionary. This was a cart-before-the-horse strategy. Part of the problem would have been that he himself was not Egyptian – nor for that matter was just about the whole of the ruling élite, which remained Turkish. He did not have the popular awareness and consciousness to mould and manipulate that the Meiji élite had; or, later yet, that Mustafa Kemal made use of in republican Turkey.[13]

But that was the paradox: the higher the source of pressure (revolution from above), the shallower the effect. Since the will to industrialize did not come from the population at large, the abandonment under European pressure of these premature programmes was as easy as their announcement. New or chastened governments renounced unachievable ambitions and reconciled themselves to the easier returns of comparative advantage and European credit. Had there been a popular interest in industry, no domestic government could have survived without maintaining some protection and no foreign government could have imposed free or almost free trade for long.

In this regard, it is worth asking why European entrepreneurs did not set up their own enterprises in countries like Egypt. The answer, in my opinion, cannot be that British policy discouraged such offshore investments by way of protecting home industry. There were people in Britain who would have favoured such a policy, but there were others, including colonial officials both at home and abroad, who were ready to encourage the industrial development of the empire. Efforts to eliminate all tariff protection for Indian manufactures failed, for example, in the face of this opposition. (The Raj was eventually prevailed upon to institute an equivalent compensatory excise on Indian manufactures, but by that time Manchester had lost most of the Indian market.) As for the sometimes-heard allegation that industrial capitalists as a group were opposed to overseas enterprise out of ideological loyalty to an imperial division of labour, I am utterly unpersuaded; and the fact that it is Marxists in particular who propagate such nonsense is a scandal to good Marxism.[14] After all, anyone who takes capitalist greed and ruthlessness seriously should be sceptical of charges of higher loyalties. These bosses are in it for the money. Why should they care if they make it by exploiting blacks and browns instead of whites?

The question may be asked, why the fascination of neo-Marxists with alleged industrial might-have-beens thwarted by European selfishness, often behind a mask of market freedom? My own sense (again) is that the effect (if not the aim) is to establish a conspiratorial thesis of world history, the better to fix blame and culpability, mobilize political if not economic resistance, and exploit the tender conscience of the haves – for what that is worth.

In that regard, it is worth noting the contrasting positions of Marx himself and his latter-day *epigoni*. Marx denounced the abuses and crimes of imperialism but saw it as objectively progressive – European intervention was necessary to pull traditional, immobile societies out of the slough of despond. Hence his approval of the American defeat of Mexico, the French conquest of Algeria, and British dominion in India. This approach does not sit well with Marxists today, especially those of the countries concerned, who prefer to blame others for their misfortune. One can understand. But as any serious observer knows, that kind of displacement of responsibility is bad for performance and achievement. If others are responsible, one may be tempted to count on these same others to save. But if these others are as mean and nasty as they are painted, why count on them at all?

1.5 Conclusion

Does it pay to be late? It can, for those who are ready. (This is clearly an untestable tautology, but what it means is no different in a way than such old saws as 'Haste makes waste'. When does one know when one has been hasty? One knows.) But getting ready is a long and difficult process, and Gerschenkron is clearly correct when he warns of the high cost of delay. All kinds of impediments may develop in the interval, the more so as the media of communication cultivate a sense of deprivation and thereby the impatience that makes for poor counsel, while intellectuals and ideologues cultivate a sense of grievance and thereby the anger that breeds foolishness.

Most of Europe in the nineteenth century was more or less ready, and that goes a long way to explain, roughly speaking, both the success and the timing of industrialization there. I say roughly speaking because there is no neat correlation and, as Gerschenkron points out, politics and policy do make a difference. Still, it is no accident that France preceded Germany and Germany preceded Russia; or that the Mediterranean lands, long pastoralized, and the Balkans, long under Ottoman rule, were the slowest of all.

Does it pay to be late? If it were not for the recent performance of such countries and 'city-states' as Korea, Taiwan, Hong Kong and Singapore, one might say it once did but doesn't any longer – that the gap between *is* and *could be* has grown with time to the point of being almost impassable. The argument would run in terms of knowledge, culture and politics, and human nature.

1.5.1 Knowledge

The new technologies are so esoteric and difficult as to be almost unlearnable, except for those who leave to study in advanced countries. This very process of study abroad is both gain and loss; for these students, once they have learned, are often reluctant to go home, if only because they can do much more with their knowledge abroad. Indeed, the better they have learned, the more reluctant they are to return, because the bigger the gap is between earnings potential abroad and at home. (Another factor, less easily verifiable is, is there not a link between adaptability on the one hand and success in these studies on the other? And do not the most adaptable find it easiest to stay?)

The brain drain is further aggravated by the material, political, and cultural gap between the West and the Rest – as the song says, 'How'ya gonna keep 'em down on the farm after they've seen Paree? ' Even in the straitened circumstances of the typical foreign student visitor, the living tends to be better in the rich countries, the social life more exciting, the politics more interesting and, very important, much safer. Most of the world's industrial nations are democracies, and students from Third World countries who learn and train there typically enjoy far more freedom than they know at home. To be sure, they also encounter the distance and hostility of racism, subtle and overt – though far more overt in such socialist countries as the Soviet Union and China than in most western (capitalist) nations. (So much for progessive sentiment and indoctrination: socialists are entitled.) On balance, though, the university years build expectations that the home country is not able, or willing, to satisfy. Hence one more good reason not to go back.

1.5.2 Political and cultural impediments

It is a fact of history that most developing countries are also new countries. They have young, untried institutions and administrative structures that fall far short of the tasks implicit in their ambitions for power and wealth. In many instances, they still have no firm identity, no sense of a national purpose, no collective identification with a common interest. On the contrary, they suffer the pains and after-effects of colonial arrangements imposed without due attention to the rational interests of population and circumstances of place. This is not the place to go into these matters in detail. Suffice it to say, whatever the economic gap that already separates many of these countries from the rich states, it is even bigger for the want of direction (in both senses) of the would-be followers.

1.5.3 'Human nature'

This includes, among other things, what economists have called the demonstration effect – seeing is wanting. For a variety of reasons related to communications technology, the poor people of the world are bombarded by testimonies of the material advantages enjoyed by others. They do not have to travel to learn these things: they see them in films and on television, and hear of them on the radio and by word of mouth. The result is a sense of impoverishment and grievance (why they and not we?) and a great impatience.

Some of this hunger finds expression in fantasy: the cargo cults of the Pacific are perhaps the best-known example. Some of it takes the form of exit. There has been a massive migration since World War II, still under way in the face of all manner of political impediments, from poor places to rich ones. But its most consequential effect, in my opinion, has been the poisoning of development efforts in the direction of haste, waste, and corruption.[15] Ask anyone in these countries if he is ready to wait a hundred years to achieve parity with the rich nations of the west and he will exclaim in outrage and indignation; and if you point out that it took the Japanese a hundred years, he will shrug in disagreement or indifference; and then may point out that the Japanese are a very patient, tenacious people.

1.6 Final thoughts

The above discussion assumes implicitly that lateness is nothing more than that – a temporal statement. Some countries industrialize earlier, some later, but all are on the same track. But that is a heavy assumption, one that reflects a certain complacency on the part of the rich that they have done right and that everyone else is destined to, and has no choice but to follow in their footsteps – that anything less is failure.

It is now clear, however, that some people (and maybe peoples) are saying that this is not the path they want to follow; that it is incompatible with older ways and values, and that self-respect requires refusal of the western way. To be sure, such hostility to change is an old story (Anglophobes in France, Slavophiles in Russia, xenophobes in China), but where once it was characteristic of the traditionalist right, it is now increasingly found on the left, where it is reinforced by fear of exploitation and 'neo-colonialism'. This is an issue, then, where far right may meet and join far left, promoting strange alliances

20 *David S. Landes*

between fundamentalist clergy and atheistic 'Marxists'. (Needless to say, these alliances do not age well – look at Iran.)

Yet even if one dismisses this growing concern as the politics of the moment, it may well reflect something deeper, namely the growing incapacity of today's late-latecomers for industrialization. Suppose what we are dealing with is a pool of candidates. Some are favoured by history; some are not. The ones most favoured go first. Others follow. And as the pool is exhausted, the hard cases remain – hard cases not only because of the misfortunes and misdeeds of history, but because, for all manner of internal reasons, they do not take to these new ways. They don't like them; they don't want them; they are discouraged from learning them; if they learn them, they want out; etc. Maybe what we are seeing here is simply that we're getting down to the hard cases.

Does it pay to be late? Sometimes yes and sometimes no. Economic history never promised neat answers. That's because it's history as well as economics.

Notes

1 The principle is actually stated conditionally: 'Assuming an adequate endowment of usable resources, and assuming that the great blocks to industrialization had been removed, the opportunities inherent in industrialization may be said to vary directly with the backwardness of the country'. Alexander Gerschenkron, 1962, *Economic Backwardness in Historical Perspective*, Harvard/Belknap, Cambridge, Mass.; p. 8. The article appeared originally in B. Hoselitz (ed.), 1952, *The Progress of Underdeveloped Countries*, Chicago University Press, Chicago.
2 Henryk Szlajfer, in his essay on Latin America and Congress Poland for the Conference of Premature Industrialization (Geneva 1989), refers to Kula's 'theory of "leaps".' I am not familiar with this theory or its source, but it sounds very much like Gerschenkron's thesis of spurts. Doesn't Kula cite Gerschenkron?
3 Gerschenkron, who based his model primarily on the nineteenth century experience of France, Germany, and Russia, argued that backward countries tended to concentrate 'at a relatively early stage of their industrialization on promotion of those branches of industrial activities in which recent technological progress had been particularly rapid', specifically in heavy industry.
4 But Gerschenkron did not do his homework on the Russian iron industry. Even with bigness, it was not so technologically advanced as the German, as German engineers and observers noted, blaming the backwardness on excessive protection. See Ulrich Troitzsch, 'Die Entwicklung der russischen Eisenhuttenindustrie im Spiegel des deutschsprachigen wirtschaftlichen und technischen Literatur (1850–1900)', in Hermann van der Wee, V. A. Vinogradov, and G. G. Kotovsky (eds), *Fifth International Conference of Economic History, Leningrad 1970*, vol. VII, 272–86.
5 See for example the data in Olga Crisp, 'The Pattern of Russia's Industrialization up to 1914', in Pierre Leon, Francois Crouzet, and Richard Gascon (eds), 1972, *L'industrialisation en Europe au XIXe siècle* [Colloques Internationaux du CNRS, Sciences Humaines, Lyon, 7–10 octobre 1970], Editions du CNRS, Paris, pp. 458–60.
6 Note that the pursuit of economic growth in the service of power was an old story; hence the policies that came to be known as mercantilism and cameralism. But the Industrial Revolution decisively altered the content of modernization and provided a model for imitation.

7 Gerschenkron concerns himself with links between hothouse growth and domestic oppression. But he notes in the case of the Soviet Union that an alleged threat from the outside can serve to justify the most painful economic squeeze, elicit self-sacrifice, and thereby obviate the need for overt, intolerable tyranny. By implication, tyrannies have an incentive to maintain a sense of danger from enemies within and without, usually alleged to be conspiratorially allied. The cultivation of a sense of insecurity works, but only up to a point, for fatigue invariably sets in. At which point, some governments are tempted to give reality to figments – that is, make enemies where they had only imagined them.

8 Patrick O'Brien and Caglar Keyder, 1978, *Economic Growth in Britain and France 1780-1914: Two Paths to the Twentieth Century*, Allen & Unwin, London. The book is not so much an analysis as an argument (nothing wrong with that), and sufficiently imaginative to merit the appellation of *roman à these*. It is the only study I know of that finds coal to have been cheaper in France than in Britain. The protectionist French industrialists of the nineteenth century, who always cited Britain's lower fuel costs as justification for tariff walls, would have been pleasantly surprised.

On Piore, Sabel, and Zeitlin, see the debate in David Landes (ed.), 1987, *A che servono i padroni: le alternative storiche dell'industrializzazione*, Bollati Boringhieri, Milan, pp. 122-78.

9 Surendra J. Patel, 1962, 'Rates of Industrial Growth in the Last Century, 1860-1958', *Economic Development and Cultural Change*, IX: 316-30.

10 There has been some lively disagreement about the sources of the so-called second serfdom in eastern Europe in the wake of Robert Brenner's interpretive essay, 'Agrarian Class Structure and Economic Development in Pre-Industrial Europe', reprinted in T. H. Aston and C. H. E. Philpin (eds), 1985, *The Brenner Debate: Agrarian Class Structure and Economic Development in Pre-Industrial Europe*, CUP, Cambridge. The traditional explanation, which I find persuasive, emphasized the influence of the west European demand for cereals, since to grow these on large estates in a land-rich frontier region required unfree labour. Cf. the Evsey Domar model, 1970, 'The Causes of Slavery and Serfdom: A Hypothesis', *Journal of Economic History*, XXX, March 18-32, itself based on the arguments of V. Kliuchevsky, 1906 and 1937, *Kurs russkoi istorii*, English transl. by C. J. Hogarth, 1960, *A History of Russia*, New York. The model was also based on an even earlier work by Herman J. Nieboer, 1900, *Slavery as an Industrial System: Ethnological Researches*, which argues that three things cannot coexist – namely, free land, free labour, and large estates. I do not find that this necessarily contradicts the Brenner emphasis on village structures (internal *vs.* external source of change; cf. the Dobb-Sweezy debate, which hinges on a similar choice), since even if one accepts the Domar model, the question still remains how to impose and enforce serfdom. Here I would argue that political arrangements matter – not only the autonomy of the village but even more the presence or absence of autonomous cities and towns. Brenner disagrees, but I submit that two things cannot long coexist, namely labour fixed to the soil and nearby places of asylum that have the right to confer liberty (*Stadtluft macht frei*).

11 An old story, especially when the wealth takes the form of a windfall. Economists today speak of the negative consequences of windfall wealth as the Dutch disease, a reference to the impact of the discovery and exploitation of gas under the North Sea. But anyone who knows the Dutch knows that that kind of thing will not keep them down long, and the choice (and success) of the name is testimony to the historical illiteracy of some economists. A better name by far would be the Spanish

disease, with reference to the deleterious effects of New World bullion on the economy and society of Spain in the sixteenth and seventeenth centuries.

12 On the question of comparative advantage, see the provocative, iconoclastic essay of Arighi Emmanuel, 1968, *L'échange inégal: Un essai sur les antagonismes dans les rapports internationaux*, Maspero, Paris, (2d, enl. edn, 1972), translated into English, 1972, as *Unequal Exchange: A Study of the Imperialism of Trade*, Monthly Review Press, New York. See also a definitive rebuttal in the form of a lesson in economics and arithmetic by Paul Samuelson, 'Illogic of the Neo-Marxian Doctrine of Unequal Exchange', in D. A. Belsley, E. J. Kane, P. A. Samuelson, and R. M. Solow (eds), 1976, *Essays in Honor of Alice Bourneuf: Inflation, Trade, and Taxes*, Ohio State Univ. Press, Columbus, pp. 96–107.

13 It is not hard, of course, to argue that Japan seems to show the opposite, namely a successful marriage of economic development and imperial expansion. In response to which I would make two remarks: first, that in the Japanese case, the national and economic preceded the imperial (it was the power derived from nationalism and industrial development that altered the balance of power in the Far East and generated military temptation); and second, that the fundamental incompatibility between these two ambitions did show in the end, and how costly it proved! Germany is another example.

On this question of the incompatibility of bellicosity and economic development, one could also cite the more sympathetic case of Paraguay, a country bordered by hostile and at the least unfriendly, neighbours and in a state of constant diplomatic conflict and war readiness. On the eve of the great war of the Triple Alliance (1865–1870: Paraguay vs. Brazil, Argentina, and Uruguay), this umbrageous but courageous little Prussia of the South American interior had an army of 80,000 in a population of, say, 750,000 – the equivalent for France of an army of over five million, or for the Unites States, of a force of over 25 million. The combination of umbrage and courage was a very costly one. Among other things, the Brazilians and Argentines got by trade and loans the modern weapons that enabled them to kill Paraguayans more efficiently than the Paraguayans, with their long-standing hostility to foreign trade, could kill them. (There are analogies in this regard to the conflict in the 1980s between Iran and Iraq.) By the end of the war, Paraguay had lost about half its people and almost the entire male population of fighting age. In his doctoral thesis, 'Cent ans de resistance au sous-developpement' (University of Geneva, 1989), Jean Batou defends Paraguayan policy as less costly than that of those Latin American countries that 'sold out' (my words) to the temptations of trade and dependency. My own sense is that the Japanese did it better and managed to reconcile trade with development and independence; also that Paraguay could have found a more sensible strategy. The problem with Paraguay is that its leaders and people believed their own slogans – that is, they turned a political ideology into a religion. That way lies faith, passion, and apocalypse.

14 I once spent three hours in a seminar in East Berlin listening and arguing against this kind of mythology. But in those days at least (this was the early 1960s), Marxist history in East Berlin was characterized by obsequious cant and knee-jerk ideological credulity.

15 Note that Gerschenkron made much of the negative consequences of dishonesty and corruption – what we might call the lack of an honest mercantile morality – in his discussion of Russian lateness. He spoke, without saying so, on the basis of his own experience in 'the old country'. The Russian pattern was of course illustrative of a wide range of cases, typically found in polities where there is no rule of law, where anything not specifically permitted is assumed to be forbidden, where office is less function than an instrument of personal enrichment (inevitable when officials are

badly paid – they have to live too), and so on. (Max Weber said it all.) In such circumstances, corruption may be an indispensable lubricant and dishonesty a rule of the game, that is, an ordering of disorder. (A cynic might even argue that systematic mendacity, for example, is a selection process for weeding out the dopes: 'He tells me he's going to Osaka because he wants me to think he's going to Kyoto; but I know he's going to Osaka.') There is no other way to do business, and the costs of corruption have to be factored in with other, 'legitimate', costs. (Hence the dilemma faced by multinationals in 'developing' countries – bribe and run foul of anti-bribery laws at home; don't bribe and don't make money.) There may even be rough 'price lists' (legitimate illegitimacy or thieves' honour), because after all, even the taker or fixer cannot afford to ask for too much for fear of killing the goose. Miscalculations can be expensive.

2 Technological innovation and structural division in the UK locomotive building industry, 1850–1914

M. W. Kirby,
University of Lancaster

In volume I of his celebrated work on *Business Cycles* Schumpeter identified the grossly uneven pace of technological change as the critical determinant of capitalist industrial development. For Schumpeter the process of 'creative destruction' was discontinuous. His emphasis centred on the jarring effects of 'strategic' innovations as existing firms and markets moved to new production functions. This image of simultaneous imitative innovation has played a critical role in the analysis of technological change and there can be no doubting the pervasive influence of the Schumpeterian legacy.[1] One industry that gives every appearance of conforming to Schumpeter's conception is locomotive building in the UK, an industry which in the decade before 1914 ranked behind the manufacture of textile machinery as the second most important of the UK engineering trades. It is certainly the case that the industry witnessed two intensive bursts of innovation; the first in the years 1829 to 1841, and the second from 1896 to 1911. The former period was marked by the emergence of three schools of locomotive engineering.[2] The least successful, as reflected in its geographic isolation and comparatively short life, was that of Timothy Hackworth. Hackworth was locomotive engineer to the pioneering Stockton and Darlington Railway and built several types of heavy freight locomotive for the company, readily identifiable by their vertical, or steeply inclined cylinders, and single return-flue boilers. Of far greater significance were the designs of Edward Bury and Robert Stephenson all of which, in combining multitubular boilers with horizontal cylinders and crank axles, laid down the basic engineering principles for subsequent locomotive development. It was Bury's passionate commitment to the diminutive four-wheeled engine which ensured the ultimate obsolescence of his designs, and following 'the battle of the wheels' in the early 1840s, Stephenson's six-wheeled, or 2–2–2 passenger type, emerged as the clear victor.[3] In this early phase of locomotive development there were few guiding principles for design, and with engineers proceeding by trial and error, Stephenson's success was a tribute to the survival of the fittest. The second burst of innovation was marked by the introduction of new types of locomotive carrying large boilers to secure improved steaming capacity. This was a pervasive movement across the home railway system, particularly in the express passenger classes, but the most decisive developments took place at the Swindon Works of the Great Western Railway (GWR). It was here, over a period of fifteen years beginning in 1903, that we can discern most of the changes in design which distinguished the express locomotive of 1950 from that of 1875.[4]

These facts of locomotive development offer an incisive comment on any assumption of even technological progress. But they also lend support to a number of serious criticisms of the Victorian locomotive building industry advanced both by contemporary observers and more recent historians of transport and technological change. In Schumpeterian terms it has been alleged that the long intervening period between the phases of accelerated innovation, from 1850 to 1895, was one of technical stagnation for the home railway workshops, when entrepreneurial impulses within the industry were at a low ebb. The consensus view has been well summarized by the doyen of railway historians, Jack Simmons:

> the railways [after 1850] seem to exemplify the qualities of mid-Victorian Britain as a whole: a continuing energy, carried over from the tremendous upsurge in the first half of the century, coupled with a serene assumption – sometimes perhaps justified, but often dangerously complacent – that the answers were known, that there was no need to look outside for anything better. The railways had become in a high degree insular, apt to brush aside suggestions for improvement with a quiet assertion that they would not work in Britain.[5]

To this can be added the accusation levelled by Rosenberg that in comparison with American practice British locomotive builders, whether in railway company workshops or private builders' establishments, indulged in 'a needless proliferation of designs and specifications' which pre-empted standardization and hence the adoption of the technology and organization of mass production.[6] These deficiencies raised the costs of domestic railways and, in the case of the private builders where batch or 'small order' production was the custom, impaired their export competitiveness. In short, in the latter half of the nineteenth century locomotive builders in both sectors of the industry were producing 'a range of products which was beyond their organizational and technical competence'.[7]

Contemporary criticisms lend support to these views. Alfred Marshall in referring to the practice of the leading railway companies in constructing their own locomotives stated that 'It is possible that British locomotives might have nearly the same commanding position in the world as is possessed by her ship and marine engines, if British railway companies adhered more closely to the general practice of British shipowners in buying their ships'.[8] In this context Marshall cited, with approval, the opinion of *The Times* that, in comparison with 'the great joint stock companies of locomotive and rolling stock manufacturers', company workshops lacked the incentive of competition and this was reflected in inferior equipment and organization of plant.[9]

The contention that railway company workshops were less efficient than their private counterparts also found reflection in the correspondence columns of the *Railway Gazette*, where it was claimed that railway company accounts failed to show the true cost of building locomotives in company workshops by omitting key items of expenditure such as the cost of new machinery, interest on capital invested, and the depreciation of machinery, tools and plant. One critic even went so far as to claim that the only plausible condition for in-house construction of locomotives was that machinery required for repair purposes could, in theory, be deployed more effectively. In practice, however, locomotive construction always required the purchase of other more expensive machinery to maintain the unit of output, a system which entailed a considerable waste of resources.[10]

Inferior equipment, competitive inertia and commercial laxity were compounded by relative technical stagnation, which resulted mainly from the failure of company locomotive superintendents to engage in the kind of exchange of ideas and knowledge of improvements that was the norm for the private builders catering for a varied international demand. In theory, the two sectors of the industry were in an oligopolistic relationship, but in practice the insularity of railway workshops, domestically and internationally, led to the neglect or delayed adoption of foreign innovations such as the steel boiler, the pony truck, and new forms of valve gear. It also encouraged the retention of obsolete designs such as the single-driver express locomotive.[11]

This assessment is a considerable indictment of a major sector of the nineteenth century engineering industry and it certainly conforms to the view of those economic historians subscribing to the 'entrepreneurial failure' thesis. However, it is possible to adopt an alternative perspective on the industry, one that is grounded in a firmer grasp of the technological imperatives of locomotive building and which denies the central proposition that the later Victorian period was marked by culpable technical stagnation. It will be argued that in the years after 1850 the steam locomotive was the subject of sustained incremental innovation, a product of the persistent demand of railway company running departments for increased haulage power and tractive effort. In particular, it will be suggested that the phase of engineering uncertainty which afflicts any technology on its introduction persisted well after 1850 in locomotive building due to the interrelatedness or 'complementarity' of technical progress on the railways. Secondly, it will be shown that the charge of excessive insularity is misplaced – that there was in fact considerable mobility of personnel within the industry, and that this was reinforced by well-established channels for the dissemination of technical knowledge. Foreign innovations were adopted, where relevant to British operating conditions, and there was no undue delay in their diffusion. Finally, it will be argued that the decision to opt for in-house construction on the part of the home railway companies was an entirely rational response to engineering uncertainty in the early phases of railway development, and also that the bifurcated structure of the industry, although detrimental to productive efficiency and export competitiveness, was the inevitable by-product of Britain's pioneering role in railway construction both at home and abroad.

2.1 The pace of technological change

If a steam locomotive designer from the mid-nineteenth century were resurrected from the grave and confronted with a 4-6-0 express passenger locomotive newly erected in the GWR workshops at Swindon in 1910, how might his reaction be characterized? It can be safely assumed that he would be struck by three things. First, he would be viewing a wheel arrangement which did not exist in his own time and which, if not startling, would at least be new. Second, he would no doubt note the basic similarities between the GWR's latest locomotive type and the products of his own design skills half a century earlier. Horizontal firetube boilers were common to both eras, as were steam powered pistons and rods, which converted the reciprocating motions so obtained into rotary power by means of main and side rods connected to coupled driving wheels. For express passenger locomotives, moreover, trailing tenders had long been in use for carrying supplies of fuel and water required in the steam generating process. In short, while the resurrected designer might be surprised by the sheer size and power of the new locomotive, in all probability he would recognise the basic constituents and understand their functions. Lastly, if he came to examine the GWR locomotive in detail he would inevitably encounter some devices that were strange to him, although in most cases he could probably deduce their function.

This exercise in speculation is hardly suggestive of rapid and radical innovation, and the lay-observer unfamiliar with the niceties of steam locomotive design could be forgiven for assuming that the period from the 1850s to the mid-1890s had been marked by technical stagnation. Yet an objective assessment of the technical record must be grounded in a firm understanding of the nature of inventive activity. One effect of the Schumpeterian legacy has been an excessive concern with the big and spectacular – the grand inventions which through their diffusion as innovations provoke major discontinuities in economic development. However, in a careful analysis of the diffusion of technology, Rosenberg has emphasised that

> inventive activity is ... best described as a gradual process of accretion, a cumulation of minor improvements, modifications and economies, a sequence of events where, in general, continuities are much more important than discontinuities
> ...
> The fact is that the period which is looked at as encompassing the diffusion of an invention is usually much more than that, it is a period when critical inventive activity (what Usher called 'secondary inventions') and essential design improvements and modifications are still going on. Although we might be tempted to dismiss this later work as much less important than the initial technological breakthrough, there is no good *economic* reason for this attitude, for it is precisely this later work which first establishes commercial feasibility and therefore shapes the possibility for diffusion. We need to approach this whole area of research with a clearer appreciation of the continuum of innovative activity, running from initial conceptualization ... to establishment of technical feasibility (invention) to commercial feasibility (innovation) to subsequent diffusion.[12]

Powerful empirical support for this view has been provided by a number of studies, notable among them being Louis Hunter's analysis of the evolution of steamboat machinery on the Western rivers of the United States. The technical record in the nineteenth century was marked by a sequence of apparently minor design improvements such as machining shafts to hundredths instead of sixteenths of an inch, or raising the effective steam pressure by applying improved forms of cylinder packing. As Hunter concludes, developments of this kind rarely enter the historical record, 'yet they are the stuff of which mechanical progress is made, and they cannot be ignored simply because we know so little about them'.[13]

The essential point to note about the steam locomotive is that its 150 year history, from its conception to its demise as the workhorse of the overland transport system, was marked by a conservative pattern of refinement to a fundamentally sound basic design. Radical changes in technology were contemplated only towards the end of the steam era, after 1930, when locomotive manufacturers in Europe and North America began to exhibit interest in multi-cylinder 'Duplex' types and geared turbines in the search for greater power and the ever-present need to limit the damage to track caused by 'hammer-blow', wheel-bounce, and slippage.[14] It was the failure to solve the latter problems, despite the development of sophisticated laboratory techniques for investigating all problems relating to rail working, fracture and other forms of failure, which destroyed the 'machine ensemble' perfected by George and Robert Stephenson before 1850, and in so doing played a critical role in the progressive abandonment of steam traction a century later. Insofar as the steam locomotive remained an experimental machine, the ongoing process of incremental innovation, punctuated by accelerated phases, served to perpetuate the uncertainty characteristic of all innovation projects in the trial production stages. As Freeman has pointed out, 'By definition, innovations are not a homogeneous class of event' and the evolution of the steam locomotive exhibits a consistency rarely found in the history of mechanical engineering.[15]

If this perspective is applied to the UK locomotive building industry in the latter half of the nineteenth century, it is apparent that there was a succession of design improvements which were undistinguished in themselves, but cumulatively significant. These included the introduction of new wheel arrangements and effective braking systems, the raising of boiler pressure, the use of new materials in the construction of both locomotives and track, the adoption of the injector, and the application of compound cylinders.

By far the most important of these developments was the substitution of steel for wrought iron in the manufacture of wheel tyres, axles, and boilers. The use of steel for motion parts was first introduced by Krupps of Essen in 1851 and, although steel components had been widely adopted in Germany and France by the end of the decade, it was not until 1880 that the new material had won general acceptance among British locomotive builders. By that year steel was also being used in boiler construction, notably by the Crewe works of the London and North Western Railway (LNWR), but general diffusion for this purpose did not take place until the 1890s.[16] This apparent innovative lag, in terms of prevailing European standards, can be explained by reference to objective factors. Initially, a majority of locomotive builders saw no reason to abandon Yorkshire iron as the traditional construction material. In its 'Low

Moor' form it was a high quality product, noted for its strength and durability. It was also cheaper than steel. Even more significant is the fact that early British steel producers were unable to manufacture a product of consistent quality. Thus axles tended to break and boilers were subject to pitting after relatively short periods of service.[17] Deficiencies of this kind acted as powerful constraints on diffusion in an industry which placed a high premium on passenger safety and operational reliability. Once these problems had been resolved by developments in metallurgy and methods of manufacture, the new steel technology diffused rapidly and enabled heavier and more powerful locomotives to be built for a given weight, operating at progressively higher boiler pressures.

The use of steel as a constructional material highlights the interrelatedness or 'complementarity' of technical progress on the home railways. This is exemplified in the diffusion of the steel rail from the 1870s onwards. Since steel rails were far more durable, lasting ten times as long as wrought iron rails and capable of bearing far greater loads, their effect was to release locomotive engineers from a critical technical constraint on the design of heavier and more powerful locomotives. In those instances where there was a lag in the rate of diffusion, special considerations conspired to prevent the more rapid adoption of steel. The North Eastern Railway (NER), for example, did not begin to re-lay its track with a majority of steel rails until 1887, primarily because of vested interests in the form of local iron manufacturers who enjoyed powerful support at board level from Sir Isaac Lowthian Bell. For the GWR, the establishment of a rolling mill for the manufacture of iron rails at Swindon in 1861 acted as a restraining influence until the plant was closed in 1878.[18]

There is little evidence of a culpable neglect of other foreign innovations. In 1859, the French engineer Henri Giffard invented the injector for the supply of feedwater to locomotive boilers. The existing technology took the form of a steam feed pump which was not only unreliable due to problems of friction and uncertainty of action, but also difficult to maintain. There was always the possibility that a boiler would run short of water without the fact being noticed, resulting in catastrophic failure. Giffard's invention resolved all of these problems and the patent rights in the UK were taken up by the private manufacturing establishment of Sharp, Stewart and Co. (then of Manchester). Diffusion throughout the home railway system was immediate and the associated improvement in mechanical efficiency was a critical factor in facilitating the growth in size of the locomotive boiler.[19]

A far more controversial innovation also emanated from France in the form of the compound locomotive revealed by Anatole Mallet at the Paris Exhibition of 1878. The principle of compounding was based upon the utilization of all the available steam via a combination of high and low pressure cylinders. The claimed results were increased cylinder efficiency, economy in fuel consumption, a more even distribution of the strain on reciprocating parts, larger bearing surfaces for axles, and finally, 'the same freedom of running as a coupled [non-compound] engine'.[20] It is a well known fact of locomotive history that compounding was taken up enthusiastically by F. W. Webb, locomotive superintendent to Britain's 'premier line', the LNWR. Beginning in 1879, Webb designed a succession of compound locomotives for virtually all classes of use, apparently attracted by the promise of fuel economies. It is generally agreed that, despite individually impressive loco-motive performances, Webb's designs were a technical failure.[21] Operational results were meticulously recorded but Webb, an unstable megalomaniac, proved incapable of learning from experience. A far more impressive approach to compounding was adopted by the NER where in the early 1890s the locomotive superintendent, Wilson Worsdell, conducted a sequence of tests extending over 32,000 miles which compared the performance of compound locomotives with the most comparable 'simple' classes. Worsdell, who had earlier collaborated with August Von Borries of the Hanover State Railways to produce a two cylinder compound engine, tested twelve classes of locomotive. The results were generally unfavourable to compounding, except when it was applied to 'through goods' traffic. Any savings in fuel were more than offset by increased maintenance charges as a result of 'broken piston rings, steam pipe joints, and excessive wear in connecting rods and slide valves'.[22] In conse-quence the NER, unlike the LNWR, lost interest in the design and construc-tion of compound locomotives, a decision which was vindicated by the rapid and widespread diffusion after 1906 of a German invention – the high-temperature superheater. The superheater, a device for adding further heat to steam after it had been created by boiling water, proved to be a far more reliable means of improving the efficiency and performance of locomotives.[23]

Similarly with the bogie and alternative forms of valve gear, diffusion was delayed primarily because of objective conditions on the home railways. The bogie, or 'pony truck', was a device widely employed by American locomotive builders at an early stage in railway development, but only rarely on Britain's home railways before 1880. Its adoption in North America can be readily explained by the relatively poor quality of the permanent way and an extra wheeled support for the locomotive frame and boiler could be deployed with advantage to improve running quality. Britain's permanent way, however, was noted for its high quality almost from the outset of construction, thus reducing the need for the kind of wheel configuration which was to become the norm in the USA. In the 20 years after 1880, however, the bogie was widely adopted by the home railway workshops – not as a device to aid smooth running, but as a necessary accompaniment to the growing weight and length of locomotive boilers. Circumstances were comparable in the adoption of new forms of valve gear after 1895, in particular the Walschaerts type invented in Belgium in 1844. The Stephenson inside valve gear had long been standard on the home railways, but by the mid-1890s axles had so increased in diameter that eccentrics required for the Stephenson gear had reached an ungainly size. In addition, there was less room available for inside valve gears placed between the locomotive frame because of the need for additional cross bracing for heavier engines. Thus, the Walschaerts and other outside gears were adopted 'more as a matter of convenience than for their supposedly superior economies in steam distribution'.[24]

If the charge of culpable innovative lags is difficult to sustain then a more valid criticism lies in the fact that, despite Britain's pioneering role in developing steam technology during the first half of the nineteenth century, the pace of subsequent *inventive* activity was more rapid abroad – notably in

France, Germany, and the USA. Yet as Mansfield has emphasised, in terms of economic and technological progress it is innovation and its effective diffusion which are of greater significance.[25] This is not to denigrate the role of the inventor, merely to point out that in distinguishing carefully between invention and innovation Schumpeter was implying that the one might not lead to the other. The reputation of Britain's most outstanding locomotive designer, G. J. Churchward of the GWR, rests not on his gifts as an inventor, but on his bold and successful application of overseas technical developments – in particular the German (Schmidt) superheater, the American tapered boiler, and the Belgian (Belpaire) firebox.[26] As Baumol has pointed out, 'aggressive and imaginative imitation . . . is a key instrument of international technology transfer' and there can be no doubting the entrepreneurial qualities inherent in Churchward's activities.[27]

Even if Britain's locomotive designers and builders had wished otherwise, the latter half of the nineteenth century and, more especially, the years after 1870 were marked by persistent demand-side pressures which placed a high premium on the search for improved locomotive performance. In 1870 the total number of passengers carried on the home railways was 336 million: by 1900 the figure had risen to more than one billion. In freight traffic, the weight of goods and minerals conveyed rose from 235 million tons in 1880 to well over 400 million tons by 1900. The reasons for this expansion are well-known. The major underlying factor was undoubtedly rising real income levels due, in part, to cheaper imported foodstuffs. Wheat grains, refrigerated meat, and dairy produce were transported from the ports to urban markets by rail and this new category of traffic was augmented on the non-freight side by a rise in the number of passenger journeys undertaken for pleasure. Weekend excursions became increasingly common in the 1870s following a reduction in Saturday working, and also as a by-product of the decline in religious worship.[28] Increasingly, the railway companies were coming to be regarded as organizations akin to modern day public utilities. This did not, however, mean the end of competition. Until the compulsory grouping of companies in 1923, the rail traveller was confronted with a choice of routes from London to the South West, Birmingham and Manchester, and north of the border to Edinburgh and Aberdeen. With the curtailment of price competition after 1870, individual companies were obliged to safeguard their share of traffic by engaging in competition in services.[29] Thus, the first Pullman car appeared on the Midland Railway in 1874, and the first dining car on the Great Northern Railway in 1878. These were followed in the 1880s by the widespread adoption of the modern bogie carriage, paving the way for the corridor train which made its debut on the Great Eastern and GWR networks in 1891–2.[30] As Simmons has pointed out, by the 1890s service could be selected for 'speed, convenience and amenity' with even the third-class passenger enjoying the benefits of upholstered seating in well-lit, heated carriages.[31] For the railway companies and their locomotive designers, these developments had major consequences which pointed to the need for greater haulage power. Increased traffic entailed either the running of more, or heavier, trains. The avoidance of excessively congested timetables pointed to the latter. Furthermore, the more lavishly appointed rolling stock of the later nineteenth century, introduced as part of the competitive scramble for business, was considerably heavier than pre-existing types. Between 1875 and 1885 average main line carriage weights increased from between 15–20 tons to 25–30 tons, with the result that passenger expresses composed of ten or more of the latter could not be hauled at scheduled speeds without fast running downhill to the detriment of safety.[32] Initially, the problem was tackled either by double-heading from the London terminus when train weights were heaviest, or by having only a small proportion of modern rolling stock attached to each train. Both solutions were unsatisfactory – the first on grounds of cost, and the second because it greatly complicated the business of the running department, with carriages of different ages and classes being scattered across the country. A striking illustration of the effects of the need for increased haulage power and greater speeds is provided by the NER which, in the decade after 1892, introduced five new classes of main-line express locomotive in rapid succession in order to maintain its share of the Anglo-Scottish traffic.[33] The fact that each class was progressively more powerful is prima facie evidence of an excessive concern for physical efficiency, but this criticism is hardly consistent with the charge of technical stagnation.

The persistent need for more powerful and heavier locomotives was a critical factor in maintaining a regime of technolgical uncertainty for locomotive designers. This need was well reflected in a leading article published in *The Engineer* in 1886. After noting the sustained increase in boiler pressures from 120 to 175lbs over the previous fifteen years, the article pointed to the increasing capacity of cylinders. By the mid-1880s diameters were approaching 19 inches and, as a result, were beginning to pose serious constructional difficulties:

> If we . . . take an engine with 19 in. cylinders the heating surface is . . . 1400 square feet, and this divided by 60 gives . . . 23 square feet of grate. But to get such a grate into an engine of the ordinary gauge can only be done by using a fire-box of uncommon length; for taking the width of the grate at 3.3 ft., it would have to be no less than 7 ft. long . . . Such furnaces can be fired readily enough, but their use involves a serious practical difficulty quite unconnected with firing. An engine with 19 in. cylinders is pretty certain to have 7 ft. wheels and to be coupled. It must be coupled either forward or backward; and no one in this country has, to our knowledge run with a 7 ft. leading wheel . . . With a 7 ft. grate and inside cylinders, this would entail a coupling rod no less than 9 ft. 6 in. long at the very least; and this is more than any locomotive superintendent would care to risk. The only way out of the difficulty would lie in pitching the grate above the trailing axle; but this involves many objectionable features, and the result hitherto has been that the English locomotive, if coupled, is objectionably restricted in grate area.[34]

The solution profferred by *The Engineer* to these dimensional problems was to recommend the re-adoption of a design which had begun to fall out of favour with locomotive superintendents as a result of its limited tractive effort in the face of rising haulage weights. This was the single driver engine (that is, with uncoupled driving wheels) which combined smooth running with fuel efficiency and ease of maintenance. The proneness of the single driver to wheel slippage, especially in adverse weather conditions, was well known. However, a recent British innovation of startling simplicity provided an effective cure for this problem – the steam sanding apparatus – which, in directing jets of sand to the point of contact between driving wheel and rail provided sufficient adhesion to eliminate slippage.[35] During the course of the 1880s, therefore, six leading railway companies resumed construction of single driver locomotives equipping them with sand boxes and large boilers, the latter development being facilitated in part by the diffusion of the steel rail which could bear up to 20 tons on the driving wheels.[36] The reinvigoration of an obsolete design as a result of complementary technical changes provides an important insight into the regime of uncertainty inhabited by locomotive designers in a era of rapidly mounting traffic demands. Ostensibly a retrogressive development, the revival of the single driver was in reality a rational response to prevailing technical conditions which was made all the more attractive in the absence of precision methods of alignment for coupling rods and axle boxes.

2.2 The social environment of innovation

A further insight into the process of technological change in locomotive building is provided by the concept of communications networks well known to students of rural sociology.[37] According to Czepeil 'Innovation, the successful application of invention is an inherently social process of information acquisition, learning and approval. Therefore to study the innovation process we must include the social environment'.[38] Empirical studies have suggested that the flow of technical information in an industrial setting is a function of four interrelated variables: first, a coincidence of production processes suggesting a commonality of interests and problems; second, a similarity in the organization of firms and divisions of responsibility; third, the bases of competition in the industry where highly competitive industries are likely to have a low frequency of informal communications; and finally, the industry's age and maturity, in the sense that the older the industry the greater the likelihood of the recognition of common problems by a core of experienced managers. If these variables are applied to the nineteenth century railway industry it becomes clear that the charge of excessive insularity is misplaced, since an effective communications network for the dissemination of technical knowledge was established at an early stage. In the first instance the career paths of locomotive superintendents in general were characterized by extensive movement around the home railway system. This pattern is well illustrated in Hamilton Ellis's seminal study of locomotive engineers.[39] Thomas William Worsdell, for example, was first employed in the carriage and wagon department at the Crewe works of the LNWR in the early 1850s. After a short period of service he was apprenticed to his uncle's mechanical engineering firm in Birmingham. He then returned to Crewe, but in 1860 was appointed manager of an engineering works in Birmingham. In 1865, he took up employment with the Pennsylvania Railroad in the USA and was soon appointed 'master mechanic' at the company's Altoona workshops responsible for locomotive construction. In 1871 he returned to Crewe as works manager, but left the LNWR for the third and last time in 1881, having been appointed locomotive superintendent of the Great Eastern Railway. In 1885 he was appointed locomotive superintendent of the NER's workshops at Gateshead and Darlington. Varied career paths, embracing periods of service outside the home railway workshops and extensive movement between them, were not unusual in the nineteenth century. They are difficult to reconcile with the charge of insularity, all the more so since analysis of the technical record of individual workshops well illustrates the crucial role of external design influences and traditions.[40] It is also worth noting that two of the most prolific innovators of the pre–1914 era – F. W. Webb of the LNWR and G. J. Churchward of the GWR – had little or no experience outside their respective workshops, yet this was entirely consistent with an unusual degree of receptivity to foreign innovations.

The reference to design traditions highlights another distinctive feature of the nineteenth century locomotive engineering profession. In structure it was remarkably cohesive in view of its close familial nature. Fathers, sons and brothers were liberally employed throughout the home railway workshops occupying, for the most part, senior positions. Prominent among these engineering dynasties were the Adams, Armstrongs, Beatties, Billintons, Drummonds, Gooches, Hackworths, Holdens, Stirlings, Trevithicks and Worsdells.[41] Unless it is assumed that family connections pre-empted informal communications and the discussion of technical issues, it seems reasonable to suppose that these family links facilitated, in some degree, the process of technological diffusion. It is important to note, however, that informal communications networks were buttressed by more formal channels for the dissemination of technical knowledge. In his study of the British engineering profession, R. A. Buchanan has focused attention on the role of professional institutions. The decisive development in this respect was the foundation in 1816 of the Institution of Civil Engineers. Its main activities were:

> the programme of weekly meetings through which, as a result of the regular publication of its proceedings, the members of the Institution continued to conduct an impressive amount of self-education. The papers presented and discussed, week by week, comprised the core function of the Institution, and there can be no doubt that they maintained a steady production of high-quality technical information on matters of great current interest to the professional engineers of the day.[42]

In 1847 the Institution of Mechanical Engineers (IME) was founded, reflecting the growing importance in the economy of the locomotive engineer and other builders of steam engines for marine propulsion and industrial power. The IME was operated from the outset on the same principles as its sister institution, with the reading of learned papers and the annual publication of proceedings. By the mid–1860s most of the senior mechanical engineering personnel employed by the home railways and the private locomotive builders were members of the IME – some were members of both institutions.[43] Similar functions were fulfilled by the Institution of Engineers and Shipbuilders in Scotland founded in 1856 by Walter M. Neilson, owner of the private locomotive manufacturing establishment of Neilson and Co. of Glasgow.[44] In a major sense these institutional developments transformed specialist engineering knowledge into a public good via procedures which were akin to academic discourse.[45] The fact that considerable income could be generated from patents acted as an incentive for engineers to use institutional lectures as a means of disseminating knowledge of technical advances. A similar function was fulfilled by the specialist engineering press which emerged after 1850. The periodicals, *Engineering* and *The Engineer*, provided an effective communications network for the dissemination of technical knowledge about current locomotive practice at home and abroad. Detailed line drawings of new types of locomotive introduced by company workshops and private builders alike were featured regularly, and *The Engineer* in particular offered informal editorial comment on both British and foreign locomotive standards and practice. The rise of international industrial and commercial exhibitions, moreover, provided locomotive engineers with a direct means of appraising differing locomotive types. There can be little doubt that it was the display of Mallet's locomotive at the Paris Exhibition of 1878 that first alerted F. W. Webb to the possibilities of compounding.

Finally, there is firm evidence of the existence by the end of the nineteenth century of a network of informal communications between the locomotive superintendents of the principal home railway workshops. Published railway company accounts reproduced a considerable amount of technical information which facilitated direct comparisons between the home railway workshops on such key indicators of performance as earnings per engine and per train mile, average repair and renewal costs, and average costs per engine. The relevant statistics were carefully tabulated by locomotive superintendents.[46] But in addition to published statistics, the surviving records of the railway companies provide firm evidence of interpersonal communications between locomotive superintendents. Thus, in 1895 Henry Matthewman, the recently appointed superintendent to the Great Northern Railway, in addressing an appeal to the company's Kings Cross management for extra locomotives based his case on 'statistical information privately exchanged by all the Locomotive Engineers of the Kingdom and which does not appear in the published accounts'.[47] Personal communications between locomotive superintendents ranged from queries concerning such comparatively minor issues as the supply and cost of yellow grease, to requests for information on the factors governing locomotive renewal and replacement.[48] These information flows certainly point to a commonality of interests in locomotive engineering, in part, the result of the non-competitive relationship enjoyed by the home railway workshops.

2.3 The structure of industry

In an international setting the distinguishing feature of the British locomotive building industry was its bifurcated structure between the home railway workshops and the private builders. It is true that foreign railway companies, such as the PLM and Est in France and the Pennsylvania Railroad in the USA, built their own locomotives, but these were the exceptions to the general rule of purchase from outside suppliers. It has already been indicated that the home railway companies were severely censured by contemporary commentators for their 'own-build' policy in the light of allegations of comparative inefficiency and high production costs.

Before examining these charges it should be noted that the decision of the leading railway companies to opt for 'in-house' construction was not the production of perverse logic or the irrational design pretensions of individual locomotive superintendents. The policy emerged in the later 1840s when the railway mania was at its height and the private builders stretched to the limit of capacity. With substantial increases in route mileage in prospect, therefore, it was only to be expected that locomotive superintendents should press the case for workshop construction, especially when the private builders were reluctant to tender for batch production or to direct capacity to the manufacture of replacement components for pre-existing locomotive classes. It is also the case that, while company workshops had originally been established for the mundane purpose of servicing locomotives, the nature of railway operations – the need to adhere to strict timetables and to offer a reliable service – soon resulted in the organization of comprehensive repair facilities focusing initially upon boiler and frame replacement. In view of the technical simplicity of the early railway locomotive, therefore, and as company workshops began to engage in the more ambitious task of re-building engines, it was but a short step to 'in-house' construction. The desire to monitor construction closely was a further incentive for the introduction of an 'own-build' policy, all the more so when design and construction together enhanced the prospect for producing a locomotive stock which was closely geared to the requirements of individual companies at a time when the quality of the permanent way was variable, and when standardization of key items of equipment such as turntables was notable for its absence.[49] Finally, there were considerations of cost. As company records reveal, the decision to opt for in-house construction could be prompted by the claim advanced by locomotive superintendents that a cheaper product of equivalent technical standard and finish could be produced in workshops than in the private builders' manufactories.[50] The extant evidence on comparative costs indicates that this claim was indeed borne out in practice with a differential in price in favour of the company workshop which could amount to £400 on the quotation price of a £2000 locomotive in the 1880s.[51] Whether the company price included a proper allowance for depreciation is open to question, although in the case of the NER where the statistical records are unusually rich, a fixed allowance was made for 'general charges' calculated as equivalent to 15 per cent of total wages per engine built.[52] On the GWR the equivalent figure, embracing 'Rates and Taxes on Factory, and Interest on Capital Outlay for land, works and equipment', was 12 per cent of total wages.[53]

Analysis of nineteenth century accounting practices is fraught with difficulty, but to the extent that the procedures of the NER and GWR were replicated elsewhere, the railway companies are exonerated from the contemporary criticism of making *no* allowance for fixed charges. Lack of statistical data, however, precludes a firm judgement on the issue. The same applies to the issue of the comparative efficiency of the company workshops and private builders. S. B. Saul, citing contemporary accounts, has described the best of the former as 'very advanced in equipment and practice', a judgement which he also applies to the private builders.[54] Such a view does not take the issue very far. What does seem certain, however, is that whatever the relative standard of technical equipment, both sectors of the industry existed in a state of mutual handicap in respect of access to scale economies. For the home railway companies effective standardization of locomotive classes could begin to take place only after the locomotive had attained technological maturity – and that was dependent upon complementary innovations else-where, in the construction of the permanent way, and in signalling and braking techniques. It was also related to some degree of traffic stability following on the sustained expansion of the later Victorian period. It is no coincidence that the first steps towards effective standardization were achieved in the Swindon workshops of the GWR after 1903.[55] Company workshops were not private empires, but there can be no denying that in the period to 1900 they conspired to produce a seemingly endless proliferation of engine types and classes constructed in quantities so small as to preclude the achievement of scale economies. Type proliferation inhibited greater capital intensity in the produc-tive process. With few exceptions the use of jigs and sophisticated machine tools could not be justified, with adverse consequences for labour productivity, and this was compounded by the limited prospects for subcontracting to specialist suppliers. Operating costs, moreover, were inflated as company workshops were obliged to service and repair non-standard types. The product may have been of superlative engineering quality, but it played its part in reducing the profitability of the home railway companies and in raising the overall cost of transport services to the detriment of the economy as a whole.[56] A promising development was the decision of the LNWR in the early 1870s to build locomotives for general sale in the UK. Of all building establishments, the company's Crewe workshops went furthest in the nineteenth century in the pursuit of standardization, and it is possible that, if the company's entry into the open market had not been frustrated by an injunction served on behalf of a consortium of private builders,[57] the Crewe experiment could have had the effect of encouraging other company workshops to build for sale – with beneficial effects on their productive efficiency.

The sensitivity of the private builders to the competitive threat posed by the Crewe works can be readily explained by the uncertainty of their market position. By the mid-1870s, in-house construction of locomotives by the railway companies had reached the point where the private builders were being treated as a reserve source of supply in times of full capacity working. Increasingly, firms such as Robert Stephenson and Co., Beyer-Peacock, and the Vulcan Foundry were becoming dependent upon overseas markets. The long term consequences were graphically portrayed in 1951 in a PEP report on the industry:

> British firms make engines to burn every grade of coal, wood and oil and to run on every type of gauge; for the South American market alone, engines have been designed for six different gauges, from 3 ft. to 5 ft. 6 in. Innumerable other local characteristics such as the quality of the water, its availability, the curvature of the track, gradients, the strength of the bridges, the height of station platforms, the climate, and the density of the traffic play an important part in determining designs ... Many railway administrations have their own consulting engineers whose

preferences and prejudices are strongly coloured by personal experience as well as by local practice. On the ground, often justified, that they are more keenly aware of their railway's needs than are the locomotive manufacturers, they sometimes insist on specifications unwarranted from a constructional point of view.[58]

If overseas orders had been for large, standard runs of locomotives the adverse effect of differing physical conditions and the irrationality of consulting engineers on productive efficiency would have been mitigated. In practice, however, overseas sales were invariably made in small batches. In the case of Beyer-Peacock, for example, in the period 1880-9 the firm successfully tendered for 272 contracts, of which 178 emanated from foreign railways. For the latter the average number of locomotives in each order was four (NRM, Beyer-Peacock Orders).[59] This experience was typical.[60] Unable to depend upon a stable home market, unlike the large American and German builders, private manufacturers failed to achieve scale economies. Specialization for particular markets made some contribution to standardization, but in general terms the wide market range, in combination with small orders and markedly divergent engineering specifications, rendered the British industry susceptible to predatory foreign competition. The amalgamation of Sharp Steward, Dubs, and Neilson, Reid and Co. of Glasgow in 1903 to form the North British Locomotive Company, far from being a sign of strength in the industry, was in reality a defensive merger prompted by increasing foreign incursions into the Indian market. It is significant that when Britain's staple industries as a whole were enjoying booming export markets in the decade before 1914, the chairman's speeches to shareholders were invariably couched in gloomy terms with recurring references to the intensity of foreign competition and short time working in the company's plants. Annual profits for the constituent companies in the five years before the merger averaged £284,000. Post-merger profits in the period 1904-12 averaged only £138,000 (exclusive of depreciation charges), with the workforce falling in numbers from 7,999 to 6,216 in the years 1907-10.[61]

Always a staunch defender of British locomotive builders, *The Engineer*, noting the rise of American competition, commented:

> In the United States the ruling principle is to turn out the largest possible quantity of work at the lowest possible price. In this country the rule is to turn out the smallest possible quantity for the highest possible price . . . We do not mean that American work is rubbish because it is cheap. What we do mean is that American locomotive builders do all they can to reduce the cost of construction . . . the great firms construct engines to certain standard patterns and they say to the purchaser, 'There are half a dozen types from which you can choose; if you find nothing to suit you among them we must ask you to try some other maker.'. One result is that it is possible to build to stock, a thing that no English or Scottish firm dares to do except on a very small scale indeed, and by building to stock they can execute orders promptly.[62]

Some American firms had the reputation for only rarely accepting export orders for less than fifty locomotives and for refusing to build to close specifications.[63] Such a strategy was clearly dependent upon the existence of a large and secure home market which conferred access to scale economies. Lacking such a market, UK builders found it increasingly difficult to quote prices low enough and delivery dates short enough to obtain the very few large orders which the export market offered. A less fragmented home railway system in which in-house construction was the rarity rather than the norm would, in all probability, have enhanced the competitiveness of the private builders and rebounded to the advantage of the economy as a whole – via lower transport costs and higher export earnings.

2.4 Conclusion

The counterfactual scenario of a more cohesive home railway system should not be taken as an implied criticism of the Victorian locomotive building industry. It is true that the rationalization of locomotive fleets which followed in the wake of the compulsory grouping of railway companies in the early 1920s, and the decision of the nationalized British Railway Board to confine new construction to twelve standard classes,[64] provide some indication of the foregone opportunities in respect of the exploitation of scale economies and the co-ordination of the locomotive stock before 1914. But such standardization was dependent, in part, on the technological maturity of the railway locomotive and, more fundamentally, the willingness of government to depart from the liberal economic order. As Sidney Pollard has argued, 'If industry is hamstrung by institutional constraints only the government can be expected to alter the institutional framework'.[65] The fact that the later Victorian state remained hostile to large scale amalgamations between the railway companies meant that access to scale economies was limited. The bifurcated structure of locomotive building, moreover, was the logical outcome of Britain's pioneering role in railway development both at home and abroad. It certainly imposed real costs on the economy, but the efficiency loss was offset to some extent by the innovative record of the home railway workshops, buttressed by effective channels for the diffusion of technology.

Notes

1 Schumpeter, J. A., 1939, *Business Cycles*, McGraw Hill, New York; Schmookler, J., 1962, 'Changes in industry and the state of knowledge as determinants of industrial innovation', in *The rate and direction of innovative activity: economic and social factors*, special conference 13, Princeton University Press, Princeton; Solow, R., 1957, 'Technical change and the aggregate production function', *Review of Economics and Statistics*, 39: 312–20; Denison, E. F., 1962, *The sources of economic growth in the United States*, Committee for Economic Development, New York; Baumol, W. J. 1988, 'Is entrepreneurship always productive?', *Journal of Development Planning*, 18: 85–94.

2 Ahrons, E. L., 1927, *The British steam railway locomotive, 1825–1925*, Locomotive Publishing Company, London, pp. 33–64.

3 Warren, J. G. H., 1923, *A century of locomotive building by Robert Stephenson*

and Company, 1823-1923, Newcastle upon Tyne, pp. 40–65; Ahrons, op. cit., pp. 34–5.

4 Westwood, J. N., 1977, *Locomotive designers in the age of steam*, Sidgwick and Jackson, London, pp. 125–32.

5 Simmons, Jack, 1978, *The railway in England and Wales:* vol. 1: *the system and its working*, Leicester University Press, Leicester, p. 177.

6 Rosenberg, N., 1970, 'Economic development and the transfer of technology: some historical perspectives', *Technology and Culture*, 11: 561.

7 Ibid, 562.

8 Marshall, Alfred, 1927, *Industry and trade*, Macmillan, London, p. 323.

9 *The Times*, 23 August 1911.

10 *Railway Gazette*, 23 July 1909.

11 Simmons, op. cit., pp. 176–7.

12 Rosenberg, N., *Perspectives on technology*, Cambridge University Press, Cambridge, pp. 7–8.

13. Hunter, L., 1949, *Steamboats on the Western rivers*, Harvard University Press, Cambridge, Mass., pp. 121–2.

14 Duffy, M. C., 1983, 'Mechanics, thermodynamics and locomotive design: the machine ensemble and the development of industrial thermodynamics', *History and Technology*, 1: 45–78; 1986, 'Rail stresses, impact loading and steam locomotive design', *History of technology: ninth annual volume*, Mansell, London, pp. 43–101.

15 Freeman, C., 1974, *The economics of industrial innovation*, Pelican, Harmondsworth, pp. 222–7.

16 Reed, B., 1982, *Crewe locomotive works and its men*, David and Charles, Newton Abbot, p. 103.

17 Ahrons, op. cit., p. 166.

18 Brooke, D., 1986, 'The advent of the steel rail', *Journal of Transport History*, 7(1): 18–31.

19 Ahrons, E. L., 1914, *The development of British locomotive design*, Locomotive Publishing Company, London, p. 132; *The Engineer*, 31 August 1923.

20 Jackson, G. G., c. 1929, *British locomotives: their evolution and development*, Sampson Low, Marston, London, p. 30.

21 Nock, O. S., 1952, *The premier line: the story of London and North Western locomotives*, Ian Allan, London, pp. 63–123; Marshall, J., 1978, *A biographical dictionary of railway engineers*, David and Charles, Newton Abbot, pp. 96–106; Reed, op. cit., pp. 83–127.

22 Public Record Office (PRO), RAIL 527/1396 (North Eastern Railway), Report with reference to the working of compound engines compared with the working of other classes of engine on the North Eastern Railway (3 vols.), November 1893.

23 Sinclair, Angus, 1970, *Development of the locomotive engine*, MIT Press, Cambridge, Mass., pp. 664–5.

24 White, J. R., 1970, 'The final years of the steam locomotive in America', in Sinclair, Angus, op. cit., p. 665.

25 Mansfield, E., 1968, *The economics of techical change*, Norton, New York, pp. 83–130, *passim*.

26 Kirby, M. W., 1988, 'Product proliferation in the British locomotive building industry 1850-1914: an engineer's paradise?', *Business History*, 30(3), p. 304.

27 Baumol, op. cit., p. 85.

28 Eversley, D. E. C., 1957, 'The Great Western Railway and the Swindon works in the Great Depression', *University of Birmingham Historical Journal*, 5(2): 180; Dyos, H. J., and Aldcroft, D. H., 1974, *British transport: an economic survey from the seventeenth century to the twentieth*, Pelican, Harmondsworth, pp. 156–8.

29 Cain, P. J., 1972, 'Railway combination and government, 1900–14', *Economic History Review*, 25(4): 623–6.
30 Behrend, G., 1962, *Pullman in Europe*, Longman, London; Hamilton Ellis, C., 1965, *Railway Carriages of the British Isles from 1830–1914*, Hutchinson, London.
31 Simmons, op. cit., p. 199.
32 Kidner, R. W., 1947, *A short history of mechanical traction, vol. 2, rail*, Oakwood Press, Chislehurst, pp. 81–104.
33 Irving, R. J., 1976, *The North Eastern Railway Company 1870–1914: an economic history*, Leicester University Press, Leicester, p. 94.
34 *The Engineer*, 13 August 1986.
35 Dow, G., 1950, *British steam horses*, Phoenix House, London, p. 29; Freezer, C. J., 1977, *Locomotives in outline: G.W.R.*, Peco Publications, Seaton, Devon, p. 15.
36 Ahrons, 1927, op. cit., pp. 294–5.
37 Rogers, E. M. and Shoemaker, F. F., 1971, *Communication of innovations: a cross cultural approach*, Free Press, New York.
38 Czepeil, J. A. (1979), 'Communications networks and innovation in industrial communities', in Baker, M. J. (ed.), *Industrial innovation: technology, policy, diffusion*, Macmillan, London, pp. 312–3.
39 Hamilton Ellis, C., 1958, *Twenty locomotive men*, Ian Allan, London.
40 Ahrons, 1927, op. cit., *passim*.
41 Nock, O. S., *Steam locomotive: a retrospect on the work of eight great locomotive engineers*, British Transport Commission, London; Ransome-Wallis, R. (ed.), 1959, *The . . . encyclopaedia of world railway locomotives*, Hutchinson, London, *passim*.
42 Buchanan, R. A., 1989, *The engineers: a history of the engineering profession in Britain 1750–1914*, Jessica Kingsley, London, pp. 73–4.
43 Ransome-Wallis, *passim*; Marshall, J., *passim*.
44 University of Glasgow Archives, UGD10/50/1 (Neilson and Co.) 'Dates and notes of the principal occurrences of my life', by Colonel Walter Montgomerie Neilson of Queenshall.
45 Noll, F. C., 1967, National associations, in Warner, W. L. (ed.), *The emergent American society, vol. 1, Large scale organizations*, Yale University Press, New Haven, pp. 276–313; Martilla, J. A., 1971, Word of mouth communications in the industrial adoption process, *Journal of Marketing Research*, 8:177–8.
46 PRO RAIL 491/880/881 (Midland Railway), Analysis of railway companies' accounts, 1871–1912; RAIL 527/1417 (North Eastern Railway), Locomotive expenses, various railways, 1875–1914.
47 PRO RAIL 254/52 (Great Western Railway), Correspondence of locomotive superintendent.
48 PRO RAIL 254/52 (Great Western Railway), Correspondence of locomotive superintendent; RAIL 527/1454 (North Eastern Railway), Correspondence of locomotive superintendent, 1885–95.
49 Kirby, op. cit., p. 291.
50 PRO RAIL 254/52 (Great Western Railway), Correspondence of locomotive superintendent.
51 PRO RAIL 236/674 (Great Western Railway), Correspondence of locomotive superintendent; RAIL 491/879 (Midland Railway), Analysis of railway companies' accounts; RAIL 527/1418 (North Eastern Railway), Cost of all new engines built by NER, 1881–1919.
52 PRO RAIL 527/1397 (North Eastern Railway), Locomotive Statistics, 1880–1904.
53 PRO RAIL 254/19 (Great Western Railway), Cost of rolling stock purchased compared with cost of constructing similar stock at Swindon works.
54 Saul, S. B., 1967, 'The market and the development of the mechanical engineering

industries in Britain 1960–1914', *Economic History Review*, 20(1): 111–30; 1970, *Technological change: the United States and Britain in the nineteenth century*, Methuen, London, pp. 148–9.

55 Kirby, op. cit., pp. 296–7; Larkin, E. J., and Larkin, J. G., 1988, *The railway workshops of Britain 1823–1986*, Macmillan, London, *passim*.

56 Kirby, op. cit., *passim*.

57 Chaloner, W. H., 1950, *The social and economic development of Crewe 1790–1923*, Manchester University Press, Manchester, p. 73.

58 Political and Economic Planning (PEP), 1951, *Locomotives: a report on the industry*, PEP, London, pp. 51–2. See also Saul, S. B., 1968, 'The engineering industry', in Aldcroft, D. H. (ed.), *The Development of British industry and foreign competition 1875–1914*, George Allen and Unwin, London, pp. 231–2.

59 Beyer-Peacock and Co., Order Books, National Railway Museum Archives, York.

60 Warren, op. cit., *passim*.

61 University of Glasgow Archives, Deloitte Papers, UGD, 109/2/5 (North British Locomotive Company), Financial Statistics, 1903–13.

62 *The Engineer*, 10 December 1897.

63 PEP, op. cit., pp. 51–52.

64 Cox, E. S., 1946, 'A modern locomotive history: ten years development on the L.M.S., 1923–1932', paper read before the Institution of Locomotive Engineers.

65 Pollard, Sidney, 1989, *Britain's prime and Britain's decline 1870–1914*, Edward Arnold, London, p. 258.

3 Destabilizing influences in the European economy in the 1920s

Derek H. Aldcroft,
University of Leicester

3.1 Introduction

On the eve of the First World War Sir Edward Grey, the then foreign secretary, observed, 'The lamps are going out all over Europe; we shall not see them lit again in our lifetime.'[1] And indeed, for the next thirty years or more the lamps remained extinguished.

The First World War shattered the unity of Europe and sapped her economic strength. Her influence in the world economy declined as the centre of gravity shifted westwards. Reconstruction and recovery in the 1920s was a painful and protracted affair. The subsequent world depression and then another world war put paid to any attempts to restore her former status. Not until the 1950s did the lights begin to shine again on the European landscape.

The decade following the First World War was, in many ways, crucial from the point of view of Europe's long-term future. Both politically and economically the situation was fluid and unstable. The 1920s have been described in a variety of terms: a period of 'false stability',[2] 'an era of illusions',[3] 'a period of surface harmony and apparent economic prosperity',[4] and 'years of hope and vigour' which 'ended in despair'.[5] All denote a failure to regain stability and composure.

Why did Europe fail to reassert herself in the 1920s? It is unlikely that the direct impact of the war can be held solely responsible for the failure despite the fact that it resulted in considerable losses and destruction, the upset of normal trading relationships, and the curtailment of economic growth for several years. After all, the even more traumatic experience of the 1940s did not leave Europe immobilised for long. In fact, a decade after the Second World War found Europe in a much stronger and more viable position than she had ever been at any time during the 1920s.

The war itself was not, we shall argue, what really mattered; rather it was what came afterwards that determined the subsequent fate of the continent. It was primarily the actions of statesmen and policymakers in the aftermath of hostilities which were to blame for Europe's weakened state and which left her vulnerable to external shocks and exposed to internal collapse. The manner in which this happened can be illustrated by examining the response to a number of key issues thrown up by the war and which were not resolved satisfactorily. In particular we shall discuss four chief policy matters:

1. The post-war settlement of Europe.
2. The reconstruction failure.
3. The treatment of Germany.
4. The currency stabilization question.

In each case the policy reaction to these issues did more to divide and destabilize than to unite Europe and, in the longer term, they provided the overture to the Second World War.

3.2 The reshaping of Europe

Keynes, in his vitriolic denunication of the peace, argued that statesmen failed to appreciate the fragility of the economic and financial mechanism that had been shattered by war, or the fact that the pre-1914 international economy had been inherently unstable. The situation, he claimed, demanded a settlement that would avert the threat of revolution by restoring international economic stability.[6] In reality, the settlement which eventually emerged destroyed the unity of Europe and hampered the progress of reconstruction.

The peacemaking exercise comprised two major features: heavy penalties were imposed on the vanquished, and extensive territorial changes were made in Central and Eastern Europe. In the latter context it was, as Thompson notes, the biggest exercise in the reshaping of the political geography of Europe ever undertaken.[7] Effectively it led to the geographic disintegration of Europe and undermined the former balance of power. Germany lost substantial territory, as did several other countries, while the Austro–Hungarian Empire was dismembered. In its place emerged several weak and uneconomic states, each with acute political and social tensions. The former Monarchy may not have been perfect but it did at least have some semblance of political and economic coherence, while at the same time acting as a bulwark between eastern and western powers. By 1920 the political and economic unity of East/ Central Europe had vanished, leaving a power vacuum in the region which effectively provided the seedbed for the Second World War. Newman, for example, stresses the crucial role of the region in determining the future distribution of power throughout the whole of Europe and, ultimately, the fate of the continent. In time, the vacuum was bound to be filled by a predator nation, since the new or reconstituted states were 'extremely weak reeds to place in the path of Germany, and they possessed few features that could lead to any hope of their being anything but satellites . . . of Germany, Hitler or no Hitler.[8] The battle for the control of the region enjoined France and Germany from almost the first moment of peace. That Germany became the obvious predator nation may be deduced from the following considerations:

1. Her rebuff at Versailles by the Allied powers;
2. Her desire to regain great power status by restoring her lost territories and

expanding eastwards, both evident in Germany's foreign policy in the 1920s; and

3. The inability or reluctance of France and Britain to tackle the Eastern question positively.

If ethnic and economic considerations were deemed to be important in recasting the map of Europe, there is precious little to show for them. Few of the emerging states in the region were really strong enough to stand alone. Nationality and territorial squabbles, together with weak administrations, raise doubts even as to their claim to national status. Economically they were far worse off than before the war. From the past they inherited 'a gigantic backlog of backwardness'[9] to which was added the chaos following hostilities, the loss of a large internal market and the impact of new boundaries. Komlos claims that the consequences, for the splintered territories, of the destruction of the Central European common market were little short of disastrous.[10] In redefining the map of Europe, short shrift was given to economic factors. For the most part the new territorial units made little economic sense, merely serving to impede reconstruction and recovery. The economic potential inherited by the successor states bore little relation to the inheritance of land and people.[11] The new states acquired various fragments of territory at different stages of development and comprising assorted ethnic minorities, which were extremely difficult to weld together into viable and cohesive political and economic units. Poland, for example, had the unenviable task of integrating three different segments previously under alien rulers into one single state. Yugoslavia inherited five diverse railway systems with four different gauges, each serving separate centres. Austria and Hungary had the problem of making sense of the remnants left to them of their Empire, shorn of some of the most valuable assets.

It may be argued, therefore, that the new territorial arrangements in East and Central Europe created more problems than they solved. They weakened Europe politically and economically at a time when a large part of the continent was already destitute. The task of reconstruction was a virtually insuperable one – given the lack of resources and backwardness, the break-up of former trading connections, the social tensions, and the clash of ethnic personalities.

3.3 The failure of reconstruction

Ironically, having caused such mischief, the major powers then soon withdrew from the scene. Apart from famine and relief deliveries in the immediate post-war period (which were totally inadequate), there was never any serious attempt to plan the reconstruction of Europe.[12] The United States had no desire to get embroiled in the affairs of Europe on a permanent basis, while Allied co-operation disintegrated soon after the war – partly as a result of Anglo-American rivalry.[13] The sharp boom followed by deflationary action in the Anglo-Saxon countries of the 1919–21 period further added to the difficulties of war-torn Europe.

Left to fend for themselves, many countries were forced to reconstruct their economies as best they could. Weak governments facing insuperable problems inevitably resorted to extreme methods, such as trade control, inflation and currency depreciation. Pre-empting private claims on resources through a price inflation tax was a convenient, albeit temporary, way of easing budgetary difficulties and the low capacity problem at a time of acute social tension. Thus, apart from Czechoslovakia who stabilized her currency quite early, East/Central Europe went in for inflationary financing and currency depreciation in a big way. There is still some debate as to how far such policies were deliberate, and even more discussion of the consequences. My own view is that the costs eventually outweighed the benefits. It is true that inflation and currency depreciation initially gave a boost to economic activity, employment and exports, but once it got out of hand it probably did more harm than good. Forced industrialization gave rise to inefficient undertakings and excess capacity as money fled into assets, regardless of their long-term productive value. Moreover, as in the case of Germany, when stabilization and financial control were finally implemented, employment and output fell. By 1925 industrial output in the region was still well down on 1913, in some cases appreciably so. The only country to show solid advance was Czechoslovakia, one of the few countries to have done well out of the peace settlement.[14]

Whether there were any real alternatives to the policies pursued is debatable, given the dire straits of the countries in question. What is clear, however, is that the drastic measures resorted to did little to solve the fundamental problems of the region. As the League of Nations noted in one of its later reports, the whole economic and social fabric of many countries was allowed to rot away and 'when it was finally faced, it had ceased to be a general problem of transition and reconstruction and had become a problem of cutting the gangrene out of the most affected areas.'[15] Eventually, therefore, when stabilization was finally achieved, reconstruction had to begin afresh – and this time with the assistance of private foreign lending. This, as we shall see, posed a further threat to the stability of the region as countries became increasingly indebted at a time of weakening commodity prices. When capital imports dried up at the end of the decade, their vulnerability was readily exposed.

3.4 The German question

Germany emerged from the war in an anomalous position. On the one hand, she had lost the war and as a consequence she had to pay the price of defeat. On the other hand, she could by no means be written off as a great power. The country still had enormous potential, and the removal of the Austro-Hungarian Empire and the nationality principle in peacemaking actually strengthened her position on the European continent.[16] Germany therefore became a destabilizing influence in Europe, not so much because of inherent weaknesses but more because of the consequences subsequently arising from the penalties imposed on the transgressor. These included

1. territorial and asset losses;
2. security provisions including demilitarization and occupation of key zones in Germany; and

3. reparations for war damages.

In time all three were whittled down by successive German governments so that Germany never fulfilled anything approaching the original demands made upon her. But in reality this was neither here nor there, since the damage had already been done. The imposition on Germany of what seemed to be an impossible burden, including a war guilt clause, meant that from the very beginning the German nation harboured a burning resentment against the victors. Germany was, therefore, determined to avenge herself for this ignominious treatment.

The most crucial issue was undoubtedly that of reparations. The subject has given rise to an enormous debate, which still goes on, much of it centred on the question of whether Germany could or could not pay the sums demanded. In a recent lengthy contribution to the subject, Bruce Kent maintains that the chief fault lay in the network of inter-allied financial claims arising out of the war, which were used as 'a diversionary smokescreen' by conservative statesmen of the time 'largely to deflect a widespread popular demand for genuine post-war reconstruction and to pre-empt confiscatory taxation'. The allies were not therefore prepared to make concessions to one another, nor ultimately to Germany, so long as the chief creditor, the United States, demanded full settlement of the sums owed to her. Thus reparations were destined to remain 'a running sore' in so far as they were used to serve the political interests of the creditors at the expense of European construction and stabilization.[17]

The implicit notion that reparations 'at any price' were untenable is not altogether convincing however. For, as Fischer points out, it is easy to overrate and misinterpret the latter problem. The apparent insolubility of the reparations issue lay not in the absence of productive potential in Germany from which to pay – as least as far as the modified schedule of payments of 1924 is concerned – but in the political and psychological unwillingness on the part of Germany to accept war guilt and reparations in the first place.[18]

The solution to the problem was further complicated in the early years by virtue of the fact that the Allied powers failed to speak with one voice when dealing with Germany's future and the burden of reparations. The initial financial stipulations under the peace treaty certainly proved exacting. Germany was to pay 20 billion gold marks by 1 May 1921, a sum which would have absorbed well over ten per cent of her national income in the years 1919–1922. The London Schedule of May 1921 reduced this to an annuity of three billion gold marks, or some five to six per cent of national income for the years 1921–23. According to Holtfrerich, the actual expenditure out-turn on reparations for 1919–22 amounted to 13.2 billion gold marks – under ten per cent of national income.[19] The latter total is probably excessive,[20] but whatever the exact figure was, it was no small sum – and not one which the Germans were prepared to accept without strong protest. When verbal onslaught failed the protest took the form, advocated by some as early as 1919, of an overt demonstration that it was impossible to pay, by resorting to the printing press. As Holtfrerich writes: '. . . threatened by Allied sanctions on the one hand and by the disintegration of the Reich on the other, no German government could have complied with Reparations demands in any way other than resort to the printing of money.[21] The final collapse of the currency came in 1923, following the Ruhr occupation by the French and Belgians on the pretext of a minor shortfall in reparation payments.

An earlier and more moderate settlement of the reparations question might have eased the situation, though it is a somewhat moot point given the bitterness in Germany about reparations. What matters however is the situation as it unfolded, that is the link between reparations and inflation and the consequences flowing therefrom. Some recent historians have been more favourably disposed to the beneficial impact of the German inflation, at least in terms of the way in which it stimulated economic activity and employment in contrast to the deflationary climate in the Anglo-Saxon countries in the early 1920s.[22] Others incline to the less optimistic view of earlier writers.[23] It is true that modest inflations can confer real economic benefits,[24] but once inflation gets out of control it probably does more harm than good. Moreover, as Gordon has demonstrated, there are very few examples of cost-free anti-inflation medicines.[25] In these respects Germany was no exception. The final stages of inflation were certainly harmful, and they were followed by recession and a stabilization crisis. For the rest of the decade Germany experienced relative stagnation and the inflationary episode did nothing to strengthen the economy or to improve its stability.[26] Indeed, in the later 1920s Germany became increasingly dependent on the inflow of American capital, which proved a further source of instability.

This is not the end of the matter however. While the economic and social consequences of inflation may still give rise to dispute, the longer-term political consequences appear to be much more certain. The political disintegration of the Weimar Republic can be linked directly to the inflationary experience. Of course, the Weimar Coalition was never a very healthy beast. It lost its absolute majority as far back as June 1920, never to regain it. It was buffeted by many problems, the most virulent of which was inflation, and which probably contributed more to the disintegration of democracy in Germany than any other factor.[27] By destroying the savings base of many middle and lower middle class families, it effectively undermined the bourgeois political consensus of Weimar. The subsequent failure to implement a fair and equitable system of compensation for creditors in the aftermath of the crisis left many middle class households extremely embittered, thereby resulting in 'a fundamental breakdown of voter identification with the traditional parties of bourgeois centre and right'.[28] This led to the emergence of splinter parties, shifting voter preferences and political instability.[29] Ultimately it was the extreme right which became the major beneficiary of the alienated middle groups who were the chief losers from inflation. Estimates suggest that members of the *Mittelstand*, which of course included most of the creditors, accounted for a very substantial part of the Nazi Party's electoral support.[30]

3.5 Currency stabilization – A lost opportunity

Not only did Allied statesmen neglect the real task of reconstruction in Europe but they also made that task more difficult to perform as a result of the peace treaty settlements and the treatment of Germany. The stability of Europe was further exacerbated by their haphazard approach to the question of currency stabilization.

In some respects this was paradoxical given the considerable attention devoted to financial and currency issues during this period and the fact that the restoration of the pre-war liberal economic order – embracing freedom from controls, free trade and, above all, fixed exchange rates under the gold standard system – was regarded, almost universally, as a basic priority of policy.[31] The virtues of the gold standard were not in question, and its restoration was seen as the key to the return of world prosperity and stability.

Whether the stabilizing properties of the gold standard were as significant as most contemporaries imagined is a debatable issue[32] but, notwithstanding any reservations on this matter, there was good reason why statesmen should have been anxious to restore the pre-war system. Apart from questions of prestige and national honour, the fact was that European currencies and international finance were in a chaotic state in the first half of the 1920s. The floating exchange rate system gave rise to large and erratic swings in currency valuations, and these tended to exacerbate inflation. They were also seen as a major impediment to European recovery and stability. Trade could scarcely flourish, as the Head of the League of Nations Economic Intelligence Service observed, when 'European exchanges for some years danced and jumped with spasmodic and tireless energy . . . That instability has not only rendered the transaction of business from day to day extraordinarily difficult and risky, but has for years excluded the possibility of laying down any elaborate economic programme for the future'.[33] More recent experience with the vagaries of floating exchange rates now affords greater sympathy with the motives of statesmen in the 1920s who were aiming to restore an orderly pattern of exchange rates.

Unfortunately, in contrast to the negotiated settlement following the Second World War, the process of currency stabilization in the 1920s was little short of disastrous. There was no systematic plan to stabilize currencies simultaneously and insufficient attention was paid to the vast changes which had taken place in world finance and the world economy throughout the 1914–20 period. In practice, therefore, currency stabilization was a long drawn-out affair, with countries acting independently of one another and stabilizing their exchange rates at different times throughout the decade, as and when it best suited their needs – which usually meant when they had managed to regain control of their domestic financial systems. Only limited recognition was given to the relative shift in costs and prices which had taken place since 1914 when choosing a new exchange rate. The chief objective was to select a rate that was thought to be defensible, though even this was disregarded when questions of prestige or honour were at stake. However, only a few countries, the UK and the Scandinavians for example, managed to regain their pre-war parities.

Stabilization took the best part of a decade, and the final outcome was far from satisfactory. Several important currencies were in disequilibrium from the start: the French and Belgian francs were undervalued, while sterling, the Italian lira and the Swedish krona were overvalued. The failure to organize a co-ordinated and viable system of exchange rates effectively undermined the new system. As the League of Nations later observed:

> The piecemeal and haphazard manner of international monetary reconstruction
> sowed the seeds of subsequent disintegration. It was partly because of the lack of
> proper co-ordination during the stabilization period of the 'twenties' that the system
> broke down in the 'thirties'.[34]

It is not altogether surprising, therefore, that the new gold standard functioned less satisfactorily than its predecessor. Not only were the conditions for its success less propitious than those obtaining before 1914, but it must be stressed that no system of fixed exchange rates can hope to survive for very long when the alignment of currencies, and especially major ones, is out of kilter from the start. The choice of the wrong exchange rates magnified balance of payments problems, calling upon the system to make adjustments on a scale far greater than previously (and for which it was never designed), and at a time when, for various reasons, the mechanism of adjustment was less easy to operate. Nearly half a century ago Condliffe argued that it was a futile gesture to restore the gold standard, largely because the conditions for its successful operation no longer held. In particular he mentioned the growing impediments to international trade: migration and capital movements, the increasing inflexibility of price systems, and the emergence of nationalistic monetary policies designed to deal with the increasing pressures on domestic economies.[35] Countries were now no longer prepared to sacrifice the stability of their domestic economies for the sake of external equilibrium to the extent that had been the case before the war. Thus the former 'rules of the game' were increasingly ignored, while the division of financial power among rival centres (London, New York and Paris) and the pyramiding of short-term claims on these centres, created further operational difficulties. The system also felt the lack of a hegemonic leader which it had had before 1914: Paris played her own game, New York was an absentee leader and London was now too weak to orchestrate the system.

The restored standard therefore provided little in the way of a solution to the instability problems of the 1920s. In fact, given the manner of its resurrection, it was only a matter of time before the system disintegrated – once subject to pressures, few countries were prepared to risk domestic stability on the altar of the exchange rate. It has also been argued that, far from imparting stability to the international economy, the new standard was itself a source of instability.[36] Indeed, in so far as it made it more difficult for adjustment to take place between creditors and debtors, together with the imbalances in reserve holdings which emerged through dishonouring the 'rules of the game', then it can certainly be seen as a destabilizing element. But whether it can also be regarded as a significant causal influence for the initial slide into depression in 1929 is another matter. On the other hand, once the depression was under way then, as Friedman and Schwartz have noted, the links forged by the gold standard reinforced the transmission and spread the effects of depression to other countries tied to the gold standard, since the only solution to external imbalance was through internal deflation. Once these pressures were deemed to be too severe then relief was sought by going off gold.[37]

3.6 The leadership problem

The European settlement as it emerged in the course of the 1920s had two main defects: it did not satisfy anyone, and it lacked firm leadership. France, Germany and Italy, for different reasons, were extremely disgruntled: France over compensation and the security issue, Germany because of the harsh treatment inflicted on her by the victors, and Italy as a result of unfulfilled promises of territory for joining the war. None of these countries was capable or willing to promote the European cause. The remnants of the Austro–Hungarian Empire, and the new and reconstituted states each in their turn had their grievances, all of which led to fragmentation rather than unity. This left Russia and Britain. The former was not particularly happy with the territorial arrangements arising from the peace settlement, but in any case her exclusion policy precluded her from playing a European role of any significance. Britain, the one country which might have been in a position to take an active role, was more concerned with her Imperial connections, which meant that she preferred to view the affairs of Europe with benign indifference when it suited her to do so.

The result of this fissiparous tendency, in contrast to the post-1945 situation, was that competitive national sovereignties dominated the scene in the 1920s to such an extent that there was little prospect of achieving unity and stability in Europe.[38] In short, 'There were', as Ross notes, 'few good Europeans.'[39]

The way in which the different outcomes post-1918 and post-1945 can be explained, in terms of the role of the United States in Europe, is worth considering. Certainly after the Second World War America played a much more active and forceful part in shaping the recovery of Europe, but then it had good political reason to do so. There was no such urgency after the First World War. There was no immediate power threat and though European recovery was regarded as important, it was never seen as being crucial to America's own well-being. This meant that when it suited her own domestic and political interests, the United States could turn a blind eye to the problems of Europe – especially if these seemed likely to entail direct involvement in the affairs of that continent. This vacillatory approach had several unfortunate consequences. It meant, first of all, that certain aspects of the post-war settlement, such as reparations and territorial rights, emerged as international issues. Secondly, it left Europe stranded in the early 1920s when American credits ceased to flow. Thirdly, it robbed Europe of the leadership it so badly needed in the 1920s. Finally, it eventually gave rise to a policy of private benefaction in the form of international lending, over which the US administration exercised little control. As Hogan comments: 'The toothless loan control program left the American government with no way to insure that capital exports really contributed to recovery.'[40]

3.7 Papering over the cracks

Despite the impediments to European stability in the first half of the 1920s, by the middle of the decade economic and political conditions had taken a turn for the better. The Locarno Pact of 1925, the revised reparations settlement of the previous year, and the negotiated agreements relating to Allied war debts did much to boost international confidence and reduce political tensions and suspicions of war. Most of the great inflations had run their course and Britain's return to the gold standard, in April 1925, helped to pave the way for the completion of currency stabilization elsewhere. Primary commodity prices had firmed considerably after the sharp downturn following the post-war boom. Above all, reconstruction and recovery had made some headway in Western Europe and 'real progress began to take the place of a painful struggle to regain a plateau of prosperity which had been lost . . .'.[41] If there were still signs of tension and weakness in the international economy, these were all but forgotten as the world looked forward to a period of sustained prosperity.

The boom in activity in the later 1920s was led by the United States. Most regions of the world shared in the prosperity and Europe regained some of the ground she had earlier lost. The relative improvement in Europe's performance prompted the observation by the author of the League of Nations' study into the world depression that the pre-war equilibrium between Europe and the rest of the world had more or less been restored.[42] This view, in retrospect, appears rather wide of the mark. Below the surface there were plenty of signs of maladjustment: notably large areas of underemployed resources in certain sectors, especially agriculture and heavy industry; the failure of some of the larger countries, for example Germany and the UK, to achieve a full recovery; the rise in primary inventories and renewed weakness in commodity prices; the patched up nature of the international currency system; and, above all, the dependence of many countries on the inflow of foreign capital. Such factors rendered the equilibrium a fragile one, leaving Europe vulnerable to external shocks.

In fact prosperity in Europe and the world at large was very dependent on the health of the American economy and the continued flow of credit from the United States, and to a lesser extent from France and Britain. But, at the same time, international lending played a crucial role in the instability crisis of the 1920s on more than one occasion. The failure of reconstruction in Europe in the early 1920s can be traced directly to the collapse of international credits, when aggregate net capital movements from the main creditors, principally the United States, declined by no less than three quarters between 1921–23. Foreign lending on a large scale was resumed only after the first major currency stabilization phase had been completed, rising from a low point of $639 million in 1923 to $2,241 million by 1928.[43] Many countries benefited from this outflow, American investment being directed mainly towards Europe (Germany being by far the largest borrower), Latin America and Canada, while Britain favoured the Dominions, Africa and Asia.

While the massive flow of lending in the later 1920s undoubtedly facilitated developments of one sort or another in many parts of the world, it also created a false sense of security. It gave an impression of soundness and stability which did not in fact exist. Yet so long as the flow of lending continued, the cracks in the international economic structure were concealed. But at the same time the lending itself helped to widen these cracks through the burdens it imposed on the borrowers. So, once the flow was turned off, the fragile stability was undermined. As Dunning comments: 'a climate of investment so radically different from that of pre-war days, combined with substantial short-term capital movements, powerfully contributed to the world economic collapse of 1931 and its aftermath.'[44]

One of the main problems was that the debtor nations, sometimes with ample encouragement on the part of the creditors, borrowed too much relative to their ability to service the loans. Post-war investments were no longer readily self-liquidating as most of them had been in the nineteenth century, largely because the borrowers were unable or unwilling to generate sufficient exchange earnings. Some borrowers, including Germany, had squandered the proceeds on prestige projects or in maintaining consumption, instead of ensuring that they went into exchange generating investments. The result was that many debtors were forced to continue borrowing simply to service past loans, thereby raising their debt burdens to intolerable levels.

Probably the worst excesses in this respect occurred in Central and Eastern Europe and Latin America. Apart from the special case of Germany, who financed both reparations and increased domestic consumption from American lending, most East European countries had incurred unmanageable debt levels by the later 1920s, with debt service payments accounting for one quarter and sometimes up to one half of the value of export receipts in some cases.[45] Moreover, since servicing foreign loans called for 'strong currency' earnings obtainable from a limited range of exports, the actual strain was much greater than these figures indicated.[46] Europe was by no means unique in this respect however. Many Latin American and African countries as well as the White Dominions (the latter had the highest per capita debt burden in the world) had seriously overcommitted themselves and were engaged in an uphill struggle to meet the obligations on past loans.[47]

In reality, therefore, the maintenance of the fragile equilibrium in both the European and the international economy was heavily dependent on the continued flow of funds from creditors to debtors. Even had conditions in the United States not determined the subsequent course of events, a reaction was bound to have come in time – simply because of the increasingly insupportable debt burdens of the borrowing nations. Indeed, by early 1928 the Governor of the New York Federal Reserve Bank, Benjamin Strong, was said to be sceptical as to the wisdom of making further loans to Europe.[48] In that year the debtors of the United States and Britain were paying $675 million a year in interest, dividends and amortization more than they received in new loans, and by the following year this burden had nearly doubled.[49] Equilibrium in external accounts was often only maintained with the help of short-term credits, which later became a destabilizing force.

Much of the increase in the relative debt burden in 1929 can be attributed to the decline in lending. Altogether net outward capital movements of the creditor countries declined by over 35 per cent (by nearly one half in the case of the United States), while in the following year the fall was even more dramatic.[50] Most debtors therefore suffered a heavy drop in capital inflows – of one half or more – in these two years. The most vulnerable areas were Central and Eastern Europe, Latin America, Australia and Germany. As Schuker comments in the case of Germany:

The Reich was singularly vulnerable to the reverse flow of capital. It had overborrowed in the 1920s and squandered much of the proceeds on public or private consumption, and it had persistently failed in the early years to adjust tax, budgetary, labour and trade policies to take account of reparations requirements added to a growing commercial debt.[51]

Many of the primary producing countries in Eastern Europe and along the periphery no doubt faced even greater difficulties. Coming on top of the weakening of commodity prices and being followed by a downturn in the American economy in the summer of 1929 and a subsequent decline in American import demand, the drying up of capital imports placed intolerable burdens on their economies and balance of payments. The way out of the impasse was eventually sought through deflation, devaluation and trade control – and sometimes through default on debts, the backwash effects of which subsequently reverberated on the metropolitan economies.

3.8 Conclusion

The sequence of events through to the crisis of the early 1930s does not form part of the subject of this paper and so we can conveniently draw the instability discussion to a close. Though the war undoubtedly caused severe dislocations and distortions to the economic system and also interrupted the normal course of growth for several years, we have argued that it was what followed in the aftermath that really upset the stability of Europe. The failure to follow through with an adequate programme of reconstruction, together with the policies relating to the post-war settlement of Europe, the treatment of Germany, and the restoration of the international currency system, meant that Europe was left in a fragile and vulnerable state – both in economic and political terms. Europe was also heavily dependent on the United States as the major creditor country. Unfortunately, the United States proved to be a somewhat unreliable backer. She did little to provide the leadership which Europe required and, throughout the 1920s, American policies posed a constant threat to economic stability: for example through withdrawal from reconstruction, a restrictive import policy, and gold sterilization measures. However, there was sufficient resilience in the European and in the international economy to withstand these setbacks so long as the American economy remained healthy and it continued to pour dollars into Europe and the rest of the world. But once these supports were removed, there was nothing left to prop up the system. In the words of the United Nations: 'The stage was thus set for the disturbances which culminated in the international financial crisis of 1931 and the subsequent disintegration of the international economy.'[52]

Notes

1 Grey of Fallodon, Viscount, 1935, *Twenty five years 1892–1916*, vol. 2, Hodder & Stoughton, London, p. 223.

2 Ross, G., 1983, *The great powers and the decline of the European states system 1914–1945*, Longman, London, p. 54.
3 McDougal, W. A., 1979, 'Political economy versus national sovereignty: French structures for German integration after Versailles', *Journal of Modern History*, 51: 4.
4 Marks, S., 1976, *The illusion of peace: international relations in Europe 1918–1933*, Macmillan, London, p. 108.
5 Beyen, J. W., 1951, *Money in maelstrom*, Macmillan, London, p. 3.
6 Keynes, J. M., 1920, *The economic consequences of the peace*, Macmillan, London, p. 1.
7 Thompson, D., 1966, *Europe since Napoleon*, Penguin, Harmondsworth, p. 626.
8 Newman, W. J., 1968, *The balance of power in the interwar years, 1919–1939*, Random House, New York, pp. 27, 58, 105–6, 201.
9 Spulber, N., 1966, *The state and economic development in Eastern Europe*, Random House, New York, p. 75.
10 Komlos, J., 1983, *The Habsburg monarchy as a customs union*, Princeton University Press, Princeton, New Jersey, p. 6; see also Jaszi, O., 1929, *The dissolution of the Habsburg monarchy*, University of Chicago Press, Chicago.
11 Berend, I. and Ranki, G., 1969, 'Economic problems of the Danube region at the break-up of the Austro-Hungarian monarchy', *Journal of Contemporary History*, 4: 170.
12 Silverman, D. P., 1982, *Reconstructing Europe after the Great War*, Harvard University Press, Cambridge, Mass., p. 230; Aldcroft, D. H., 1977, *From Versailles to Wall Street*, Allen Lane, London, pp. 55–64.
13 Artaud, D., 1973, *La reconstruction de l'Europe 1919–1929*, Presses Universitaries de France, Paris, p. 17.
14 Ránki, G., 1983, 'Inflation in post-World War I East-Central Europe', in Schmukler, N. and Marcus, E. (eds), *Inflation through the ages*, Brooklyn College Press, New York, p. 483.
15 League of Nations, 1943, *The transition from war to peace economy: report of the delegation on economic depressions*, League of Nations, Geneva, p. 70.
16 Weinberg, G. L., 1969, 'The defeat of Germany in 1918 and the European balance of power', *Central European History*, 2.
17 Kent, B., 1989, *The spoils of war: the politics, economics and diplomacy of reparations 1918–1932*, Oxford University Press, Oxford, pp. 9, 286, 373.
18 Fischer, W., 1974, 'Die Weimarer Republik unter den weltwirtschaftlichen Bedingungen der Zwischenkriegszeit', in Mommsen H., *et al.* (eds), *Industrielles System und politische Entwicklung in der Weimarer Republik*, Droste Verlag, Düsseldorf, p. 74.
19 Holtfrerich, C.-L., 1986, *The German inflation 1914–1923*, Walter de Gruyter, Berlin, pp. 149–50.
20 Schuker, S. A., 1988, *American reparations to Germany 1919–33: implications for the third world debt crisis*, Princeton University Press, Princeton, pp. 106–8.
21. Holtfrerich, *The German inflation*, p. 153.
22 Feldman, G., 1983, 'The historian and German Inflation', in Schmukler, N. and Marcus, E. (eds), *Inflation through the ages*, Brooklyn College Press, New York, p. 388; Holtfrerich, *The German inflation*, chs 7–9.
23 Hardach, G., 1984, 'Banking and industry in Germany in the interwar period, 1919–1939', *Journal of European Economic History*, 13(2): 210.
24 Eichengreen, B., 1986, 'Understanding 1921–1927: inflation and economic recovery in the 1920s', *Rivista di Storia Economica*, 3: 34–66.
25 Gordon, R. J., 1982, 'Why stopping inflation may be costly: evidence from fourteen

historical episodes', in Hall, R. E. (ed.), *Inflation: causes and effects*, University of Chicago Press, Chicago, ch. 1.

26 Petzina, D., 1977, *Die deutsche Wirtschaft in der Zwischenkriegszeit*, Franz Steiner Verlag, Wiesbaden, pp. 13–15.

27 Carsten, F. L., 1983, *Britain and the Weimar Republic: the British documents*, Batsford, London, pp. 96, 141–2.

28 Childers, T., 1983, 'Inflation and electoral politics in Germany, 1919–29', in Schmukler, N. and Marcus, E. (eds), *Inflation through the ages*, Brooklyn College Press, New York, p. 382.

29 Jones, L. E., 1979, 'Inflation, revaluation and the crisis of middle class politics: a study of the dissolution of the German party system, 1923–8', *Central European History*, 12: 148; Abraham, p., 1981, *The collapse of the Weimar Republic: political economy and crisis*, Princeton University Press, Princeton.

30 Hughes, M. L., 1988, *Paying for the German inflation*, University of North Carolina Press, Chapel Hill, p. 164; Childers, T., 1983, *The Nazi voter: The social foundations of fascism in Germany, 1919–1933*, University of North Carolina Press, Chapel Hill.

31 Arndt, H. W., 1944, *The economic lessons of the nineteen–thirties*, Oxford University Press, London, p. 223.

32 Yeager, L. B., 1966, *International monetary relations: theory, history and policy*, Harper & Row, New York; Triffin, R., 1968, *Our international monetary system: yesterday, today and tomorrow*, Random House, New York.

33 Loveday, A., 1931, *Britain and world trade*, Longmans Green, London, p. 31; League of Nations, 1920, *Currencies after the war: a survey of conditions in various countries*, League of Nations, Geneva, p. ix.

34 League of Nations, 1944, *International currency experience: lessons of the interwar period*, League of Nations, Geneva, p. 117.

35 Condliffe, J. B., 1941, *The reconstruction of world trade: a survey of international economic relations*, Allen & Unwin, London, pp. 102–3.

36 Fearon, P., 1979, *The origins of the great slump*, Macmillan, London, p. 25.

37 Friedman, M., and Schwartz, A. J., 1963, *A monetary history of the United States, 1867–1960*, Princeton University Press, Princeton, New Jersey, p. 359; Choudhri, E. U., and Kochin, L. A., 1980, 'The exchange rate and the international transmission of business cycle disturbances: some evidence from the great depression', *Journal of Money, Credit and Banking*, 12.

38 Jacobson, J., 1983, 'Is there a new international history of the 1920s?', *American Historical Journal*, 88: 630, 644.

39 Ross, *The great powers*, p. 53.

40 Hogan, M. J. 1977, *Informal entente: the private structure of cooperation in Anglo-American diplomacy, 1918–1928*, University of Missouri Press, Colombia, p. 224.

41 Loveday, *Britain and world trade*, p. 47.

42 Ohlin, B., 1931, *The course and phases of the world depression*, League of Nations, Geneva, p. 17.

43 North, D. C., 1962, 'International capital movements in historical perspective', in Mikesell, R. F. (ed.), *U.S. private and government investment abroad*, University of Oregon Books, Eugene, p. 48.

44 Dunning, J. H., 1970, *Studies in international investment*, Allen & Unwin, London, p. 20.

45 Aldcroft, D. H., 1988, 'Eastern Europe in an age of turbulence, 1919–1950', *Economic History Review*, 41: 597.

46 Raupach, H., 1969, 'The impact of the great depression in Eastern Europe', *Journal of Contemporary History*, 4: 80.

47 United Nations, 1955, *Foreign capital in Latin America*, United Nations, New York, p. 15; Schedvin, C. B., 1970, *Australia and the great depression: a study of the economic development and policy in the 1920s and 1930s*, University of Sydney Press, Sydney, pp. 2–3, 68, 75.
48 Schuker, *American reparations to Germany*, p. 43.
49 Royal Institute of International Affairs, 1937, *The problem of international investment*, Oxford University Press, Oxford, p. 284.
50 North, *International capital movements*, p. 40.
51 Schuker, *American reparations to Germany*, p. 123.
52 United Nations, 1949, *International capital movements during the interwar period*, United Nations, New York, pp. 66–77.

4 Textiles and regional economic decline: Northern Ireland 1914–70[1]

Philip Ollerenshaw,
Bristol Polytechnic

In the long debate on the decline of the British economy, increasing attention has been given recently to a 'matrix of rigid institutional structures' in industrial relations, enterprise and market arrangements, education (especially technical and higher), finance and government–industry relations that evolved in the nineteenth century and persisted in many cases until the recent past. In contrast to the neo-classical view that atomistic market structures and competition offer the 'best guarantor of economic well-being', those who stress institutional rigidities hold that it was precisely those same structures that militated against widespread adoption of modern, mass produced methods and corporate managerial hierarchies.[2] Hitherto, research has concentrated, unsurprisingly, on the staple industries, and in textiles has been typified by a series of powerful surveys of the British cotton industry by William Lazonick. Lazonick suggests that institutional rigidities effectively prevented the emergence of corporate organization until the 1960s and inevitably produced chronic technological backwardness and long-term industrial decline.[3]

This essay focuses primarily on the decline of another textile industry, linen, which was mainly located on the north east of Ireland and which, 'until the outbreak of war in 1939, probably remained the closest of all British industries to the free competitive ideals of the nineteenth century.'[4] The industry comprised firms involved mainly or exclusively in flax spinning, linen thread manufacture, weaving and finishing piece goods made wholly or mainly from linen, and the making up of household linen products. In the first section we examine the long term structural problems of the industry, and then proceed to consider some other aspects of its decline, including research and advertising and its relationship with government.

Industrial structure and regional problems

In some of his recent writing, Sidney Pollard has emphasized the role of the region in the industrialization of modern Europe and, with other scholars, has redirected our attention to the perpetual process of regional advance and decline. In his major work on this theme he concentrates explicitly on

Table 4.1 Regional Unemployment in the United Kingdom 1939-54*

Region	1939 July	1946 July	1948 June	1950 June	1952 June	1954 June
London and S.E.	4.9	1.0	1.5	1.0	1.2	0.8
Eastern	4.8	1.0	1.0	0.9	1.1	0.9
Southern	2.9	1.0	1.5	1.1	1.2	0.8
South West	4.0	1.0	1.5	1.2	1.2	1.1
Midland	5.3	1.0	0.5	0.5	1.0	0.5
North Midland	6.4	1.0	0.5	0.5	1.1	0.5
E. and W. Riding of Yorks	8.0	1.5	1.0	0.9	2.3	0.8
North Western	10.9	3.0	2.0	1.5	4.9	1.3
Northern	12.3	5.0	3.0	2.6	2.3	2.0
Scotland	10.2	4.5	3.0	2.7	3.2	2.4
Wales	14.2	8.5	5.5	3.4	2.6	2.1
Great Britain (average)	7.5	2.5	2.0	1.4	2.1	1.1
Northern Ireland	20.2	8.8	6.5	5.5	10.6	6.3

*The figures are percentages of all insured workers aged 14 and over unemployed in industry and agriculture.
Source: Isles, K.S., Cuthbert, Norman, 1957, *An economic survey of Northern Ireland*, HMSO, Belfast, p. 18.

industrialization, and once a region became industrialized, it fades from view.[5] From the First World War, however, the manifold problems of traditional industrial regions loom large in the UK experience and nowhere was the intractable nature of 'the regional problem' demonstrated more forcefully than in Northern Ireland – a low wage region with a poor stock of natural resources and a highly specialized industrial base dominated in 1914 by linen and shipbuilding.

The partition of Ireland in 1920 cut twenty-six counties out of the UK and created Northern Ireland as a six county state, with its own regional government in Belfast. Over the next fifty years, Northern Ireland established its reputation as the most economically backward region within the UK. It had no monopoly of intractable economic problems, but most indicators confirm the province's position as the most disadvantaged part of a national economy that was itself in relative economic decline. For example, expressed as percentages of the UK average, net output per employee was 84.6 in 1968 and per capita income was 72 in 1972.[6] In the latter year, unemployment was three times the national average. Indeed, since 1936, unemployment in the province has been higher than in any other UK region,[7] and it failed to achieve full employment even in the favourable economic environment after 1945 (see Table 4.1).

Central to any account of the economic history of Northern Ireland is the contraction of its textile industry, and this survey is intended to provide a necessarily brief examination of this important aspect of deindustrialization down to about 1970. Within Northern Ireland textiles dominated the manufacturing sector and, as late as the mid-twentieth century, accounted for more than a third of manufacturing employment – a much greater proportion than even in north west England. Textiles also contributed more than a third of net manufacturing output in the province. From this it follows that the performance of the textile industries, which were dominated by linen until the 1950s, was a key influence on the economy of Northern Ireland generally and its manufacturing sector in particular.[8] Some general data on the industry's output, capacity and employment are provided in Table 4.2.

On the eve of the First World War, the north east of Ireland was the world's leading linen producing area, and had been so since at least 1870. Regional specialization, so characteristic of textile industries since the early industrial revolution, became more emphatic after 1860. In the linen industry, the small Yorkshire output centred on Barnsley declined further while in east-central Scotland, jute increasingly replaced linen, though in 1914 there was still a significant Scottish linen industry specializing mainly in coarse goods.[9] Ulster accounted for some three quarters of UK linen output and specialized in the medium and fine end of the market, a fact that helped to protect it from foreign competition before 1914.

The most serious challenge in the home market came from Belgium, which successfully undercut relatively coarse yarn prices in Ulster and led directly to Irish spinners moving to the higher ground of finer yarns. Even if foreign competition in linen did become more evident from the later nineteenth century, a far more serious threat came from other textiles, most notably cotton. A number of early twentieth century observers noted that, as a result of increasing competition, the European linen industry stagnated between 1870 and 1914 – or even contracted, 'a fact that seems to show that the volume of the world's linen trade has fallen absolutely'.[10]

The significance of this trend did not become fully apparent until after 1914. Until then, Ulster linen production benefited from the decline of the industry elsewhere in the UK, and took advantage of cheap foreign flax, tow and yarn to keep costs down. It was also assisted by the fact that wages were lower than in any other UK textile industry, even jute.[11] Clearly related to this was the extremely low rate of unionization and the low rate of labour productivity. In the British cotton industry, where almost half the labour force was unionized by 1910,[12] the strength of trade union organization is sometimes cited as an important reason why managers could not invest significantly in more capital intensive machinery, even had they wished, and so were forced to retain traditional labour intensive techniques.[13]

In linen, there was no similar constraint since it is doubtful whether unionization exceeded ten per cent by 1914, or even by 1920, and it remained at a low level unitl the 1940s.[14] Whereas organized labour in British cotton may have held the 'balance of power', in the linen industry sectional and sectarian conflicts, the lack of alternative employment for a largely female labour force, and an unsubtle blend of paternalism and repression,[15] all meant that employers in Ulster were typically in a stronger position than their Lancashire counterparts. On the issue of productivity it might be noted here that data from the 1907 Census of Production indicated that output per worker in flax, hemp and jute at £61 per annum was significantly lower than either the £70 in

Table 4.2 Output, Capacity and Employment in the Linen Industry of Northern Ireland, 1912–51

Year	Flax Yarn Production Tons	Linen Thread Production Tons	Linen and Union Cloth Production Millions Sq Yards	Spindles	Powerlooms	Employment Thousands
1912	31,017	2,440	211	926,000	34,000	76
1924	28,050	2,060	161	930,000	37,000	75
1930	20,050	1,550	116	866,000	31,000	56
1935	28,850	1,450	146	868,000	28,000	57
1951	22,200	2,360	99	775,000	22,000	56

Source: Black, William, 1957, 'Variations in employment in the linen industry', unpublished Ph.D. thesis, Queen's University of Belfast, pp. 232, 235.

the woollen or the £79 in the cotton industries. If the cost of labour was relatively low in Ulster linen, the cost of technology was relatively high and this too discouraged labour saving techniques. One estimate in 1913 suggested that a cotton mill with mule spindles could be completely equipped for about 27s 6d per spindle, and a mill with ring spindles for 32s 6d. A flax mill using flyer spinning would cost about £7 per spindle. Similarly, a cotton weaving shed making medium grade goods could be built and equipped for some £36 per loom whereas the medium grade linen weaving shed would cost £45.[16]

Apart from a few vertically integrated concerns, most firms specialized in a single process, though the degree of vertical specialization in 1914 was not as great as in British cotton.[17] There was only limited movement towards greater integration before the 1950s. Each section of the industry had its own representative bodies which dealt with a range of issues including, for example, the implementation of short term working during recession, or the level of wage rates. Clearly, with a high degree of specialization within the industry, there was considerable scope for friction between different firms whose interests did not coincide. In an effort to overcome this problem the Council of the Irish Linen Industry, comprising representatives from all the main sections, was established, though it tended to be dominated by the most powerful sections: the Flax Spinners', the Irish Powerloom Manufacturers' and the Linen Merchants' Associations.

In terms of its sources of raw material, linen was typical of UK textile industries in its heavy dependence on overseas supply. Irish flax acreage had declined on trend since the late 1860s, and the 1912 figure was only 28 per cent of that for 1870. More than 80 per cent of the raw material for Irish linen came from Russia and Belgium.[18] As long as there was peace in Europe, this dependence was not a problem, though the implications for the linen industry of large-scale conflict in north west Europe were indeed serious.

Another feature which made linen characteristic of UK textiles was its export dependence. Ulster specialized in medium and fine linens and found its customers in relatively affluent markets, especially the USA – in contrast to the market orientation of British cotton. As a contemporary noted in 1913: 'While British cotton manufacturers look East for their customers, selling most largely in India and China, flax manufacturers look to the West, for with the exception of a diminishing amount shipped to Europe, the linen exports go west, and the US alone takes half the total'.[19] Market conditions in the US were thus a key determinant of linen production in Northern Ireland and had been so since at least the 1830s. High quality, strength and durability had been the characteristics that had enabled linen to hold out against the repeated incursions of cotton products, but the danger was that changes in tastes or fashion might mean that those same qualities which had once been indispensible assets would turn into chronic liabilities.

It was the First World War, rather than the inter-war depression, that first brought home to linen manufacturers the precariousness of their position, and nowhere was this more obvious than in the supply of raw material. Given that medium and fine linen goods were essentially luxuries, it might be expected that they would have low priority as war materials, and at the start of the war this seemed to be the case. Three developments, however, transformed the military importance and competitive position of the linen industry. First, the capture of key flax growing and flax spinning areas and the ability of Germany to prevent other governments from exporting flax and yarn, had serious adverse consequences in Ireland.[20] The export of high quality Belgian flax effectively ceased from an early stage in the war and Russian flax, hitherto exported through the Baltic states, had to be directed through the inconvenient and ice-prone port of Archangel. Second, and of much longer term significance, was the disruption to Russian flax exports caused by the 1917 revolution. Imports of flax and tow into the UK held up remarkably well until the revolution, but collapse was rapid thereafter: 77,280 tons in 1917; 23,696 in 1918; and a mere 3,895 in 1919.[21]

This curtailment of the principal sources of raw material as a result of war and revolution would have been bad enough under normal demand conditions, but it was compounded by a third development which had a profound short-term impact – the massive increase in military demand for linen products. As a government report of 1918 noted:

> The military importance of such textile raw materials such as flax, wool and cotton is at first sight less obvious than that of such hardware materials as steel or timber. At the present stage of the war, however, it is impossible to avoid recognition of the importance of the raw material of aeroplane linen fabric, whilst the national need of the heavier classes of Flax Textile products is obvious on consideration of the inevitable Naval and Military demands for canvas covers, sail cloth, tent duck, machine gun belts etc; there is also the universal demand for linen sewing thread.[22]

The need to secure raw material supplies, curtail exports, stimulate domestic flax production, encourage substitutes, and meet tight government deadlines all led to increasing government control of the linen industry which culminated in the establishment of the Flax Control Board[23] in 1917. After that the industry was controlled 'from the flax field to the cloth store'.[24] In general the military orders, which included some 50,000 miles of aeroplane cloth, were delivered remarkably successfully.

An inevitable result of demand pressures and supply constraints, however, was rapid inflation – which created a more serious problem for linen than for any other textile industry in the UK.[25] Indeed the ratio of cotton to flax prices increased markedly during the inter-war period and this must be seen as one of a number of factors which diminished the competitiveness of the linen industry in the long term.[26] To some extent, and with government encouragement, the raw material problem was offset by an almost threefold increase in Irish flax acreage between 1914 and 1918, but this was purely temporary. Shortage of flax was also partly overcome in the First World War, as in the Second, by the substitution of other fibres to make 'unions'. So widespread did this practice become that as early as 1915, a Belfast linen trade report pointed out that 'cotton is now a very big feature in the local trade, and enters into the composition of almost everything that is made here'.[27]

In the light of the above, it is clear that the First World War demonstrated the insecurity of the linen industry's position, and even the short post-war boom enjoyed by so much of British industry was far more muted in Ulster.

The raw material problem drove up prices to such an extent by 1918 that linens were 'only compatible with a millionaire's tastes.'[28] The difference in experience between Britain and Ulster is indicated by the fact that at the same time as the British economy reached a cyclical peak, in March 1920, the Flax Spinners' Association reduced the hours worked by its members' mills to 25 per week. In fact, short time working had been typical of most spinning mills ever since the cyclical downturn which began just before outbreak of war.[29]

Even before the armistice was signed, however, a small number of informed commentators had begun to identify the formidable range of problems that the linen industry would have to overcome if it was ever to regain anything like its former levels of activity. These problems included the uncertain supply and high price of flax, the high degree of vertical specialization and frequency of internecine disputes within the industry, the threat of cotton-based substitutes, the rising tide of protection in overseas markets, the lack of research and development and inadequate marketing policies.[30] In addition to these problems there was some evidence of fundamental ignorance on the part of businessmen of cost accounting techniques. This last weakness has been identified as a common problem in British business in the early twentieth century,[31] and seems to have been typical of the linen industry. According to one accountant speaking in Belfast in 1918, 'not five per cent of those engaged in manufacturing linen knew really with any exactitude the cost of producing their goods'.[32]

Historians have appreciated some of these problems but have stressed that solutions to them, certainly in the inter-war period, were not within the grasp of linen manufacturers since the world demand for linen was contracting.[33] To some extent this was undoubtedly true. At the end of the 1920s it was clear that changes in tastes and fashion had adversely affected the demand for linen:

> Entertaining is now largely done at hotels or clubs in preference to the home and this has resulted in a virtual abandonment of the tradition whereby a generous supply of linen was regarded as a necessity in every well furnished household. Moreover, the unsatisfactory treatment of linen by laundries and the expense of laundering are not without influence on the Purchaser.[34]

A more general point was made at the same time: 'the public today as a rule prefer to buy the cheaper article and renew it at an earlier date rather than expend a somewhat large sum in order to obtain an article of lasting worth.'[35] This trend had particularly serious effects on the use of linen damasks, bed linen, bedspreads, dress linens and shirting cloths.

It remains the case, however, that recent historiography has not given sufficient attention to the shortcomings of the industry itself, and has therefore been somewhat fatalistic in tone and tended to argue that the industry performed creditably in the face of uncontrollably adverse demand conditions. Although accepting that market conditions were far from promising, it will be suggested that certain steps could have been taken to improve the industry's performance, but that ultimately these steps were not taken or were taken too late to be of benefit.

One of the most important features of the linen industry in Northern Ireland

Table 4.3 Paid Up Capital in Private and Public Joint-Stock Companies, 1953 (£000s)

	Paid up capital in private cos.	% of total	Paid up capita in public cos.	% of total
United Kingdom	2,391,000	37	4,088,000	63
Northern Ireland	41,443	61	25,790	39
Linen industry (spinning and weaving)	5,682	66	2,882	34

Source: Black, 'Variations in employment in the linen industry', p. 20.

has been the resilience of the small or medium size private family firm. Indeed, as late as the 1950s the ratio of paid up capital in private to public companies in this industry was two to one. Private firms figured much more prominently in the economy of Northern Ireland than in the UK as a whole and their prominence was especially marked in the linen industry (see Table 4.3). In a region where there were few immediate or obvious alternative industries into which entrepreneurs or workers might transfer, where unemployment was chronic, and whose textile industry faced secular decline and a weak degree of unionization, the temptation to plod on regardless was one to which most firms succumbed. Also important is the fact that the industry really lacked any external influence which could force the pace of rationalization or amalgamation. But it should be emphasized here that no linen enterprise was sufficiently dominant to take the initiative in industrial reorganization,[36] and neither the banks nor the Northern Ireland government took it upon themselves to offer such a lead. Under these circumstances it was perhaps surprising that the question of rationalization found its way onto the agenda at all.

In the immediate aftermath of the First World War, however, there were several indications that firms in the linen industry did co-operate in order to promote price stability and financial liquidity in the face of severe economic fluctuations. The issue of prices did not become prominent until the sharp downturn of spring 1920, and the lengthy discussion of price fixing arrangements which continued over the next eighteen months reflected the difficulties facing single process firms in different sections of the industry whose interests were not the same.[37] Fixing minimum prices for yarn helped spinners, but might place weavers at a disadvantage by increasing their input costs. Similarly, fixing minimum yarn prices for firms in an open economy such as the UK might be a futile exercise if cheap foreign yarn was available to undercut the domestic product.

A minimum price yarn agreement between Scottish and Irish spinners was hammered out in 1920, and strenuous and briefly successful attempts were made to extend the scope of the agreement to include French and Belgian spinners.[38] Although the agreement held for a few months in late 1920, the European spinners, whose raw materials supply position was much more favourable than for those working in the UK, flatly refused to continue it from January 1921.[39] As the need for minimum prices – or at least more price stability – intensified, so the ability of the industry to achieve that goal diminished.

Rather more success in furthering co-operation seems to have been achieved by the Irish Linen Society, established in 1920, which embraced various trade associations and organizations associated with research, flax supply, manufacturing and marketing, and was overseen by a central council. As far as individual firms were concerned, the advantage of the Irish Linen Society was that it did not threaten their independence but held out the prospect of a greater degree of intra-industry collaboration than ever before. According to the *Textile Recorder*:

> More good for the advancement of the linen trade as a whole has been effected [by the ILS] than was ever achieved during the last half century prior to its progress. It has meant that narrow inter-firm prejudices and rivalries have been totally abolished in favour of a broad progressive principle, based on co-operation and a whole hearted desire.[40]

Unfortunately this optimism was wholly unwarranted and the 'narrow inter-firm prejudices' continued for decades afterwards, but at least the industry now had a representative forum into which various sections had an input.

One of the most pressing problems facing linen firms from 1920 was the accumulation of unsold stocks, and, in an industry where the small and medium size firm was the norm, this was bound to affect liquidity sooner rather than later. In order to meet this particular difficulty, the Irish Linen Trade Corporation was formed in 1921 as a limited company, with an initial nominal capital of £500,000. Established with the 'goodwill and co-operation' of the banks in Northern Ireland, the LTC was essentially a warehousing operation which provided cash (at Bank Rate plus a small commission) to firms on the security of stocks deposited with the LTC and valued by its board of directors, who were leading figures in the industry. This initiative was thought to be largely responsible for the fact that there were very few failures in the industry following the downturn and severe depression of the early 1920s.[41] It is important to note, however, that both the ILS and the LTC left the structure of the industry intact, though as hopes of a full recovery faded a number of commentators began to argue the case for full blown rationalization.

There were two stimuli to the discussion of rationalization. First, there was the problem of excess capacity. Between 1921 and 1928, while spinning and weaving capacity declined only slightly, an average of 44 per cent of spindles and 43 per cent of looms were idle, and many more worked short time.[42] The second stimulus was the well publicized attempt, beginning in the late 1920s, to rationalize the British cotton industry – an attempt which was led by the Bank of England and other banks with an obvious interest in bolstering the stability of the banking sector in the face of the huge indebtedness of hard pressed cotton firms.[43] Between 1928 and 1930 the linen industry in Northern Ireland, under the auspices of its newly formed Remedies Committee, actively considered rationalization and called in expert advice in the person of Sir Gilbert Garnsey of the leading London-based firm of accountants, Price Waterhouse. Garnsey produced a preliminary scheme for rationalization[44] but believed that it was inadvisable to proceed further unless firms indicated their willingness to entertain the idea. Those most closely involved with canvassing opinion on this question discovered the main difficulty was that 'firms who are in a fairly comfortable financial position, and successful in their daily business, would feel some diffidence in proposing to go into full amalgamation with firms not quite so successful'.[45] In the event, nothing came of the proposed rationalization scheme and so the best opportunity to effect radical structural change was lost. Moreover, if such a scheme foundered in the profound depression of 1930 its chances of success at a later date were, to say the least, remote.

In the later 1930s and 1940s proposals for greater inter-firm co-operation were normally limited to the promotion of price control, standardization of products, or the establishment of a central selling organization. Comparatively few argued the case for rationalization, and the recommendation of the 1944 Post-War Planning Working Party Report on this issue was vague and tepid. As one critic noted, 'although the Committee appear to be half convinced of the desirability of some reduction in the number of small independent firms, they appear content to wait upon some obscure process of natural evolution.'[46]

In fact, 'natural evolution' rather than government or bank-led reorganization remained the order of the day throughout the twentieth century history of the linen industry. From the 1920s onwards there was some increase in both horizontal and vertical integration, though neither process accelerated significantly until after the Second World War. Although in 1954 five composite firms (i.e. those that were both horizontally and vertically integrated) controlled some 30 per cent of the industry's capacity, single process firms remained the form and 'rugged individualism was still a matter of pride'.[47]

Over the next decade, however, fundamental structural change did occur and one in three large firms disappeared (see Table 4.4). Horizontal integration, particularly in the spinning section, increased as firms sought to reap economies in both purchasing and handling, diversification of product lines and in order to use capital equipment more fully – an especially important consideration in an industry where short time working was so common. Similarly, vertical integration was motivated by the greater assurance of inputs, the abolition of intermediaries, the greater potential for efficient stock control, and the increased control over marketing strategy and distribution channels. The growth of composite firms, which in theory were in the best position to achieve maximum benefit from both types of integration, also typified the period. Integration was, of course, still no guarantee of survival as was demonstrated by the symbolically important closure in 1961 of the York Street Flax Spinning Company Ltd, one of the oldest, largest, most integrated and recently modernized firms in the industry. At industry level, perhaps one of the most enduring legacies of the single process firms which had dominated the industry for so long was that there was a clear shortage of managers to run the integrated concerns – very few knew how to 'think vertically'.[48]

Table 4.4 Large Plants in the linen complex of Northern Ireland, 1954 and 1963/4

Industry	Employment 1954	1964	Establishments 1954	1963
Spinning*	21,952	12,304	53	37
Weaving	15,360	8,045	74	43
Making up	8,144	6,747	67	55
Trade hemstitching	4,911	2,902	54	35
Textile finishing**	6,047	3,959	50	31
Total	56,414	33,957	298	201

NB   Data refer to establishments employing 25 or more persons
*   includes threadmaking
* *   includes textile printing

Source: Steed, G.P.F., 1971, 'Internal organization, firm integration and locational change: The Northern Ireland linen complex, 1954–1964', *Economic Geography*, 47: 373.

The profound structural changes in the later 1950s and the 1960s took place after the onset of much tougher competition in international textile markets, and failed to stem the decline of the linen industry. If the paucity of management skills to run vertically integrated concerns was a factor in slowing down the rate of structural change and perhaps impeding the success of those concerns, the belated nature of the effort to integrate at all seemed to point to management's 'inclination to adjust after the event'.[49]

Research and Advertising

The structural problems of the linen industry remained apparent until after the mid-twentieth century and, as we have suggested, managerial failings were also apparent. We now consider the industry's policies in two areas to which economic historians have recently paid increasing attention – research and advertising.

Several writers have pointed to the poor innovative record of British industry, emphasizing firms' reliance on government funded co-operative research associations and also focusing upon the frequently tenuous links between academic and applied industrial research. A major new initiative in the United Kingdom, during and after the First World War, was the establishment of Research Associations under the auspices of the Department of Scientific and Industrial Research. The initial budget to finance these projects amounted to £1m. The aim was to promote co-operative research at industry level to compensate for the perceived lack of research facilities in individual firms. It was originally envisaged that the government and the relevant industry would finance RAs jointly for an initial period of five years, after which the industry itself would take over funding. Despite the fact that tax benefits accrued to firms making contributions to RAs, the response to this government initiative was generally disappointing. In the event, subsidies had to be continued beyond the original five year period, since private funding proved inadequate in all but one of the twenty-four RAs.[50]

The Linen Industry Research Association (LIRA) was one of those set up under the scheme, but both the short and long term responses of the industry to it were weak. By 1927 it was estimated that firms representing between only one-quarter and one-third of the capital in the industry had joined the RA, compared with two-thirds and eighty-five per cent in the RAs which served the woollen/worsted and cotton industries respectively.[51]

Before the formation of LIRA in 1919, the efforts of the linen industry to engage in research were confined to a tiny number of atypical large firms – so much so that at the inaugural meeting of the Association, James Crawford (Managing Director of the York Street Flax Spinning Company) believed that 'the idea of research at all . . . marked an epoch in the history of the trade'. Linen manufacturers had been willing to rest on their reputations for far too long 'with little or no concern beyond their next balance sheet, without an idea of the wider vision of those who had gone before and without taking time to look ahead or to consider the questions which lay at the very basis of industry and commerce.'[52] Even on so basic a question as knowledge of the flax plant, they knew appallingly little. Crawford's reasoned plea for both pure and applied research, his emphasis on the need for patience in achieving results, and his optimism about the ultimate benefits seem not to have been generally shared within the industry. This might be explained by the fact that his firm was not only vertically integrated but also the largest in the industry, with far more resources to devote to research than the typical, small, single process enterprise.

A further possible indicator of the general lack of interest in scientific methods was the low membership of the Irish section of the Textile Institute, which stood at a mere 25 at the end of the First World War – a figure which seemed to confirm that 'the old methods . . . are still in vogue'.[53] Yet another sign of weakness was the apparent absence of research facilities for the linen industry at the Queen's University of Belfast. A series of lectures on the industry organized by the university's Faculty of Commerce towards the end of the war was described as a 'very momentous innovation',[54] but as far as research effort was concerned, unfavourable comparisons were made between Queen's and the University of Leeds. Despite the tiny size of the English linen industry, Leeds had a long-established research and experimentation capability within its Textile Department, including a flax farm at Selby. The Belfast area, notwithstanding its 90,000 linen workers, received 'no special university attention, but merely the continuance of the haphazard "what-was-good-enough-for-grandad-is-good-enough-for-us" policy'.[55] Similarly, while the importance of fabric design was acknowledged in the linen industry, there appear to have been few contacts between this industry and the municipal College of Art in Belfast.[56] This may well have contributed to a conservatism in design, and emphasized the fact that competitors gave more attention to 'the production of novelty goods and attractive designs at popular prices'.[57]

Once underway, the work of LIRA impressed even the most vocal of the industry's critics. Led by Dr Vargas Eyre, a highly qualified and experienced research chemist, the Association set about improving flax yields and the consistency and resilience of linen dyeing and finishing.[58] Given the fundamental importance of this type of work, the Belfast Chamber of Commerce found itself at a loss to understand why so few firms actively supported its efforts, 'especially as the cost when distributed falls so lightly on the individual concern'.[59]

The problem of inadequate funding and organization of research was one which persisted into the later twentieth century. In the major report of 1928 into the causes of depression in the linen industry, lack of research is not mentioned. In contrast, in the Report of the Post-War Planning Working Party of 1944, it was suggested that LIRA take control of all flax and linen research, its organization be strengthened and its emphasis be switched more to the problems of flax production and processing in addition to the 'more strictly industrial problems' of linen manufacture on which it had previously concentrated. While this was a welcome recognition of the significance of research, the working party still envisaged that half of the projected £50,000 research expenditure would be provided by government.[60] After the Second World War LIRA diversified its activities in several directions, including the implications for the linen industry of the introduction of spun rayons into Northern Ireland, though it still felt its work was not sufficiently appreciated by its members.[61] Further extensions of its work came through efforts to improve technology and the formation, in 1965, of a Merchanting Research Sub-committee. As the industry contracted, the traditionally low rates of subscription to LIRA declined still further to the point where it was in danger of losing its eligibility for any government funding.[62] Indeed, looking at the half century from 1919 it must be doubted whether, in the absence of sustained government assistance, the linen industry would have been willing to undertake *any* significant research effort.

If research into flax cultivation and linen manufacture was belated and poorly financed, the advertising techniques of the industry were also wanting. Before 1914 there was no concerted initiative to advertise linen products, and this was attributed to Ulster manufacturers' 'possession of a virtual monopoly' especially in the high quality end of the market.[63] The loss of civilian markets during the First World War, together with intensified competition from cotton, encouraged a reappraisal of advertising policy and marketing policy in general.

An obvious difficulty facing the linen industry was the finance and co-ordination of an advertising strategy for dozens of small and medium size firms. A related problem also arose from the atomistic market structure of the industry, namely the multiplicity of product lines inevitably produced by large numbers of specialist firms. After the First World War, some of the most informed commentators pointed to the urgent need to cut down on the number of products offered by individual firms. As one such commentator put it in 1918: 'An inspection of the catalogues of even moderate size linen manufacturing concerns will show that each of them is attempting to make almost every class of linen. The aim, in each case, is to put on the market a complete range of cloths which shall comprise everything demanded by a linen consumer.[64]

The results of this were damaging, both to individual firms and to the industry as a whole. Lack of standardization meant that short runs of production were far too common and changes of setting to machinery too frequent, leading inevitably to idle capacity. In 1918, a year of very strong demand in the linen industry, it was estimated that some 25 per cent of machinery lay idle because of the 'evil of short runs', and this contributed significantly to the relatively poor productivity of linen workers compared to those in cotton.[65] Despite this, the prospects for persuading linen manufacturers of the benefits of standardization were not thought to be good, and indeed seem not to have made much headway ten years later.[66]

However, a decision to undertake a concerted advertising campaign was made in 1919 and can be viewed as one of the earliest signs that the industry in general had begun to appreciate its lack of effort in the past. Co-ordination of the new initiative was undertaken by the Irish Linen Society, and the main aim was to improve sales in the US market. An initial budget of £30,000, later increased to £90,000 over three years, was raised by requesting Society members to contribute subscriptions according to their annual turnover.[67] Another part of the sales drive, aimed particularly at distinguishing linen products from close substitutes, was the introduction in 1921 of the 'True Irish Linen' hallmark, which was designed to instil a 'true guild spirit of salesmanship and pride of products into all associated, whether spinner, weaver or merchant'.[68]

Welcome though such initiatives were, their utility was diminished by the unprecedented price instability of linen goods after 1918. Stable supplies of raw material and stable market conditions had meant that linen prices had been fairly predictable before 1914. After the war, this was no longer the case. Once the economic downturn began, from mid-1920, retail buyers simply ordered the absolute minimum – in the firm expectation that prices would fall lower still. Neither the advertising campaign nor the one third reduction in the prices of linen goods in New York succeeded in achieving much beyond 'limited purchasing by those who were really in need of certain articles'.[69]

A further obstacle for linen in the American market during the 1920s was the highly effective advertising campaign mounted by one of its most serious competitors – US-made, linen finish cotton damasks. According to the Belfast Chamber of Commerce, linen manufacturers and merchants were simply not effective enough in promoting their products and had no answer to the Americans, thus 'they are letting the case go by default, and they are losing business thereby'.[70] What contemporaries could not fail to notice was that the extreme buoyancy of the US economy in the years after 1921 was not reflected in a strong demand for linen. In 1928, for example, the US took 78 per cent less linen (by weight) from the UK than it had in 1912.[71]

Frequent criticisms of its advertising efforts at home and abroad, together with the possibilities offered by the apparently endless economic boom in the US, led to a belated decision by both Irish and Scottish linen manufacturers and merchants to mount a more intensive campaign. In the home market, by 1928 the Irish Linen Guild had organized the distribution of trademarked and standardized goods (table damasks, bed linen and face towelling) at uniform prices to 700 firms in 300 locations throughout Britain and Ireland.

Standardization of size, price and quality was welcomed by the major retail
outlets such as Selfridges 'and others of the great London stores'.[72] In the US, a
delegation from Irish and Scottish linen industries arrived to promote their
products at the end of the 1920s, but their arrival coincided almost exactly with
the collapse of the New York Stock Exchange on Wall Street in October
1929.[73] If linen exports to the US had been disappointing in the 1920s, their
prospects after 1929 were far worse.

While in the United States, however, the delegation received confirmation of
a number of respects in which the linen industry was considered to be old
fashioned or inefficient. These included obsolescent styles and designs, the fact
that there was still too little standardization of quality, unnecessary duplication of distribution effort and excessive internal competition between firms
in the same industry.[74] None of these criticisms was new, but the failure to
tackle them effectively meant that the linen industry consistently failed to take
advantage of its most important and prosperous if increasingly tough market
during the 1920s.

The clear message was that a co-ordinated marketing and distribution
strategy was essential to revive demand. The need to rethink marketing
strategy, and in particular to anticipate demand through market research,
continued to be stressed into the 1950s. As a leading linen manufacturer put it
in 1954, 'To me, one of the peculiar features of the Irish linen trade has always
been its patient waiting for the customer to state his needs rather than a
"commencing-upon-manufacturing" and aggressive sales policy based upon a
study of the consumer markets and the catering for their potential demand in
advance.'[75]

The role of government

The various problems confronting the linen industry from the 1920s onwards
and the growing pressure for some kind of protection inevitably raises an
important long term issue: the relationship of the new devolved government of
Northern Ireland with the region's most important manufacturing industry. It
is sometimes suggested that at Westminister in the earlier part of the twentieth
century industrialists, compared with the City, 'were less well integrated into
the policy making structure and could never manage to speak with one voice
on major issues'.[76] The position of industrialists in the Northern Ireland
government was, however, very different from that at Westminster.

During the Home Rule debate from the 1880s until the partition of Ireland
in 1920, most of Ulster's industrial, commercial and agrarian élite was firmly in
the Unionist camp, and the creation of a regional government enabled them to
exercise a degree of political power that would have been almost inconceivable
under any other circumstances. The first general election in 1921 produced
forty unionist MPs and a dozen nationalists/republicans. Of the unionists, no
fewer than ten were connected with the linen industry.[77] As far as the executive
was concerned, the roll call of ministers 'read like an executive committee of
Northern industry and commerce',[78] and they retained their business interests
throughout their usually long spells in office. A classic example was J Milne

Barbour, chairman and managing director of the Linen Thread Company, who also served as unpaid Minister of Commerce from 1925 to 1941, after which he became Minister of Finance.

Even if it would be perverse to suggest that the Northern Ireland government had an anti-industrial ethos, or that there were no conflicts between ministers, it can be claimed that in the long term the government showed itself unimaginative in economic policy and, perhaps predictably, keen to prop up the traditional textile industry of the province. To a large extent, of course, Northern ministers were no different from those at Westminster in their commitment to strictly limited state intervention in industrial affairs, and in this they clearly had the support of the Belfast Chamber of Commerce, the oldest and largest organization of businessmen in the province. In 1920, for example, the Chamber 'once more' and unanimously passed a resolution calling on Lloyd George to reduce public expenditure to balance the budget, to reduce the national debt, and for 'Government control of business [to] . . . be terminated as soon as possible'.[79] However, even had the Northern government wished to pursue an independent and positive economic policy, its scope for doing so was limited by the ultimate supremacy of the Westminster government. A further obstacle to decisive action was the fact that although the Minister of Commerce was in theory responsible for assisting industry and trade, virtually all other ministers had a 'finger in the pie', thus making inter-departmental confusion and conflict more likely.[80]

In the 1920s the Northern government did attempt to assist the linen industry in a rather negative way by lobbying for it to be included under the Safeguarding of Industries legislation.[81] This attempt, the result of increasing linen import penetration from European producers, was unsuccessful – much to the disappointment of the prime minister, Sir James Craig, who in 1926 confessed himself a firm believer in protection for home industry.[82] One possible area in which the government might have played a positive role was in the rationalization of the linen industry, but it was clear that no government-led initiative would be forthcoming. Craig, while deeming it desirable that the industry secure expert opinion on the feasibility of any rationalization scheme, also judged it preferable for industrialists to perceive and act on this need for themselves, rather than being forced into it by government.[83] At the same time, J. M. Andrews, Minister of Labour, took a strictly short term view of the impact of rationalization, and thought it unlikely to lower unemployment since it would necessarily involve the disappearance of some firms and the scrapping of excess capacity.[84] During the debate on rationalization in the late 1920s and early 1930s the Ministry of Commerce indicated that they 'would not take any part in negotiations'.[85]

In the 1930s, most policy actions which were considered to benefit the linen industry came not from the Northern but from the Westminster government, and none of them addressed the problems that continued to characterize the industry. The abandonment of the Gold Standard, together with the introduction of tariffs were seen as significant for the industry, with one leading commentator going so far as to say that their combined effect 'has been to save the Irish linen trade from very great peril'. Further optimism was engendered by concessions won at the Ottawa Conference in 1932, especially with regard to the Canadian market which took ten per cent of total UK linen exports. The UK clearly dominated the Dominion market for linen goods: in 1930 its share of total linen imports into Australia was estimated at 87 per cent, Canada 95 per cent, New Zealand 96 per cent and South Africa 78 per cent. Even so, contemporaries warned that neither simplification nor reduction of Dominion tariffs would guarantee that the linen industry would benefit unless manufacturers advertised their products 'more intensively in the Dominion trade and general press.'[87] Well into the 1930s, then, the old complaint about ineffective advertising was still being voiced.

The fourth area of government policy that was widely expected to be advantageous to the linen industry, perhaps more than to any other UK industry, was the Anglo-American Trade Agreement of 1938. The US remained the largest single export market for linen goods and this market was worth about as much as the combined exports of the UK cotton and woollen industries to the US. The significance of linen as a dollar earner, to the tune of around £1.5–2 million in the late 1930s, was not lost on contemporaries.[88] It is not surprising then that reductions ranging from ten to twenty per cent *ad valorem* on virtually all classes of linen goods were widely welcomed by the industry and by the Northern Ireland government, and seemed to offer some respite from decades of rising tariff barriers in this crucial market.[89] Any potential benefits, however, soon evaporated on the outbreak of war in the following year.

Although protection and the Ottawa agreement had inevitably increased the significance of the home and Dominion markets, the departure from Gold (at least in the short term) had increased export competitiveness[90] and the 1938 agreement offered some hope in the US market, the fundamental and long-appreciated problems of raw material supply and price instability were still acute. As an example, raw material prices in the linen industry rose by about 70 per cent during 1934, and at the same time the UK depended on foreign sources for some 95 per cent of its raw material.[91]

Given the overwhelming dependence on imported raw materials, it is no surprise that between 1939 and 1945, as in the First World War, disruption of flax supplies together with strong government demand quickly 'raised the price level of all grades to a point that must inevitably preclude the use of flax fibre in the production of any but essential government supplies'.[92] The raw material problem became acute after the German invasion of Belgium in 1940. UK textile industries were quickly brought under government control, though the economy of Northern Ireland generally was slow to mobilize, apparently because of the reluctance of its government to become integrated into the national structure of area boards under the Ministry of Supply.[93]

In the case of the linen industry, an important opportunity for introspection might have been afforded by the appointment of a Post-War Planning Committee whose unanimous report was presented in March 1944. Ten of the Committee's eleven members were directly involved in the linen industry and it would seem that in the interests of unanimity they took care to 'recommend nothing that would disturb any existing interest in the industry'. While not hesitating to ask for more government financial assistance, their argument, in the words of one impartial expert, was that 'the industrialists' pre-war sovereignty should not be challenged in any way'. All in all, the 1944 Report was 'a most disappointing document'.[94] Although it contained some positive proposals on the organization of flax buying and appreciated the need for co-ordinated research – supported, as ever, by considerable government finance – it seemed to assume that the industry was highly efficient and therefore played down or ignored the potential for structural change or modernization of machinery.

The 1944 Report signally failed to explore the extent to which the industry could use non-flax fibre, or extend production runs through standardization, or eliminate excess capacity. In short, there was little in the report to indicate that the industry intended to change direction in the post-war world. In any case, because the economic climate was generally buoyant in the six years after 1945, the need to change direction at all seemed much less pressing. Exports of linen goods from the UK increased by nine per cent between 1947 and 1951, and it was not until the severe slump of 1951–2 that the industry relapsed into its familiar pattern of unemployment, short-time working and depressed profit levels.[95]

Between 1939 and 1951, however, while the fortunes of the linen industry temporarily improved, the shortage of raw material forced manufacturers to experiment with the use of man-made fibres – though the initial opportunity for Ulster linen manufacturers to do this owed more to luck than to skill. In 1941 the government imposed a system for the allocation of rayon. This meant that the purchase of all rayon yarn was under government control, with the exception of yarn from staple more than three inches long when spun on woollen or linen machinery. This loophole, which was not closed until 1945, enabled rayon staple to establish itself quickly as a major new raw material in the textile industry of Northern Ireland. Moreover, the price of rayon was both lower and more stable than that of flax. If after 1918 linen had become more expensive relative to cotton, so after 1939 it became more expensive in relation to rayon.[96]

Before the end of the Second World War no rayon was actually spun in Northern Ireland, and the province received the bulk of its supplies from spinners in Yorkshire. After the war, with indispensable government assistance, the development of man-made fibre production became extremely important in Northern Ireland – and within twenty years its contribution to net manufacturing output in the province was double that of linen (see Table 4.5). If the loophole of 1941 had enabled Ulster's textile industry to substitute man-made fibres into their production process more easily than cotton manufacturers, the province was also fortunate in its ability to offer financial inducements to industry that were more wide-ranging and more generous than in Britain.[97] This relative generosity became a permanent feature from the later 1940s onwards, and by the early 1970s it was estimated that Northern Ireland was able to provide assistance to new projects to the extent of 62.9 per cent of capital costs, as against 50.6 per cent in Development Areas and 31.4 per cent in other British regions.[98]

This special position was largely due to the province's exclusion from the 1945 Distribution of Industry Act, the cornerstone of post-war British regional policy.[99] Even before the end of the war, however, discussions had taken place between Sir Basil Brooke, Prime Minister of Northern Ireland, and Courtaulds

Table 4.5 Net output of the textile industry as a percentage of total net manufacturing output in Northern Ireland 1949–75

Year	Textiles	Textiles other than linen	Linen
1949	31.5	2.9	28.6
1954	24.9	5.4	19.5
1958	18.7	4.7	14.0
1963	18.6	7.5	11.1
1968	20.5	13.6	6.9
1972	20.6	15.1	5.5
1975	16.6	11.3	5.3

Source: Reports on the Census of Production, Ministry/Department of Commerce (Belfast)

which centred on the possibility of securing a site for a staple fibre factory in the province.[100] Availability of labour and materials, argued Brooke, would enable work on a new site to begin immediately – even in wartime. Despite the fact that building costs were higher and the local market obviously much smaller than in Britain, the opportunity to start construction without delay was the clinching argument in favour of a Northern Ireland site for Courtaulds. In the event, the immediate start did not prove feasible, Northern Ireland therefore no longer seemed so attractive, and the claims of alternative sites increased in strength. The Courtaulds board, however, decided to keep its promise to Brooke and the company went on to build a plant at Carrickfergus which opened in July 1948.

Courtaulds' move into Northern Ireland brought prestige and employment, and it turned out to be the first of several instances of inward investment by British, European or American multinationals. Courtaulds opened a second plant in 1953, and within ten years others followed including Monsanto in 1958, Du Pont in 1960, and British Enkalon and ICI in 1963. The rising trend of inward investment in textiles was reflected in the ever more extensive financial assistance provided to industry by the Northern Ireland government. From a level of £600,000 in 1951–2, government direct assistance increased to £40 million by 1969–70 and totalled £230 million during the period 1945–70.[101]

In a region which found it impossible to achieve full employment, it might be expected that the arrival of such major companies as Courtaulds would have been universally welcomed. At first, however, there were several important voices within the linen industry and the Northern Ireland government which regarded new firms almost entirely as a threat. Criticism of the Industries Development Acts (1932, 1937 and 1945) centred mainly on the argument that they paid insufficient attention to the track record, current requirements and future prospects of firms in traditional industries which, it was claimed, were now losing labour to new firms.[102]

Moreover, many still considered it axiomatic that it was the traditional industries which 'in the testing time ahead would allow Northern Ireland to avoid large scale unemployment by their ability to adapt and sell in competitive world markets.'[103] Accordingly, a series of financial packages beginning with the Re-equipment of Industry Act (1951) was designed to provide traditional industry with every opportunity to modernize technology and buildings. The need for modernization was indeed acute. By 1948, no new flax mills had been built for over forty years, while in many mills the average age of machinery in active operation was forty or fifty years. Any new machinery 'was installed to suit existing housing with the result than in many instances conditions extant today are far removed from those required to ensure maximum output at minimum cost'.[104]

The demand for re-equipment grants was strong, and of 160 applicants for assistance by 1954, about half came from the textile industries. Government assistance enabled Ulster firms to re-equip with modern automatic looms for weaving rayon to such an extent that by 1957 the region had the most modern machinery of any UK textile region using rayon.[105] Many mills, however, continued to operate obsolete plant and informed opinion pointed to other problems which still needed to be addressed, not least cost accounting and production planning.[106] Within the linen industry, less attention apparently went into solving these problems than was devoted to airing complaints about the allegedly punitive levels of taxation and the adverse impact this had on private investment, and indeed significant concessions were made by the government in response to these complaints during the 1950s.[107] Moreover there were some who claimed that the scope for technical change in the linen industry was small because of the difficulties inherent in processing the flax fibre, and for this reason the industry was bound to retain its 'craft' character. In the view of one linen manufacturer, government grants were too easily available and rather than spending vast sums on re-equipment firms would be well advised to pay more attention to training the labour force:

> Far too many Northern Ireland linen manufacturers still employ rule-of-thumb methods in determining matters, and supposed economies are too often more than discounted by the higher overheads which pile up when the older craft methods of manufacturing give way to so-called modern ones. In successful linen weaving, as in spinning, patience, dexterity, indeed inherited skill, can play a greater part than anything else in making for success . . . In the past there has been too much "leaving it to chance" to provide recruits who in many cases received only indifferent training, and as a result took too long in becoming proficient operatives . . .[108]

Although there was some truth in this, there was a danger that it would be taken to extremes and used as an argument against technical change *per se*, and there were some informed critics who took linen manufacturers to task for their 'craft obsession'.[109]

Notwithstanding all the government aid and the buoyancy of the international economy, Northern Ireland still failed by a considerable margin to achieve full employment during the period after 1945. The chronic difficulties faced by the linen industry were reflected in its continuing decline as an employer: 58,300 in 1949, 25,300 in 1968, and also in the emphatic collapse in its contribution to net manufacturing output in the province (see Table 4.5).

As the decline accelerated two Queen's University economists, K. S. Isles and Norman Cuthbert, compiled *An Economic Survey of Northern Ireland*, commissioned in 1947 by the then Minister of Commerce, Sir Roland Nugent, and published ten years later. Apart from being arguably the finest survey of any UK region ever published, the report contains in places a penetrating critique of the province's industrial structure. Its authors analysed in great detail all the problems involved in sustaining innovation and expansion that stemmed from a predominance of small, family-run private firms in the linen industry – though they did note that in the 1930s such firms may have persevered when other types of enterprise would not.[110]

Though it was not part of their brief to recommend possible courses of action, the authors amply fulfilled their wish to provide data and numbers which would be beneficial in the formation of economic policy. Indeed, their criticisms of the structure of the province's traditional industries and government industrial policy, and their suggestion for a Development Corporation, were more soundly based and better argued than anywhere else. Perhaps for that reason, the reception to the *Economic Survey*, on the part of the very Ministry that had commissioned it, was distinctly cool. Lord Glentoran, Minister of Commerce at the time of the report's publication was particularly unimpressed with the argument for a Development Corporation since it 'showed a sorry lack of faith in the vitality of Ulster industry'.[111] That lack of faith was largely justified.

The history of government relations with the textile industries in Northern Ireland in the decades after 1921 is a mixture of 'negative' intervention, such as pressure for safeguarding or protection between the wars, combined with 'positive' financial assistance, which played a crucial role in sustaining both research and advertising effort throughout the period down to 1970. If both those efforts were lacking, the fault lay far more with the industry than with the government. After the Second World War government assistance played a more important role, not only in research and advertising, but also in the finance of modernization at firm level and in actively promoting inward investment. As far as the latter was concerned, the policy seemed to succeed until the early 1970s. The arrival of many large man made fibre and other manufacturers helped to divert attention from the decline in linen, but it also increased the province's dependence on corporations controlled from elsewhere. By 1975, 45 per cent of Northern Ireland's largest industrial enterprises, employing 500 or more workers, were controlled from Britain, 20 per cent from the United States, and ten per cent from other European Community countries.[112] The ability to attract inward investment began to decline sharply following the outbreak and continuance of political conflict in Northern Ireland after 1969. Moreover, the province was far more dependent on oil for energy than the rest of the UK and the oil price shocks after 1973 posed a major problem for the energy intensive man-made fibre industries. These factors, coupled with huge overvaluation of sterling between 1979 and 1983,[113] led to a dramatic collapse of the man-made fibre industries in Northern Ireland, with the closure of many plants including Courtaulds, ICI, British Enkalon and others, and massive redundancies at those plants that remained. This collapse, together with the longer term decline of linen and the province's other staple industry, shipbuilding, are crucial elements in one of the most acute cases of deindustrialization in Western Europe since the Second World War.

Conclusion

In this paper we have tried to highlight the problems encountered by a traditional industry in a peripheral region. If some of these problems stemmed from forces that were outside the industry's control, others did not. Some, but by no means all, of the latter were a direct consequence of the competitive nature of the industry and the predominance of small, family firms. We have noted weaknesses in research, advertising and marketing, cost accounting techniques, production planning, fabric design and, perhaps, an overemphasis on the 'craft' aspects of production at the expense of technology.

Furthermore, though the Northern Ireland government helped to compensate for the industry's lack of effort in some areas, it did nothing to promote structural change. It was also unmoved by independent criticism of the organization and strategy of the industry itself. The fact that from 1921 to 1972 Northern Ireland was governed by one party with little opposition, together with the fact that leaders of the linen industry actively supported and were integrated into the government, greatly reduced the scope for debate and the critics' chances of a sympathetic hearing.

From the evidence presented here, two conclusions might be drawn. First, the decline of the linen industry had many more causes than a contracting world market, and the shortcomings of the industry itself need to be emphasised far more than they have been hitherto. Second, while there is no doubt about the tenacity and strength of structural and institutional rigidities in the linen industry and the economy in which it operated, there is, as both Alford and Coleman have recently stressed, a need to recognize the limitations of explanations of industrial decline that rest on institutional or structural factors. In particular, such explanations play down or ignore the attitudes and commerical practices of businessmen.[114] Certainly our evidence points to the need to give very considerable weight to the latter in explaining the decline of the linen industry during the twentieth century. As one of the more reflective linen manufacturers put it in 1954: 'many of our industry's past troubles are the result of lack of courage, imagination and enterprise'.[115]

Notes

1 Financial assistance to undertake research for this paper was provided by the Economic and Social Research Council and the Pasold Research Fund, to whom I am most grateful. I would also like to thank Hilary Ollerenshaw for her comments on an earlier draft.
2 Elbaum, Bernard, and Lazonick, William (eds), 1986, *The decline of the British economy*, Oxford University Press, Oxford, ch. 1, esp. p. 2.
3 See in particular ibid., pp. 18–50 and Lazonick, 1983, 'Industrial organization and

technological change: the decline of the British cotton industry', *Business History Review*, 57(2); 195–236.
4 Beacham, A., 1945, 'The Ulster linen industry', *Economica*, 11(2): 205.
5 Pollard, Sidney, 1981, *Peaceful conquest: The industrialization of Europe 1750–1970*, Oxford University Press, Oxford, p. v.
6 Keeble, David, 1976, *Industrial location and planning in the United Kingdom*, Methuen, London, pp. 207, 218.
7 Murie, A. S. *et al.*, 1969, 'A survey of industrial movement in Northern Ireland between 1965 and 1969', *Economic and Social Review*, 4(2): 231.
8 Thomas, M. D., 1965, 'Economic geography of manufacturing industry in Northern Ireland', unpublished Ph.D. thesis, Queen's University of Belfast, pp. 15, 31, 40.
9 Durie, Alastair, 1979, *The Scottish linen industry in the eighteenth century*, John Donald, Edinburgh, p. 169.
10 *The Statist*, 4 August 1917: 194.
11 Clark, W. A. G., 1913, *Linen, jute and hemp industries in the United Kingdom*, Department of Commerce, Washington D.C., Special Agents series number 74, p. 61.
12 Clegg, H. A., Fox, A., Thompson, A. F., 1964, *A history of British trade unions since 1889, Volume I, 1889–1910*, Oxford University Press, Oxford, p. 468.
13 Lazonick, W., 1986, 'The cotton industry', in Elbaum and Lazonick (eds), *Decline of the British Economy*, pp. 24–28.
14 Black, William, 1957, 'Variations in employment in the linen industry', unpublished Ph.D. thesis, Queen's University of Belfast, p. 110.
15 Ibid.; Patterson, H., 1985, 'Industrial labour and the labour movement 1820 to 1914', in Kennedy, L., Ollerenshaw, P. (eds), *An economic history of Ulster 1820–1939*, Manchester University Press, Manchester, pp. 175–6.
16 Data on productivity and costs are taken from Clark, *Linen, jute and hemp industries*, pp. 9, 12.
17 Ibid., p. 21.
18 *Flax supply association report for 1919*, Belfast, 1920, p. 19.
19 Clark, *Linen, jute and hemp industries*, p. 19.
20 Notes on flax control, May 1918, P.R.O. MUN 4/6506. See also *The Statist*, 15 September 1917: 445–6.
21 *Flax supply association report for 1919*, p. 19; *Textile Recorder*, 15 May 1918: 31–2; *Textile Manufacturer*, 15 July 1918: 182; *The Statist*, 22 February 1919: 315.
22 Notes on flax control, para 1.
23 Government control ceased on 31 August 1920, but the Flax Control Board was revived early in the Second World War to meet similar problems.
24 *Textile Recorder*, 15 January 1918: 316.
25 On prices before and after the war see *The Statist*, 17 Febuary 1923: 43; Report of the committee appointed to investigate the principal causes of the depression in the linen industry, 1928, P.R.O.N.I. COM 27/1: 16–21, (hereafter cited as 1928 report on depression).
26 Black, 'Variations in employment in the linen industry': pp. 213–4.
27 *Textile Recorder*, 14 August 1915: 123.
28 Ibid., 15 May 1918: 31.
29 *Northern Whig*, 7 February 1914; flax spinners association minute book 1912–20, P.R.O.N.I. D.2088/29/4, *passim*. Short time working began on 2 March 1914.
30 See in particular *Textile Recorder*, 15 November 1917: 213; 15 January 1918: 315–6; 15 March 1918: 402; 15 May 1918: 3–4; 15 July 1918: 86–7.
31 Alford, B. W. E., 1986, 'Lost opportunities: British business and businessmen

during the first world war', in McKendrick, N., and Outhwaite, R. B., (eds), *Business life and public policy: essays in honour of D. C. Coleman*, Cambridge University Press, Cambridge, p. 220.

32 *Textile Recorder*, 15 November 1918: 249.

33 See for example Johnson, D. S., 1985, 'The Northern Ireland economy 1914-39', in Kennedy and Ollerenshaw, *An economic history of Ulster*, pp. 196-7.

34 1928 report on depression, p. 9.

35 Ibid.

36 Beacham, 'The Ulster linen industry': 205.

37 Flax spinners association minute book 1912-20, 18 June 1920.

38 Ibid., 16-18, 25 June 1920; ibid., 1920-34, 2, 30 July; 6 August 1920. Irish powerloom manufacturers' association minute book of the association and council, P.R.O.N.I. D.2088/30/3, 4 June; 9 July; 13 August; 19 October; 16 November 1920.

39 Flax spinners association minute book 1920-34, 7 January 1921.

40 *Textile Recorder*, 15 November 1920: 54.

41 Ibid., 15 February 1921: 70; 15 March 1921: 52.

42 1928 report on depression, pp. 1-2.

43 Bamberg, J. H., 1988, 'The rationalization of the British cotton industry in the inter-war years', *Textile History*, 19(1): 83-102.

44 Memorandum by Sir Gilbert Garnsey KBE dealing with a proposed scheme of amalgamation, 19 March 1929, P.R.O.N.I. COM 25/8. This memorandum estimates that in Northern Ireland there were 50 firms engaged in spinning, some 100 in weaving and over 130 in merchanting.

45 Flax spinners association minute book 1920-32, meeting of the spinning trade, 11 April 1930, evidence of H. R. Ross, a member of the Linen Industry (Remedies) Committee.

46 Beacham, A., 1945, 'Post-war planning in the Ulster linen industry', *Economic Journal*, 55(1): 119.

47 Steed, G. P. F., 1971, 'Internal organization, firm integration, and locational change: the Northern Ireland linen complex, 1954-64', *Economic Geography*, 47(3): 375. The following paragraph is based on this excellent study.

48 Ibid.: 376.

49 Steed, G. P. F., Thomas, Morgan D., 1971, 'Regional industrial change: Northern Ireland', *Annals of the Association of American Geographers*, 61: 348.

50 Mowery, David, C., 1986, 'Industrial research 1900-50', in Elbaum and Lazonick, *Decline of the British economy*, pp. 189-222, esp. 205-7.

51 Committee on Industry and Trade [Balfour Committee], 1927, *Factors in industrial and commercial efficiency*, pp. 308-23.

52 *Textile Recorder*, 15 October 1919: 208.

53 Ibid., 15 May 1918: 4.

54 Ibid., 15 December 1917: 253.

55 Ibid.

56 Ibid., 15 February 1919: 366; 15 August 1919: 146.

57 1928 report on depression, p. 15.

58 *Textile Recorder*, 15 January 1920: 363; 15 April 1920: 456. In the long term it did not prove possible to increase flax yields significantly. See Black, 'Variations in employment', p. 249.

59 *Belfast Chamber of Commerce Journal*, April 1923: 10.

60 *Textile Recorder*, June 1944: 28.

61 Ibid., February 1952: 96.

62 Ibid., March 1959: 52; May 1959: 34; May 1965: 34.

63 *The Statist*, 1 March 1919: 365.
64 *Textile Recorder*, 15 November 1918: 251.
65 Ibid. and 15 July 1926: 51–2.
66 1928 report on depression, p. 15.
67 *Textile Recorder*, 15 March 1919: 435.
68 Ibid., 15 September 1921: 58.
69 Ibid.: 67.
70 *Belfast Chamber of Commerce Journal*, I, April 1923: 10.
71 *The Statist*, 17 August 1929: 26.
72 *Textile Recorder*, 15 November 1928: 55–7; *The Statist*, 5 October 1929: 482.
73 *The Statist*, 7 December 1929: 986.
74 Ibid.
75 Larmor, Sir Graham, 1954–5, 'Mechanization and productivity in the Ulster linen industry', *Journal of the Statistical and Social Inquiry Society of Ireland*, 19(3): 334.
76 Cain, Peter, Hopkins, A. G., 1987, 'Gentlemanly capitalism and British expansion overseas II: new imperialism, 1850–1945', *Economic History Review*, 40(1): 4–5.
77 *Textile Recorder*, 21 June 1921: 105.
78 Farrell, Michael, 1976, *Northern Ireland: The Orange state*, Pluto Press, London, cited in Buckland, *Factory of grievances*, p 12.
79 Belfast chamber of commerce letter book 1919–20, P.R.O.N.I. D.1857/1/BA/12, B.C.C. to the Rt. Hon. David Lloyd George, 28 March 1920.
80 Buckland, *Factory of grievances*, pp. 9–36, 105–29.
81 Irish power loom manufacturers' association minute book of the association and council, P.R.O.N.I. D.2088/30/4, 11 May 1928.
82 *Textile Recorder*, 15 January 1926: 10.
83 Buckland, *Factory of grievances*, p. 118.
84 Ibid.
85 Meeting of the spinning trade 11 April 1930, cited above, see note 45.
86 *Textile Recorder*, 15 January 1933: 27.
87 Ibid., and 15 November 1932: 21.
88 Beacham, 'The Ulster linen industry', p. 199.
89 *Textile Recorder*, 6 December 1938: 16.
90 Although depreciation of sterling was expected to boost exports, it did increase the price of imported flax and yarn.
91 *Textile Recorder*, 15 January 1935: 18.
92 Ibid., 6 June 1940: 26.
93 Bew, P., Gibbon, P., Patterson, H., 1979, *The state in Northern Ireland 1921–72: political forces and social classes*, Manchester University Press, Manchester, p. 104.
94 Beacham, 'Post-war planning', 121.
95 Black, 'Variations in employment', pp. 47–9; *Textile Recorder*, June 1952: 122; August 1952: 96; October 1952: 118.
96 This account is based on Hague, D. C., 1957, *The economics of man-made fibres*, Macmillan, London, pp. 272–8.
97 The best account is McCrone, G., 1969, *Regional policy in Britain*, George Allen & Unwin, London: esp. pp. 139–42.
98 Murie *et al.*, 'Survey of industrial movement in Northern Ireland': 232.
99 See McCrone, *passim.*; Edwards, R. S., Townsend, H., *Business Enterprise*, Macmillan, London, pp. 424–31.
100 Coleman, D. C., 1980, *Courtaulds: an economic and social history; volume III, crisis and change, 1940–65*, Oxford University Press, Oxford, pp. 7, 42–3. The ease

of effluent disposal, not mentioned by Coleman, was also seen as a factor in Courtaulds' decision to go to Carrickfergus. Thomas, 'Economic geography of manufacturing industry': 39.
101 Ministry of Commerce, Belfast, 1970, Facts and figures about industrial development in Northern Ireland: 10.
102 Bew, Gibbon, Patterson, *The state in Northern Ireland*, p. 137.
103 Ibid.
104 *Textile Recorder*, July 1948: 45.
105 Hague, *Economics of man made fibres*, pp. 276-7.
106 *Textile Recorder*, January 1952: 106.
107 Bew, Gibbon, Patterson, *The state in Northern Ireland*, p. 141.
108 Larmor, 'Mechanization and productivity', p. 33.
109 Steed and Thomas, 'Regional industrial change', p. 349.
110 Isles, K. S., Cuthbert, N., 1957, *An economic survey of Northern Ireland*, HMSO, Belfast.
111 Bew, Gibbon, Patterson, *The state in Northern Ireland*, p. 144.
112 Keeble, *Industrial location and planning*, p. 237.
113 Kennedy, K., Giblin, T., McHugh, D., 1988, *The economic development of Ireland in the twentieth century*, Routledge, London, pp. 108-9.
114 Alford, 'Lost opportunities', pp. 225-6; Coleman, D. C., 1988, 'Review of Elbaum and Lazonick', *Decline of the British economy, Business History*, 30(1): pp. 130-1.
115 Larmor, 'Mechanization and productivity', p. 34.

5 An economic background to Munich revisited: British investment in inter-war Czechoslovakia

Alice Teichova,
Girton College, Cambridge

5.1 Introduction

In the first place I should like to say how much I welcome the opportunity to contribute to this volume in honour of Sidney Pollard whom I met for the first time twenty-five years ago when he visited Prague and gave a lecture at my Department of History at the Paedagogical Faculty of Charles University. Indeed, he was the first prominent British economic historian I was able to meet personally and to talk to about the results of my many years of research on foreign investment in Czechoslovakia. When in 1969, after twenty years of absence, I returned to Britain – taking refuge for the second time – Sidney Pollard became not only a colleague but also a friend. While seriously interested in my claims that British investment in Czechoslovakia was considerable he – like many others of my colleagues, half teasingly and half seriously – was doubtful whether there was anything of *economic* interest to Britain in Central Europe, especially with regard to Czechoslovakia, until I was able to put forward convincing evidence in my book, *An economic background to Munich; International business and Czechoslovakia 1918–1938* published by Cambridge University Press in 1974. It was my aim to show that this country in the heart of Europe was not so 'far away', not so unknown,[1] and economically not as insignificant as this view would imply.[2]

In the second place I welcome the opportunity to contribute to this *Festschrift* because it offers me a chance to revisit the topic of *An economic background to Munich*. This book has a rather unusual pre-publication history because I delivered the first manuscript written in Czech to Academia, the publishing house of the Czechoslovak Academy of Sciences in Prague, on the afternoon of 19 August 1968. On the next day the troops of the Warsaw Pact countries invaded Czechoslovakia and, as a result of the repressive political period which followed, my book was struck from the publication list of Academia. When six years later the book appeared in print in England it was, like all other of my publications, banned in Czechoslovakia. Two months ago I received a letter from Academia apologizing for unjustifiably cancelling my contract of 1968 and offering to include my book, *Zahraniční kapitál v československém hospodářství 1918–1938* (Foreign Capital in the Cze-

choslovak Economy 1918–1938) in their publication plan of 1990–1992. To this
I wholeheartedly agreed, especially since my book has been out of print since
the early 1980s and Cambridge University Press has generously agreed to
waive its rights in order to let the Czech publication go ahead. Thus I am in the
process of *revisiting* the problem of international business in Czechoslovakia.

In the third place, the theme of international investment is highly topical as –
since November 1989 – the Czechoslovak economy, like the economies of other
Central and South-Eastern European countries, is arousing intense interest
among foreign investors. Indeed, for instance, the famous Škoda-Works are
considered to be 'a prize catch for the West'.[3] The Czechoslovak government
seeks now, as it did after the First World War, economic partnership with the
West and wishes to revitalize its role as a door to Eastern and South-East
Europe.

The new and unexpected phenomenon of the opening up of the Eastern half
of Europe serves only to increase the scramble for markets which has
accelerated in preparation for a single common European market in 1992. In
addition, the struggle between large companies, mainly based in the leading
industrial powers, is marked by the growth of mergers and takeovers within
and across national borders, in order to gain an increasing share of international investment.

Historically, foreign direct investment is closely bound up with the
development of international business and has become the most effective
instrument in establishing the dominance of giant multinational enterprise in
the international economy. In the 1980s, the decisive share of the total stock
of foreign direct investment is owned, controlled and operated by multinational companies whose headquarters are situated in their various home countries. Geographically the giant companies of the USA, the European
Community and Japan have established a veritable triangular power base
which, so far, has not been seriously challenged. The industrially developed
economies not only export the largest share of total direct foreign investment
(97.3 per cent in 1983) but they also absorb its greatest share (74.2 per cent in
1983) investing in each other's enterprises, while the developing areas receive
a relatively small percentage of total direct foreign investment (25.8 per cent
in 1983) and obviously they are only marginally engaged in exporting capital
(2.7 per cent in 1983).[4]

Economically and politically, foreign investment became one of the crucial
factors in the international capitalist economy and in international relations.
Thus the changes in the rank order of the leading countries of origin of
foreign direct investment over time represent also some measure of their
power and influence; at the same time they reflect the economic strength of
the big companies radiating their direct investments from those countries.

Just as we are witnessing a redistribution of spheres of influence without a
war in Europe at the present time, a shift in the balance of power in politics and
economics occurred after the October Revolution in 1917 and after the First
World War in 1918. To quote the opening paragraph of *An economic
background to Munich*:

Just as the First World War resulted in a new division of territories between victors and vanquished, it also led to significant transfers in foreign long term investment throughout the world.

Until 1914 Great Britain, France and Germany had been the main investors of capital, drawing interest and profits from the majority of nations in the world. After her defeat in the First World War Germany ceased to be a creditor country and became one of the most indebted states, not only in Europe but in the world as a whole. Great Britain still held first place in the world statistics of foreign investment, but the United States of America – a debtor nation before 1914 – took second place . . . With a much smaller amount of capital investment abroad, France became the third largest creditor in the world. Although other countries also exported capital, on balance their indebtedness was greater than their credits and they were in one way or another tied to the creditor states.[5]

This balance of power essentially characterized the inter-war period until the Munich Agreement of 30 September 1938.

5.2 Foreign capital in Central and South-East Europe

Historians have time and again come back to the problem of Munich and a large literature exists offering many different interpretations. Nevertheless, the Munich Agreement 'about Czechoslovakia but without Czechsolovakia' has become a byword for betrayal in international affairs. My research has led me to see it as an attempt at bridging the differences between the West European Powers and the Third Reich, above all between Britain and Germany, on the basis of the sacrifice of Czechoslovak independence and the prospect of an anti-Soviet, and possibly also anti-American, alignment. In my book I was concerned with the economic background to Munich which has not received the same attention as other political and international aspects. Indeed, since it was published in 1974, there has been no further work or publication in Czechoslovakia or anywhere else on this aspect.

I came upon the topic when I began to question assumptions prevalent in post-1945 Czechoslovak historiography for which I felt there was not sufficient empirical evidence. Already my first attempt at questioning them involved me in the first and only polemic publicly carried out in the pages of the Czechoslovak Historical Journal of the 1950s.[6] They concerned three generally accepted judgments. Firstly, it was assumed that German capital was predominant in the Czechoslovak economy. Secondly, it was assumed that the Czech bourgeoisie was, in the last analysis, responsible for the surrender of Czechoslovak independence at Munich, as these circles had plotted the sell-out to Germany for their own gains. But at the same time, quite in contradiction to the above evaluation of the Czech bourgeoisie, it was assumed that Western capital, especially British interests, had withdrawn voluntarily and obligingly from Czechoslovakia long before Munich to make room for German penetration into Central and South-East Europe. This interpretation maintains that there was an *economic Munich* before the *political Munich*. It is formulated thus: the dismemberment of Czechoslovakia resulted from 'the decision of the West in the years before the political Munich to retreat voluntarily from

Central and South-East Europe, which was to become an exclusive sphere of influence of German imperialism'.[7]

This interpretation has remained an integral part of Czechoslovak historiography and is part of all outlines and textbooks of inter-war history.[8] The evidence presented in my book *An economic background to Munich* shows, on the basis of empirical research, that this concept is untenable.

Drawing mainly upon *An economic background to Munich: International business and Czechoslovakia*, I shall deal with these assumptions in turn.

5.2.1 Changes in the distribution of international investment and the question of the predominance of German capital in pre-Munich Czechoslovakia

Central and South-East Europe was the main area of German and Austrian influence before the First World War. However, after the victory of the Entente the whole area was drawn into the financial and capital orbit of the Allied Powers, especially France, Britain and also the USA. It constituted one of the three most important world markets for capital investment – the other two being the British Empire and Latin America.

The shift of interest towards Central and South-East Europe was primarily connected with the defeat of the Central Powers (Germany and Austria-Hungary), and also with the loss of the Russian market after the Soviet government nationalized and confiscated foreign holdings at the end of 1917. Since the greater part of French long-term investment in Europe and half of the total of British capital export to Europe had been placed in Tsarist Russia,[9] the newly established successor states provided a potential field for trade and investment which could substitute, to some extent, the losses suffered in Russia.[10]

The Western Powers accepted the political reality of the newly established states on the territory of the former Hapsburg Monarchy; they regarded them as a *cordon sanitaire* with a double function: on the one hand, to immunize the Danube Basin against the infiltration of bolshevism from Soviet Russia, and on the other hand, as a barrier against renewed German *Mitteleuropa*-aspirations. Yet, with relation to their *economic* interests, they looked upon the area as a single unit.

Specifically Britain's increased interest in Central Europe emanated from her generally changed position in the international economy. British investment took on a more defensive character *vis-à-vis* the United States after 1918 by concentrating on the British Empire and also by acquiring a share in the German and Austrian spheres of interest in Central and South-East Europe. The relative importance of the Danubian region rose as a comparatively new field of activity for Britain because of the increased competition which British goods and capital faced from the USA and Japan in overseas markets. Capital injections from Britain to these weakened economies were considered necessary in order to rebuild trade connections. Considerations of this nature led to Britain's increased economic activity in Central Europe and the Balkan countries in the 1920s.

The Versailles Peace Treaty of 1919, by which Germany and her allies

88   *Alice Teichova*

Table 5.1 Comparative data of long-term foreign investment in six East-Central and South-East European countries, 1937

Percentages of totals

		Direct foreign participation in equity			
	Foreign holdings of public debt	Joint-stock companies	Other limited companies	Banks	Insurance companies
Romania	89.2(a)	83	–	75	70
Yugoslavia	82.5(a)	61	–	75	–
Hungary	81.1(a)	c.25	–	–	–
Bulgaria	72.3(a)	48	–	–	–
Poland(b)	63.0	44	90	29	–
Czechoslovakia(c)	17.5	29	3	15	26

(a) 1931/2
(b) 1936
(c) Czechoslovakia also exported capital, see Table 5.3.
– = data unknown

Source: A. Teichova, 'East-central and south-east Europe, 1919–1939', in P. Mathias and S. Pollard (eds.), *The Cambridge Economic History of Europe*, VIII, Cambridge, 1989, p. 924.

formally accepted responsibility for causing the War, created favourable conditions by means of their financial and economic clauses for the expansion of business interests from the victorious to the defeated economies. Thus a massive shift took place during which the states of Central and South-East Europe became increasingly dependent upon the capital resources of France and Britain and also of the United States.

In Germany there was strong awareness of this shift in the balance of economic power. In official records, not only in sources of irredentist organizations, the post-1918 situation is denoted as unacceptable from the very outset of the Weimar Republic. Irritation about the eclipse of German power in Eastern Europe occurs with remarkable continuity in documents of the Auswärtiges Amt throughout the inter-war period and, as has been widely written about, with rising aggressiveness after Hitler came to power. A recurring nationalist-revisionist sentiment runs like this: that the Peace Treaty of Versailles has severed Germany from world markets; that the successor states were established mainly to hem in the German economy; and especially that the state of the Czechs was blocking Germany's way to the South-East into the Balkans and beyond, barring her access.

As a result of my calculations (see Tables 5.1 and 5.2), it is apparent that foreign capital participated substantially in all economies of Central and South-East Europe. The only state in this region which not only imported but also considerably exported capital was Czechoslovakia. Table 5.1 shows the

Table 5.2 Origin of foreign investments in joint-stock capital of Czechoslovakia, Poland, Bulgaria, and Yugoslavia, 1937 (percentages)

Country of origin	Czechoslovakia(a)	Poland(b)	Bulgaria(c)	Yugoslavia(d)
Britain	30.8	5.5	1.1	17.3
France	21.4	27.1	9.2	27.5
Austria	13.1	3.5	—	—
Holland	8.8	3.5	0.4	2.1
Germany	7.2	13.8	9.3	6.2(e)
Belgium	7.1	12.5	20.5	5.3
Switzerland	4.5	7.2	25.1	7.3
USA	3.5	19.2	11.1	12.0
Italy	2.2	—	13.2	3.1
Sweden	0.9	2.7	—	1.2
Hungary	0.5	—	2.3	2.0
Czechoslovakia	—	1.6	7.4	8.5
Other countries		3.4	0.4	7.5(f)
Total	100	100	100	100

Notes: (a) Industry and banking.
(b) Industry and trade.
(c) All joint-stock companies in private enterprise.
(d) Industry in private enterprise.
(e) Includes Austria.
(f) Includes: Monaco 2.9%, Poland 0.3%, Liechtenstein 0.3%, Luxemburg 0.5%, Swiss mixed capital 2.6%, Anglo-Dutch capital 0.8%, USA-French capital 0.1%.

Source: As in Table 5.1, p. 923.

amount of foreign capital invested in the individual countries and Table 5.2 lists the countries of origin of foreign investment. Accordingly, on the eve of the Second World War direct foreign participation in the total joint-stock capital ranged in rounded figures from 30 to 80 per cent: 30 per cent in ČSR, over 40 per cent in Poland, around 50 per cent in Bulgaria, over 60 per cent in Yugoslavia, and around 80 per cent in Romania. Its position was strongest in the producer goods industries (iron and steel, engineering, chemicals, mineral and vegetable oils) and in banking. Of the entire foreign capital invested in all the Central and South-Eastern European economies, at least 75 per cent originated in Western industrial countries with Britain and France taking up either first or second place in the rank order of international investors, while Germany, which was leading in this area before 1914, held on average fifth or sixth place. This distribution of international investment had developed from the 1920s, had reached its highest volume of the inter-war period in 1930, and from then, because of the impact of the world economic crisis and the general stagnation in international investment, it remained practically stable until the

Table 5.3 Direct foreign long-term investments in Czechoslovak industry and banking, 31 December 1937

Origin of foreign investment	Total foreign investments, Kč 3,191,904,000 – 100% (foreign investments amount to 27% of the total capital investments in Czechoslovak industry) %
Great Britain	30.8
France	21.4
Austria	13.1
Holland	8.8
Germany	7.2
Belgium	7.1
Switzerland	4.5
USA	3.5
Italy	2.2
Sweden	0.9
Hungary	0.5
Total	100.0
West European long-term Investments	68.1

Source: A. Teichova, *An economic background to Munich: International business and Czechoslovakia*, Cambridge, 1974 (compiled from Table IV, p. 48).

Munich Agreement in 1938. In this distribution of international investment Germany had lost its predominant place.

5.2.2 The myth of the 'voluntary' withdrawal of Western, especially British, capital investment from Czechoslovakia 'long before Munich'

Czechoslovakia played a critical role as a vital link between British and French economic interests on the one side, and the South-East European region on the other. Her role as a juncture of, and intermediary between, Western and South-East European business is of utmost importance for a deeper understanding of the interplay of politics and economics at Munich.

As in the other countries of this region, a transfer of foreign capital holdings had been taking place in Czechoslovakia after the victory of the Entente in which Austrian and German capital had to withdraw in favour of domestic Czechoslovak capital (*nostrification*)[11] and of financially powerful groups from Britain, France, Belgium and the United States (cf. origin of foreign investment in Table 5.3). Czechoslovakia attracted foreign capital investment not so much because its economy was less developed, as was the case with other states of the area, but because of the relatively high degree of concentration in industry and banking (cf. the distribution of foreign investment according to branches of industry in Table 5.4), the comparatively low level of wages, the

Table 5.4 Foreign long-term investments in Czechoslovak industry as a percentage of the total share capital in the various branches of industry, 31 December 1937

Branches of industry	% of total share capital
Mineral oil and synthetic fats	97
Mining and metallurgy	64
Electrotechnical industry	52
Chemical industry	46
Engineering	40
Textiles	29
Building materials	22
Glass, procelain, ceramics	18
Food industry	17
Paper industry	16
Commercial companies	9
Transport companies	5
Insurance societies	26
Banking	15
In industry as a whole	32

Source: As in Table 5.3 (Table III, p. 46).

stable political conditions of a democratic republican system of government, and also because of its geographical position in the very heart of Europe. Czechoslovakia was important because it ranked in the top seven armament suppliers and the ten leading producers of industrial goods in the world at that time. In addition, Czechoslovak government policy actively encouraged British and French involvement in its economy, for it sought to cement its military and political alliances with close business ties. The strong tendencies towards combination in finance and industry enabled British and French capital to penetrate into the centre of the largest banks and industrial concerns of the country. The pyramidal business structure which arose in the process of concentration provided opportunities for wide-reaching connections in the economy of Czechoslovakia herself as well as favourable conditions for further expansion, through subsidiary companies of Czechoslovak banks and industrial enterprises, into the economies of South-East European countries. Thus, much of the outwardly Czechoslovak capital export was not purely of Czechoslovak origin, but participated under specific conditions in the capital export from France and Britain.[12]

The influx of Western capital was consciously supported by the Czechoslovak government with the overwhelming consensus of the business community, above all by Czech industrial and banking circles, in accordance with the orientation of its foreign policy towards the Entente Powers. Throughout the existence of the independent Czechoslovak Republic and with the active support of Czech bankers and industrialists, the government tried to achieve political and economic consolidation with the help of Entente capital

Table 5.5 British and German direct foreign investment in Czechoslovak banks and companies – 31. 12. 1937*

Banks and companies	Great Britain mio Kč	%	Germany mio Kč	%	Total mio Kč	%
Banks	54,425	24.2	—	—	224,817	100
Mining & metallurgy	706,912	61.0	117,694	10.1	1160,858	100
Mineral & vegetable oil	5,638	1.4	—	—	414,521	100
Chemicals	76,615	24.8	25,475	8.2	309,060	100
Textiles	56,929	25.0	2,020	0.8	227,937	100
Engineering	9,596	4.4	4,900	2.1	223,106	100
Sugar refining	8,710	4.9	—	—	176,149	100
Electrical industry	14,409	10.8	44,376	33.3	133,204	100
Glass, porcelain, ceramics	22,322	30.2	11,993	16.1	74,008	100
Food	3,716	6.4	—	—	58,395	100
Paper	2,483	7.0	—	—	35,510	100
Commercial companies	249	0.7	—	—	33,621	100
Insurance companies	—	—	8,014	24.4	32,810	100
Wood	2,270	8.5	—	—	26,859	100
Transport	7,731	30.5	12,160	48.0	25,307	100
Building	12,170	58.2	3,360	16.0	20,934	100
Distilleries	64	0.5	—	—	13,678	100
Miscellaneous**	—	—	—	—	1,130	100
Total	984,239	30.8	229,932	7.2	3191,904	100

*Enterprises irrespective of their legal status.
**Musical instruments and leather industry.
Source: Excerpted from *An Economic Background to Munich*, Table IV, p. 48.

investments by complicated capital transfers in order to dislodge German and Austrian economic influence from key positions. The main direction of the Czech entrepreneurs' economic interests aimed at meeting the challenge of German competition. Thus the idea of a deliberate sell out by the Czech bourgeoisie to the German competitor cannot be substantiated.[13]

British interests held the single largest share of total foreign investment in the inter-war Czechoslovak economy. For comparison Table 5.5 shows the amount and distribution of British and German foreign direct investment in Czechoslovakia at the end of 1937.

British participation in banking can be traced to the immediate post-war years when the Bank of England under the auspices of the Treasury and the Foreign Office devised a scheme to provide British capital with a foothold in Central Europe through some big Viennese bank.[14] The Bank of England's interest focused on the Anglo-Austrian Bank which had built up a diversified and sound business structure throughout the whole Austro-Hungarian Empire. Indeed, the bank's most valuable assets were located in Czechoslovakia: in addition to 30 branches its combine consisted of enterprises in

1919

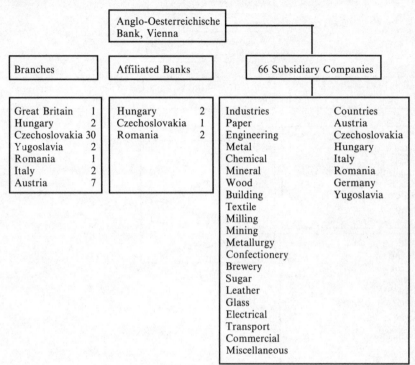

Figure 5.1 Anglo-Oesterreichische Bank of Vienna, 1919

the sugar, textile, paper, porcelain, glass, iron and steel, and metalworking industries, that is in the main export industries. This whole banking–industrial conglomerate was integrated into the business structure of the Bank of England by 1922 (cp. Figure 5.1). Its head office in London, later known as the Anglo-International Bank, had its main Central and South-East European interests concentrated in branches in Vienna and Prague. Figures 5.1 and 5.2 illustrate the branch network and the industrial combine of the Anglo-Oesterreichische Bank of Vienna in 1919 and the Anglo-Austrian Bank as a subsidiary of the Bank of England in 1926. The Czechoslovak part, as an entity independent of the Viennese branch, functioned as the Anglo-Czechoslovak Bank. While the Viennese connection ceased, mainly because of the *misère* affecting the Austrian economy, that with the more buoyant economy of Czechoslovakia proved more lasting and rewarding. The Anglo-Czechoslovak Bank formed a point of intersection for British capital throughout the inter-war period.

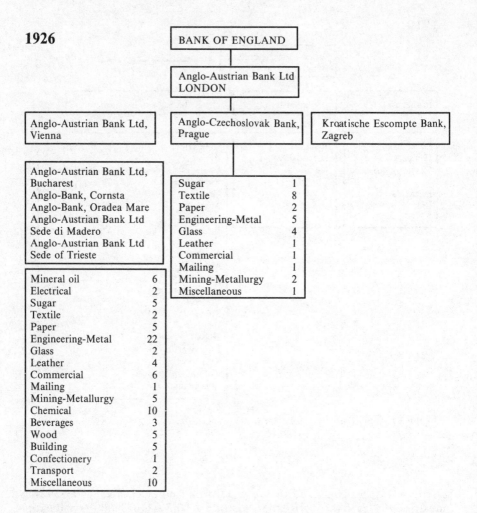

Figure 5.2 Anglo Austrian Bank, as a subsidiary of the Bank of England, 1926

The significance of direct foreign investment in the big commercial banks of Czechoslovakia which exclusively originated in the West was greatly enhanced by their wide-spread industrial subsidiary companies. There was not a single German capital holding in the Czechoslovak banking system. This fact was monitored with considerable attention by the Deutsche Bank and the Dresdner Bank. German efforts to gain a hold over Czechoslovak banking succeeded only after Munich.

Much more prominent than in banking were British interests in the iron and steel industry of Czechoslovakia in the 1930s. They consisted of the British-based Rothschild-Group's 100 per cent holding of the Vítkovické horní a hutní těžířstvo, the single largest combine in the whole Czechoslovak economy and

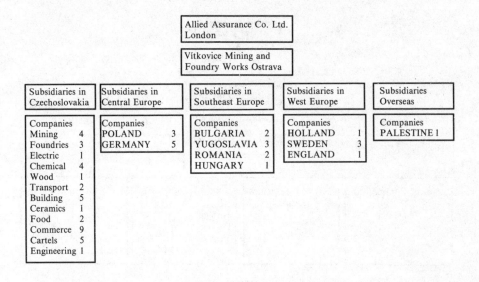

Figure 5.3 Combine of the Vítkovice Mining and Foundry Works, Ostrava, 1937

in the heavy industry of Central and South-East Europe. Its structure was that of an integrated and diversified multinational company which occupied an important position in the European steel industry (cf. Figure 5.3). The British connection was also well known in London government circles, especially when German pressure was applied after the *Anschluß* of Austria to force the Rothschild-Group to transfer the Vitkovice combine into German hands. The Rothschilds agreed to negotiate only after the Gestapo had arrested Baron Louis Rothschild – a member of the Viennese branch of the family – and threatened him with physical violence. Even so, the British government did not give its approval and informed the German government through diplomatic channels of this. The value the National Socialists attached to the Vítkovice combine is evident from Hitler's order to General Keitel, issued on 14th March 1939, to occupy the Vítkovice mines and plants one day before the general military invasion of the Czech Lands, in order to prevent the Poles from taking over the rolling mills before the arrival of the German army.

Czechoslovakia's chemical industry was the largest east of Germany. The British chemical industry established its Central and South-East European interests by first gaining and sharing with French partners a 30-year monopoly concession from the Prague government to produce explosives in the Czechoslovak firm *Explosia*, and then extending production to Hungary and Romania. These connections began with Nobel Industries Limited and were strengthened when their multinational combine was merged into Imperial Chemical Industries (ICI) in 1926. About that time German producers in the international explosives cartel had to undertake to abstain from any activities threatening British interests in the Danube Basin. ICI's position was further reinforced in the early 1930s in the face of German competition.

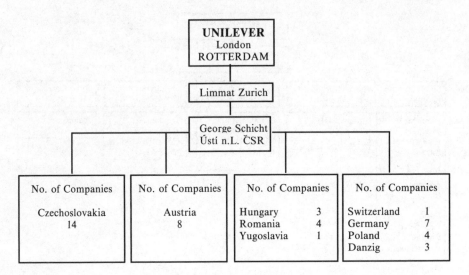

Figure 5.4 The Georg Schicht Group and the Unilever Combine

Also the interests of Unilever in Central and South-East Europe centred on Czechoslovakia where the leading manufacturer of soap and margarine, the Schicht combine, had become the pivot of the Unilever Trust in this region. Schicht's whole Central and South-East European structure was merged into the British-Dutch combine (cp. Figure 5.4). These ties also remained unchanged until the Munich Agreement. Quite contrary to any signs of voluntary withdrawal, the Chairman of Lever Bros. and Unilever, Francis d'Arcy Cooper, saw advantages in a future 'Greater Germany' as a large number of Unilever companies would then be situated in a homogeneous customs territory.[15]

In view of the distribution of international investment on the eve of the Second World War, the question of competition in the 1930s is in my opinion of the utmost importance. The tables and figures show that direct foreign capital investment in the pre-Munich Czechoslovak economy was mainly divided between Britain and France, and that this provided a jumping-off point for widely ramified business links in South-East Europe. Czechoslovakia's Anglo-French orientation in international relations corresponded on the whole to the reality of economic conditions. Thus in the field of foreign investment, German business encountered entrenched British and French positions in its efforts for economic expansion and political revision which intensified in the 1930s with regards to the countries of Central and South-East Europe.

As the balance of forces established after Versailles began to crumble during the world economic crisis, Czechoslovakia became an area of complicated competitive struggles in international business, in which the competition between Czechoslovak and German groups took place within the framework of West European and German competition. In its drive for expansion,

German capital was forced to penetrate the Czechoslovak economy in ways other than through direct capital investment.

In the first place, German big business tried to tie important Czechoslovak industries to their own by way of cartel agreements (for a detailed analysis, see *An economic background to Munich*, Chapters 2.2, 3.2, 4.2, 5.2). The most numerous and influential German cartels were able to make inroads into the trade of those industries in which British and French capital was strongly present. Through cartels, German business groups attempted to gain greater influence in the economic life of Czechoslovakia and thus to weaken the position of their British and French competitors.

In the second place, Hitler's German trade offensive into South-East Europe endeavoured to undermine the capital structure and the political alliances which rested on the axis: Britain and France in the West, Czechoslovakia as the centre point, linking them to Souh-East Europe. After 1935, Czechoslovakia was the centre of the remains of efforts at achieving collective security in Europe through the Franco-Czechoslovak-Soviet Pact of mutual assistance in case of aggression which was broken in Munich.

The next question is how successful was German economic policy in this competition?

5.2.2.1 In the sphere of international investment
Here, Germany made hardly any headway at all before 1938. Historical evidence shows that German companies and banks were unable to dislodge Britain and France, and with them Czechoslovakia, from the leading positions in South-East Europe, even in the decade after regaining their economic strength – that is between 1929 and the outbreak of the Second World War. Only the violent intervention *after* Munich, followed by the occupation and dismemberment of Czechoslovakia and the attack on Poland, changed the relations of forces between Western and German capital holding. A measure of this change can be gained by comparing the results of a statistical survey of the presence of direct foreign investment on 31 December 1940 conducted by the German Occupation Authority in the 'Protectorate of Bohemia and Moravia' (see Table 5.6) with the results presented in Table 5.3 concerning the origin of direct foreign investment in Czechoslovakia on 31 December 1937. Within less than two years of German occupation, the rank order of foreign investors was reversed: while at the end of 1937 Britain took up first place among the countries of origin of foreign investment, by the end of 1940 the German Reich ranked first. Even the 34 per cent of British foreign investment in Table 5.6 had been taken over by German administrators of enemy property, mainly by the Hermann Göring Works.[16]

5.2.2.2 In the sphere of international cartels
In this area, Germany's policy was relatively more effective, because the Hitler regime used the cartel system as an instrument for furthering German trade expansion. Since in the most important international cartel agreements either the whole or part of the South-East European market had been allocated to Czechoslovak concerns, German cartel partners tried to get Czechoslovak cartel partners to agree to revise conditions in a way that would enable them to

Table 5.6 Direct foreign investments in industry and banking in the 'Protectorate Bohemia and Moravia' (31.12.1940) (Areas occupied by National Socialist Germany on 15 March 1939.)

Country of origin of investment	In per cent of total foreign investment
German Reich	47
England	34
Switzerland	7
USA	4
France	1.5
Slovakia	1.3
Sweden	1.2
Other countries	4
Total foreign investment	100.0

Source: Archiv Státního úřadu statistického – Koncernové šetření (Archives of the Czechoslovak State Statistical Office – Inquiry into Concerns conducted by the German Occupation Authority).

gain bigger shares of the traditional Czechoslovak export markets, as well as, wherever possible, a stake in the domestic market of Czechoslovakia. But even in this field German expansion was kept within limits because the Czechoslovak firms were often go-betweens, and behind them stood the stronger partners in international cartels from Britain and France. Within the cartel mechanism German business competed for higher production quotas and larger shares in the Central and South-East European markets, but their demands were not met to their satisfaction before Munich.

5.2.2.3 The question of Germany's trade drive into South-East Europe as part of her Grossraumwirtschaft plans
Under the special circumstances of depressed trade conditions in the 1930s, Germany's policy of bilateral trade agreements with the weak agrarian economies of South-East Europe succeeded in substantially increasing her share in the foreign trade of these countries and drawing them more effectively into the German sphere of influence. As it became more obvious that German influence ever more limited the economic moving space of the South-East European states, they tried to extricate themselves from the German trade ensnarement and appealed to Britain for support.[17]

By 1938 a wide gap had developed between the dominance of Western finance and industry in the field of capital investment on the one side, and the rising share of German trade in the area of South-East Europe on the other.

5.3 Was there an economic Munich?

In conclusion, the assumption (maintained by Czechoslovak historiography since the late 1950s) that there was an economic Munich before the political Munich will be discussed. This is connected with the question of how relevant the sacrifice of Czechoslovak independence at Munich was to the distribution of spheres of economic influence among the Great Powers in general, and to the distribution of international investment in particular.

The Agreement, which was signed by Chamberlain, Daladier, Mussolini and Hitler in Munich on 30 September 1938, is – in historical context – identified with the betrayal of a weaker country by its stronger allies, with sacrificing a democratic country's independence to appease a Fascist aggressor. The politician most responsible for Munich was Neville Chamberlain who regarded the actual agreement on the cession of Czechoslovak frontier districts to Germany as a means to a 'greater' end. He is quoted as saying that he could not care less where the Sudeten Germans lived. Indeed, two days before flying to Munich Chamberlain said, totally untruthfully, in a broadcast that this was 'a quarrel between people in a far away country of whom we know nothing'. When he returned from Munich to London he waved a piece of paper crying 'Peace in Our Time'. This piece of paper was not the Munich Agreement, but it was the Anglo-German Declaration signed by himself and Hitler *after* the night of the Munich Conference in which they promised each other 'to settle all outstanding questions by co-operation, and never to go to war with each other'. It became known as a 'scrap of paper' because, only six months after it was signed German troops marched into Prague and, eleven months after it they invaded Poland.

Keeping in mind that Czechoslovakia was the key to South-East Europe, it is not a mere intellectual exercise to prove the fictitiousness of the assumption that long before the Munich Agreement there was a voluntary withdrawal of West European and particularly British capital investment from Central and South-East Europe. Up to the Munich Agreement, there is no convincing evidence to support the assumption that Western direct foreign investment was withdrawn from Czechoslovakia voluntarily in order to facilitate the German economic advance into South-East Europe. That there was no deliberate economic Munich before the political Munich is essential for the understanding of the economic and political impact of the Munich Agreement, for it was this Agreement which broke all European political pacts and, as a consequence, disrupted economic links.

In conclusion let us come back to the foreign policy of Neville Chamberlain and the calculations which led him to abandon Czechoslovakia to Hitler in Munich. Internationally, there were three areas which gave cause for particular concern to Chamberlain after he became Prime Minister in May 1937: the Soviet Union, the United States, and Germany. Faced with this complicated situation, and in view of Britain's relatively weakened international position, the Birmingham businessman's calculation was alarmingly simple. He believed that he could strike a bargain with Hitler on the basis of the sacrifice of Czechoslovak independence and with the prospect of maintaining British economic interests as well as Britain's position as a major world power. After the signing of the Munich Agreement Chamberlain, at his own request, saw Hitler alone. The result was that they signed the joint-Anglo-German Declaration which Chamberlain read out at the airport in London after his return:

We regard the agreement signed last night and the Anglo-German Naval Agreement as symbolic of the desire of our two peoples never to go to war with one another.

Chamberlain thought that he had achieved his aim, and that is why he waved the document containing the Anglo-German Declaration at the waiting crowd at home.

Far-reaching economic adjustments between Britain and Germany were intended to take place after Munich. Negotiations were mainly secretly conducted on all levels – economic, political and military – after Munich, lasting until the very outbreak of the Second World War.[18] Indeed sources in the Public Record Office which are so far closed to researchers may reveal more than is known at present about these discussions. However, London and Berlin were not able to overcome their differences. The division of capital investment and foreign trade in Central and South-East Europe was the subject of intensive negotiations, but Britain was not prepared to withdraw from her positions to the extent demanded by Hitler. However, *after* Munich she was not able to protect them without war.

Notes

1 Neville Chamberlain, 27 September 1938.
2 This I set out to do in Teichova, A., 1988, *The Czechoslovak Economy 1918–1980*, Routledge, London and New York.
3 How great the interest of the global multinational companies is in acquiring a stake in this largest enterprise in engineering on the territory of the Eastern European states is substantiated by competing take-over bids.
4 Teichova, A., 'The giant company – a legacy of *fin de siècle* capitalism', in Teich, M., and Porter, R. (eds), 1990, *Fin de siècle and its Legacy*, Cambridge University Press, Cambridge, p. 13
5 Teichova, A., 1974, *An economic background to Munich: International business and Czechoslovakia 1918–1938*, Cambridge University Press, Cambridge, p. 1.
6 *Československý časopis historický* (Czechoslovak Historical Journal) (1959), VI, 3, 542–544; (1959), VII, 1, 114–121; (1959), VII, 3, 473–478.
7 Král, V., 1958, *Otázky hospodářského a sociálního vývoje v českých zemích 1938–1945* (Questions of the Economic and Social Development of the Czech Lands 1938–1945), II, Academia, Prague, p. 10.
8 Only after the 'velvet revolution' are the results of my research being integrated into the evaluation of the Czechoslovak inter-war economy, as in V. Lacina, 1990, *Formování československé ekonomiky 1918–1923* (The Formation of the Czechoslovak Economy) Academia, Prague.
9 Royal Institute of International Affairs, 1937, *The Problem of International Investment*, London, New York, Toronto, p. 145.
10 The evidence produced in my book was reinforced by Claud Beaud, 'The interests of the Union Européenne in Central Europe' in Teichova, A. and Cottrell, P. L. (eds), 1983, *International Business and Central Europe, 1918–1939*, Leicester University Press, Leicester, New York, p. 377.
11 Cf. Teichova, *The Czechoslovak Economy*, p. 68.
12 P. Marguerat finds a similar development in South-East Europe while studying the Romanian case. Cf. Marguerat, P., 1977, *Le IIIᵉ Reich et le pétrol roumain. Contribution à l'étude de la pénétration économique dans les Balkans à la veille et au début de la Seconde Guerre mondiale*, Geneva, and the same, 'Le protectionisme financier allemand et le basin danubien a la veille de la seconde guerre mondiale: l'exemple Roumanie', *Relations internationales*, 16 (1978): 351–64.

13 Teichova, A. and Waller, R., 'Der tschechoslowakische Unternehmer am Vorabend des Zweiten Weltkriegs', in Dugoborski, W. (ed.), 1981, *Zweiter Weltkrieg und sozialer Wandel*, Vandenhoeck and Ruprecht, Göttingen, pp. 292–93.

14 The story of the Anglo-Czechoslovak Bank's connection with the Bank of England after the First World War is told in greater detail in my article 'Versailles and the Expansion of the Bank of England into Central Europe', Horn, N. and Kocka, J. (eds), 1979, *Law and the Formation of Big Enterprises in the 19th and Early 20th Centuries*, Colloquium Verlag, Göttingen, pp. 366–87.

15 In his speech to the shareholders at the Annual General Meeting of Lever Brothers and Unilever Ltd. on 13 May 1938 the Chairman tried to calm anxieties about German expansion in Europe after the *Anschluss* of Austria by maintaining that production and transfers of profits could continue as before and that even the threat of a European war had diminished after the integration of Austria into Germany. (Works Archive of the North Bohemian Fats Industry, Ústí nad Labem, Box 859.)

16 The ruthless expansion of the Göring Works into Central and Eastern Europe has been described and assessed by many authors. With regards to Czechoslovakia, V. Král's, *Otázky*, II, (1958) gives an account based on evidence from the Nuremberg Trials, and R. J. Overy deals with the methods and consequences of this expansion in his study, 'Göring's "Multi-national Empire" ', in Teichova and Cottrell (eds), *International Business and Central Europe*, pp. 269–306.

17 I discuss the complex problem of bilateral trade with Germany in the second half of the 1930s in an article in memory of György Ránki, 'Bilateral trade revisited: Did the South-East European states exploit National Socialist Germany on the eve of the Second World War?', in the memorial volume for György Ránki: Glatz, Ferenc (ed.), 1990, *Modern Age – Modern Historian. In Memoriam György Ránki (1930– 1988)*, Institute of History of the Hungarian Academy of Sciences, Budapest, pp. 193–209.

18 A virtually day-by-day analysis of the officially conducted Anglo-French-Soviet negotiations and the parallel British-German negotiations conducted secretly can be found in Teichova, A., 1961, 'Great Britain in European Affairs', *Historica* III.

6 Towards the liberalization of the Spanish economy, 1951–9*

Joseph Harrison
University of Manchester

Before the remarkable burgeoning of manufacturing industry from the 1950s onwards, Spain was generally considered a prime example of economic backwardness, dominated by its huge and largely archaic agricultural sector. As late as 1910, two out of every three active Spaniards were employed on the land. Recent research indicates a hitherto unsuspected progress in the Spanish countryside during the first third of the present century, not least in livestock farming, fruit and horticulture. Even so, on the eve of the Spanish Civil War, cereals and legumes still accounted for three-quarters of the cultivated surface and generated 45 per cent of the agricultural income.[1]

Spain could also stake a claim to possessing the most closed economy in Western Europe. After a brief flirtation with free trade, initiated by the Figuerola reforms of 1869, the final years of the nineteenth century witnessed a pronounced drift in the direction of autarky. The protectionist tariff of 1891, enacted in response to lobbying from the wheat farmers of Old Castile, Catalan textile manufacturers and Basque ironmasters, was further strengthened in 1906 and 1922. As José Luis García Delgado argues, a prevailing mood of economic nationalism, which aimed to reserve the Spanish market for domestic producers, gave rise to a plethora of interventionist measures.[2] Writing in 1936, the distinguished Valencian economist Román Perpiñá contended that Spain was 'among the civilized countries, the only one with a complex and significantly autarkic economy'.[3]

Following his military victory over the Second Republic in 1939, General Franco, urged on by an army fearful of foreign invasion and the xenophobic, semi-fascist Falange, the single party of the new regime, pressed ahead with the long-standing goal of economic self-sufficiency with renewed vigour. As we shall see, the Francoist pursuit of autarky *à outrance* was to have disastrous consequences.

6.1 The quest for autarky

The first decade of Franco's new order was characterized by almost unmitigated economic stagnation. Shortages of basic foodstuffs and raw materials

* The author wishes to thank the Nuffield Foundation for an award to carry out research in Barcelona and Madrid.

resulted in widespread hunger and perennial bottlenecks to production. A drastic reduction in real wages led to a drop in living standards unparalleled in contemporary Spanish history. The spectre of mass starvation was only narrowly averted after 1946 by huge imports of foodstuffs from the sympathetic pro-axis regime of Juan Domingo Perón in Argentina. Albert Carreras's reworking of national income estimates for 1941-5 shows an average increase of one per cent a year, with substantial fluctuations over the period. Yet this was less than adequate compensation for an average fall of six per cent per annum during the period 1936-40, which covered the civil war. The same author's index of industrial production for 1946-50 reveals a ten per cent rise. However, compared with the performance of other Mediterranean economies at this time, Spain's modest achievement appears far from impressive. Over the same quinquennium the indices of industrial production of Italy, Greece and Yugoslavia show increases of 70, 100, and 110 per cent respectively.[4]

Official explanations of Spain's poor economic performance in the 1940s invariably seek to pin the responsibility on factors beyond the control of Spain's policy makers. Above all, they stress such factors as the damage wreaked upon the Spanish economy by three years of bloody civil war, the so-called enduring drought (*la pertinaz sequía*) which persisted throughout the 1940s and the United Nations' resolution of December 1946 for member states to recall their diplomats from Madrid and to suspend economic relations with the erstwhile ally of Nazi Germany and fascist Italy.[5] Not surprisingly, the great majority of Spain's economic historians reject these explanations as mere *post hoc* excuses. The civil war of 1936-9 was considerably less destructive on the Spanish economy than were the effects of the Second World War on many of the belligerents. In the absence of sufficient rainfall south of the Pyrenees, a more realistic irrigation policy and the allocation of a larger amount of foreign currency reserves to purchase fertilizers might have gone some way to tackle the drought. Meanwhile the United Nations' boycott merely reflected that organization's reaction to Franco's refusal to introduce democratic reforms – the price which the *Caudillo* was not prepared to pay in order to share in postwar economic reconstruction.[6]

Scholarly accounts of Spain's undistinguished record at this time invariably emphasize Franco's ignorance of economic matters, together with the incompetence and frequent venality of ministers and civil servants. An economic system founded on arbitrary bureaucratic controls down to even the most trivial decisions was bound to engender favouritism. Sometimes bribery was adjudged the only effective way to secure adequate supplies of raw materials. In contrast, the dispassionate advice of Spain's tiny and beleaguered band of academic economists was rarely sought and, when proferred, more often than not rejected. Put bluntly, Franco's Spain throughout the 1940s and beyond was obsessed with ill thought out, interventionist schemes whereby economic recovery was subordinated to the political survival of the regime. Many of its economic institutions were inspired by models which were formulated in Hitler's Germany or Mussolini's Italy. Thus, by the end of the decade, it was the dictatorship's half-baked interventionism rather than coincidental conjunctural factors which brought Spain to the brink of disaster.[7] Carlos Barciela's account of Francoist agricultural policy (1939–59) demonstrates how state interference in the countryside, aimed at regulating prices and production, served only to generate a thriving black market (*estraperlo*). In the case of wheat, the black market became even larger than the official one. At the same time, livestock farming received little official backing while such products as citrus fruit, where Spain enjoyed a comparative advantage in the newly-emergent export markets, were discouraged.[8] Meanwhile, despite the regime's strident advocacy of rural values (designed to mollify ex-combatants from Franco's overwhelmingly peasant army), state intervention after 1939 was primarily concentrated on encouraging industrial development. The corner-stone of industrial policy was import substitution which attained its apogee between 1946 and 1951. Spearheading the messanic quest of industrial self-sufficiency was the *Instituto Nacional de Industria* (INI), a state holding company founded in 1941 and modelled on the Italian organization IRI (*Istituto per la Riconstruzione Industriale*). Presided over until 1962 by Juan Antonio Suanzes, a naval engineer and boyhood friend of the *Caudillo*, INI's brief, set out in Article One of its founding Act, was to 'encourage and finance in the service of the nation, the creation and resurgence of our industries, especially those whose aim is the resolution of problems imposed by the requirements of the defence of the country or those aimed at the development of our autarky'.[9]

Champions of the institute argue that during the late 1940s and 1950s its component companies, pre-eminent in the fields of electricity supply, chemicals, iron and steel, non-ferrous metals, engineering and automobiles, built up the necessary infrastructure for the subsequent process of development (*desarrollo*) which followed Spain's Stabilization Plan of 1959.[10] In contrast, INI's detractors protest that many of its projects were undertaken with scant regard to their opportunity cost. Suanzes and his supporters were resolutely convinced that if it were technologically feasible to produce a particular commodity in Spain, then it should be produced. Public sector borrowing to finance some of INI's white elephants was, by the end of the 1950s, to exert strong inflationary pressures on the Spanish economy.[11] Protectionism, already in the ascendancy before the outbreak of the Civil War, was augmented after 1939 by an arsenal of interventionist measures. Despite the recognized narrowness of the domestic market, the satisfaction of internal demand was given a clear priority. Exports were discouraged by a markedly overvalued peseta, while the option of devaluation was repeatedly rejected. At the same time, the import of raw materials that were to be found in the Peninsula – irrespective of their quality or their cost of extraction – was generally prohibited. To tackle Spain's commercial deficit the authorities resorted, with increasing enthusiasm, to the use of import licences. After 1948, bilateral trading agreements further restricted international trade by allocating quotas for specific countries and products. Despite the introduction of multiple exchange rates in October 1948, Spanish exporters were still disadvantaged. According to a recent calculation by Jordi Catalán, even the rate of exchange which most favoured exports overvalued the peseta by more than 80 per cent.[12] As late as 1959, Spain's export and import to Gross Domestic Product ratios remained as low as five per cent, considerably below the external trade ratios of other nations with similar population size and per capita income.[13]

Even though the policy of autarky reflected the political ideology of the Franco regime, official sources maintained that, because of the adverse international climate after 1939, no alternative course of action was available. That view, however, has not gone unchallenged. In an article on Spanish manufacturing industry during the Second World War, Jordi Catalán contends that the European conflict presented non-belligerent nations with a golden opportunity to expand and diversify their industrial sectors. Yet Spain, whose manufacturers amassed considerable fortunes during the First World War thanks to the country's neutrality, fared less well during the 1939–45 conflict than other non-belligerents (Portugal, Switzerland, Sweden and Turkey), whose economies were more open. The inability of the Franco regime to derive greater benefit from the seemingly insatiable appetites of the warring factions for strategic goods has to be ascribed, first and foremost, to myopic and counterproductive government policies. Not least, the Spanish authorities refused to provide manufacturers with adequate amounts of foreign currency to purchase essential raw materials and other inputs. In addition, the dictatorship's repressive treatment of the industrial labour force, which had remained loyal to the Republic, drove tens of thousands of skilled workers into exile.[14]

A dispassionate and succinct analysis of Spain's economic situation in the late 1940s was provided by Britain's commercial counsellor in Madrid, John Walker. In his report for 1948 Walker stated:

> The outbreak of the world conflict soon after the civil war ended greatly impeded rehabilitation, for foreign supplies of coal, fertilizers, raw materials, machinery and other essentials required to restore a war-shattered economy were greatly restricted, almost to the point of extinction in some cases. At the same time difficulty was experienced in finding markets even for the reduced exportable surpluses of agricultural products. Competitive purchasing of certain essential war materials by the belligerents was, however, an important compensating factor, enabling Spain not only to keep her balance of payments on a fairly even keel, but also to build up again some modest reserves of foreign exchange. At the end of the war this fortuitous support disappeared and the development anew of traditional exports, complicated by the rise of many local prices above world levels, has consequently emerged during the last three years as a major economic problem. It has brought into relief others, all inter-related, such as marked inflationary trends, basic shortages of foodstuffs, materials and equipment, declining efficiency of road and rail transport and, lastly, economic nationalism.[15]

Walker was impressed by the advice offered to the Spanish authorities by the Banco Urquijo, the country's only significant industrial bank. Anticipating official thinking, the bank argued that there could be no recovery either in agricultural or industrial production without a substantial expansion in the import of basic raw materials and capital goods. It calculated the cost of the 'special' imports required over the next few years to put the Spanish economy on a sound footing at over £170 million. This total comprised £100 million to be spent on machinery and industrial equipment, £30 million on raw materials and £40 million on other materials and agricultural equipment. Without foreign credit and allowing for some duplication, the Banco Urquijo estimated that an additional annual expenditure of between £30 and £35 million in foreign currency would be needed. This figure represented more than half of the value at which Spanish imports had been running in 1947 and 1948.[16] At this juncture, despite rumours of impending dollar credits, funds to purchase such imports did not appear to be in sight. Notwithstanding the frantic machinations in Washington on Spain's behalf by a well-orchestrated 'Spanish Lobby' of influential American catholics, anti-communists, military planners and businessmen with interests in the peninsula, the Franco regime remained firmly excluded from the European Recovery Program (Marshall Aid). Fortunately for Spain, between 1947 and 1949 the Iberian power received $264 million in credits from Argentina, which were used mainly to acquire cereals and other foodstuffs. However, in January 1950 Argentina, itself in crisis, suspended all credit sales to Spain.[17]

In his report to London, Walker argued that three options were available to Spain's policy makers:

1. to economize on less essential imports, i.e. a more rigorous application of the failed policy of import substitution;
2. to restrict consumption;
3. to stimulate exports.

Of these, the third option seemed at this stage to offer the best prospects.[18] Nevertheless, three years later Walker's successor noted the continuing shortage of foreign exchange which still placed severe restrictions on raw materials and capital goods. On the positive side, exports of fruit (especially oranges), vegetables and other foodstuffs were rising. An important factor in this respect was a sharp increase in imports of fertilizers in the intervening years. Imports of phosphates rose from an average of 278,000 tonnes in 1945–8 to 534,000 tonnes in 1949–52.[19] Meanwhile the Korean war, which broke out in June 1950, brought increased international demand for wolfram, pyrites, iron ore and mercury. Despite the well-known antipathy of President Truman and his Secretary of State, Dean Acheson, for General Franco, the conflict in Asia led to a growing rapprochement between Spain and the United States, which culminated in the bilateral military and economic agreement of 1953.

Even so, by the summer of 1951 when the *Caudillo* reshuffled his cabinet, the inability of Spain's exports to earn larger amounts of foreign currency appeared to have thwarted any possibility of economic reconstruction. The suspension of Argentinian aid proved a setback for the Spanish authorities. In September 1950, as the Cold War deepened, the United States Congress finally approved a modest loan of $62.5 million to a regime which consistently stressed its antipathy to the Red Menace. Nevertheless, following a series of famine years, a bumper harvest in 1951 offered the main source of relief to Spain's delicately balanced economy.[20]

6.2 Economic growth and instability

After the disappointing performance of the Spanish economy in the 1940s, a number of indicators bear witness to the high degree of economic growth and structural change which took place in the following decade. Between 1950 and 1959 national income, measured at constant 1964 prices, rose by 54 per cent from 425,000 million pesetas to 653,000 million pesetas. Over the same period the proportion of the active labour force employed on the land fell sharply from 49.9 per cent to 42.5 per cent.[21] Albert Carreras's index of industrial production shows an average increase of 6.6 per cent a year for the period 1951-5. For the next quinquennium it indicates an average annual rise of 7.4 per cent, in spite of a marked deceleration in 1959-60 as a result of the Stabilization Plan of July 1959. According to Carreras's calculations, the rate of growth of industrial production south of the Pyrenees in the 1950s compares favourably with those of Italy, Yugoslavia and Greece. However, unlike those other Mediterranean economies, Spain's industrial expansion was not achieved without a sharp rise in inflation from 1954 onwards, and a serious deterioration in the balance of payments after 1956. The latter especially threatened the very survival of the Franco regime.[22] Moreover, Spain's commendable rates of industrial growth could not obscure important structural weaknesses in the manufacturing sector. As late as 1958, enterprises employing under five workers accounted for 85 per cent of the total number of companies. Small firms predominated even in such sectors as chemicals, basic ferrous metals, machinery and equipment, where the optimal size was reckoned to be over a thousand employees. Many factories, not least in the textile sector of Catalonia, had hardly been modernized since their construction. In consequence, Spain's manufacturing sector was plagued by low productivity, a lack of competitiveness, and a pitiable export performance.[23]

The improvement in the country's economic fortunes after 1951, albeit precarious, coincided with a decision by the *Caudillo*, in the throes of popular protests in the large cities and a deteriorating Cold War situation abroad, to alter the composition of his cabinet. Among the key appointments were Rafael Cavestany to the agriculture portfolio and Manuel Arburúa at the Ministry of Commerce, now separated from the Industry Ministry. The new administration also sought improved diplomatic relations with the United States. In September 1953 General Franco signed a mutual defence agreement with the United States by which, in return for permission to construct military bases on Spanish soil, the Eisenhower administration guaranteed Spain a package of economic aid.

Of the new ministers, possibly Cavestany has received the most critical acclaim.[24] He went on to implement a string of progressive measures in the countryside, including the reconstruction of landed plots, irrigation, reafforestation and the provision of financial support to farmers for the purchase of such items as seeds, fertilizers, tools and machinery. Yet his policies continued to afford excessive protection to wheat, rice and the vine, while paying insufficient attention to rising domestic demand for animal products. Contemporary commentators, such as Spain's most respected economist Manuel de Torres, reproached Cavestany for permitting unnecessary imports of foodstuffs which could have been produced at home without great sacrifice.[25]

Greater controversy surrounds the contribution of Arburúa, who took over from Suanzes, the arch exponent of autarkic development, at Commerce. While some writers see him as the originator of a Spanish NEP, struggling to put an end to the prevailing orthodoxy of economic self-sufficiency,[26] others stress his confusion (all too apparent in his policy statements), his indecisiveness, and his loss of momentum after pushing through a spate of legislation during his first two years in office. Moreover, the latter was only undertaken, they argue, to win over offers of credit from the Americans.[27] Yet even Arburúa's detractors acknowledge his entrepreneurial flair. He soon achieved notoriety in government circles for fixing deals with businessmen over the ministerial telephone on such matters as the granting of import licences. When Franco sacked him in 1957 it was amidst widespread accusations of corruption and maladministration.[28]

The cornerstone of Arburúa's policy was a self-proclaimed attempt to facilitate an increase of specific types of import. First, in an endeavour to remove the worst excesses of the *estraperlo* in the countryside as well as to stabilize food prices, he launched a crash programme of foodstuff imports. Luckily for Arburúa, this initiative coincided with a succession of good harvests at home, apart from 1953. Hence this aspect of his plans did not end up draining away foreign reserves as some had feared.[29] Secondly, the minister sought to tackle a series of problems (low industrial productivity, energy shortages, and the dilapidated railway system) via imports of much-needed raw materials and capital equipment. Between 1951 and 1955 imports of machinery, including vehicles, and metals rose by 70 per cent to stand at 36 per cent of total imports. After 1955 there was a steep rise in imports of semi-manufactures, itself a reflection of the consolidation of manufacturing. Even so, Arburúa's goal remained that of import substitution. Spain's industrialization policy continued to be underpinned by an assortment of protectionist policies, exchange manipulations, etc. Moreover, during his six-year tenure of office the increase in Spanish imports was far from spectacular. At the time of his dismissal in February 1957, imports were still below their 1929 peak, while foreign trade was approximately one-sixth of the average value per capita of other West European nations.[30]

For his part, Arburúa recognized that the creation of new export products, especially manufactures, might prove a lengthy and difficult process. Nevertheless, the minister's early forecasts of export growth proved hopelessly optimistic. Despite official emphasis on industrialization policy, agricultural products (fruit, vegetables and wine) accounted for three-fifths of all exports. In addition, foreign sales of perishable foodstuffs were irregular, due to Spain's unpredictable climate, while prices received in highly competitive markets fluctuated dramatically. More worryingly in the long run, the terms of trade continued to move against providers of foodstuffs and raw materials. The failure of Spain's industrialists, moreover, could be gauged by the fact that when Arburúa left office, exports of manufactured goods were falling in absolute terms. No amount of manipulation of the exchange rates and other artificial stimuli could compensate for the lack of competitiveness of Spanish manufactures.[31]

6.2.1 American aid

Spain's inability in the 1950s to generate a significant increase in export earnings only underlined the importance of United States' support for the Spanish economy, especially during the middle years of the decade (1953-6). Between 1951 and 1957, the United States provided the Iberian nation with $625 million of aid. It is commonly agreed that America's generosity provided a vital breathing space for the ailing Franco regime which could well have collapsed.[32] Yet, given the magnitude of Spain's requirements, the extent of the United States' aid that she received was not always fully appreciated. Moreover, much of the aid took the form of agricultural surpluses (olive oil, cotton, tobacco), which might otherwise have been destroyed. On the positive side, the Spanish railways (RENFE) received $60 million of aid consisting of locomotives, rails, sleepers and other material, while electricity supply and the iron and steel industry saw their investment programmes boosted. INI, nevertheless, complained that American aid contributed next to nothing to the country's industrial growth.[33]

There can be little doubt that Spain would have derived greater benefits from US aid had it been more concentrated on the provision of capital goods for the modernization of industry and improvements in the transport infrastructure. Even so, in spite of the smallness of the sums involved, American aid contributed to Spain's economic development in a number of important ways. Above all, it offset part of the current account deficit caused by the failure of Arburúa's export drive.[34] United States representatives in the peninsula also emphasized that US aid was a crucial factor in securing higher living standards and combating inflation.[35] In addition, the terms and conditions of American support to Spain were aimed at strengthening the position of economic liberals within the Spanish cabinet. Article Two of the Defense Support Program, for example, committed the recipient nation to stabilize its currency, establish a realistic exchange rate, balance the budget, eradicate monopolistic practices, stimulate competition in the domestic market and encourage international trade. These were fine sentiments. Indeed, such ideals were to inspire the architects of the 1959 Stabilization Plan, if not their successors. However, before 1956, when the United States' ambassador openly criticized Spain's restrictive attitude to foreign investment, the Eisenhower administration appeared more concerned with the military and strategic implications of the bases agreement than in opening up the Spanish market to greater competition.

6.2.2 Tourism

Before the 1950s, given the prevailing orthodoxy of autarky, scant regard was paid in government circles to the beneficial effects for the Spanish economy of encouraging foreign tourism. External influences also played a part. After the United Nations' diplomatic boycott of Franco's Spain in March 1946, the French government closed its borders with the neighbouring country. The crossing points were not reopened until February 1948. On the Iberian side, the Falangists' suspicion of outsiders as potential *agents provocateurs*, along with the prudishness of the Catholic church – bikini-clad females on Spanish beaches often faced arrest and a subsequent fine – did little to attract foreign holiday-makers to the *costas*. More importantly, Spain lacked a modern and efficient infrastructure of arterial roads, main-line railways, docks and airports to cope with mass tourism. Nor was there an adequate supply of moderately-priced hotels in which to accommodate large numbers of incoming visitors.

A pioneering study published under the imprimatur of Spain's newly-created Ministry of Information and Tourism showed that in 1952 the country came a poor ninth in the European tourism league, measured by earnings. Foreign visitors, it was calculated, spent a mere $37 million in Spain, compared with $188 million in France, an equal amount in the United Kingdom, $140 million in Switzerland and $100 million in Italy. Encouragingly, the survey pointed out that Spain's receipts from foreign tourism in 1952 (1,563 million pesetas) more than offset the nation's trade deficit (1,307 millions). Expenditure by Spanish tourists abroad was not calculated. Yet, bearing in mind Spain's perennial trade deficit and the difficulties encountered by Spanish emigrants in Latin America in remitting their savings home, earnings from foreign tourism were viewed as an important factor in future economic development.[36]

In the short and medium term, however, it would have been premature to entertain inflated hopes for foreign tourism. The sums involved in the early 1950s were tiny, while Spain's industrialization programme envisaged heavy and sustained increases in imports. Moreover, visitors to Spain generally belonged to lower income groups who were attracted by its cheapness and who rarely remained as long as visitors to, say, the Alps or the French and Italian rivieras. Without a far-reaching commitment to the provision of infrastructure for the tourist trade, its potential for expansion was severely limited. Press reports in 1956 indicated that saturation level had already been attained. Even so, earnings from foreign tourism surpassed $100 million in 1957 – at a time when US aid began to diminish.[37]

6.2.3 Foreign investment

By the winter of 1956, Arburúa's much-vaunted plans to liberalize the Spanish economy were in deep trouble. His export drive had manifestly failed to earn sufficient foreign currency to pay for imports vital to Spain's industrialization programme. American aid, which saw Spain through the middle years of the decade, was fast running out. Earnings from foreign tourism and emigrant remittances, while not insignificant, had to await the so-called Spanish Economic Miracle of the 1960s before they were to play leading roles in national economic developments.

To a growing array of bankers, industrialists (especially in Catalonia), and sections of the economic press, the only answer to Spain's economic misfortunes lay in encouraging foreign investment. Imports of capital from more advanced economies would not only tackle Spain's balance of payments difficulties but would also bring about crucial injections of new technology into Spain's outmoded industrial sector, thereby helping to make Spanish products more saleable in international markets. Unfortunately for the revisionists, as the future Finance Minister Mariano Navarro was later to realize, many members of Franco's administration – including the *Caudillo* himself and his second-in-command, Rear Admiral Luis Carrero Blanco – were deeply imbued with an almost allergic mistrust of foreigners.[38] Such xenophobia was responsible for the restrictive attitude to foreign investment that was strikingly condemned by the United States ambassador in June 1956. American capitalists, he informed his audience of Catalan entrepreneurs, were well disposed to contribute to modernization of the Spanish economy when the political climate became more welcoming.[39]

This diplomatic overture coincided with the near exhaustion of the Franco regime. During the final months of 1956, labour unrest in the main industrial zones, along with nationalist manifestations in Catalonia, preoccupied the authorities, bringing the social order to the verge of collapse. Added to this, severe frosts almost ruined the citrus harvest, one of Spain's main export earners. Rumours circulated in Madrid of a report, written by Arburúa, claiming that Spain's gold and currency reserves had fallen as low as $40 million. Faced with the possibility of national bankruptcy, the minister proposed a package of severe austerity measures – a sure sign that the old model of mild autarky and interventionism was now thoroughly exhausted. Even his faithful admirer, General Franco, saw that he had little alternative but to replace Arburúa and his discredited policies.

6.3 The technocrats in power

Spain's economic policy during the period 1957-9 has been much commented upon.[40] Having demoted the Falangists in his administration, the Caudillo turned to a new team of economic technocrats closely linked to the Catholic lay group *Opus Dei*. Mariano Navarro, a director of the Banco Popular, became Minister of Finance and Alberto Ullastres, a Catalan economics professor, took over the Commerce portfolio from Arburúa. They were supported by an able team of professional economists, including Juan Sardà at the Bank of Spain, Manuel Varela at Commerce and Juan Antonio Ortiz García at Finance.[41] Together they embarked, timorously at first, on the path from autarky to the introduction of market mechanisms. Their reforms were not matched by the concession of greater political freedoms, the legalization of trade union activity, nor even a more progressive taxation system. For two years the Spanish authorities pursued a series of cautious initiatives, largely through the modification and adaptation of existing instruments. This period is sometimes referred to as 'pre-stabilization', though it is difficult to discern any deliberate line of policy. In April 1957, the system of multiple exchange rates was simplified and the peseta was devalued, though not by enough. Large amounts of short-term capital flowed out. Moreover, a plethora of controls remained. To protect industry from the effects of inflation, new subsidies and deposit techniques were introduced. In an attempt to peg prices, July 1957 saw the rediscount rate raised from 4.25 to 5 per cent, while interest rates on deposit accounts were frozen. To bring in additional revenue, in December a series of tax reforms were enacted. Thereafter, in 1958, as the policy makers began to run out of steam, attempts were made to attach Spain to a number of international institutions which were later to underwrite the Stabilization Plan. In January 1958 Spain joined the Organization for European Economic Co-operation. Six months later she also became a member of the International Monetary Fund and the World Bank. The latter institutions provided help and encouraged the acceptance of new ideas. This was especially important since many powerful figures, not least Franco and Carrero Blanco, still opposed the dismantling of autarky. Suanzes and the Industry Ministry also showed a marked preference for industrialization and inflation as against stabilization and economic liberalization. Indeed, General Franco only backed down when briefed by Navarro on the profound balance of payments crisis which had beset Spain.

The Stabilization Plan of July 1959 was introduced against a background of near insolvency. Spain's balance of payments, in perpetual crisis since 1957, gave cause for extraordinary concern in the first half of 1959 when the central bank's gold and foreign exchange reserves, net of short-term liabilities, were in fact negative. The Plan itself, Spain's first great liberalization measure (including the Figuerola reforms of 1869), was wide-ranging.[42] A first series of measures set out to eliminate excess demand. The public sector deficit was substantially cut, while direct advances by the Bank of Spain to public institutions were frozen at their end-of-1958 level. Yet, the most far-reaching measures concerned Spain's foreign trade and payments system. Multiple exchange rates were abolished and the peseta fixed at a par of 60 to the US dollar. Quotas and other restrictions were removed from about 50 per cent of Spanish imports from OEEC countries. In addition, legislation was introduced which offered substantial incentives and guarantees to foreign investors. Among other undertakings, proposed or implied in the 1959 Stabilization Plan, were a long overdue revision of Spain's outmoded tariff legislation, measures against restrictive practices, a reform of the inadequate taxation system and the introduction of long-range economic planning. However, although all these proposals were to pass into legislation, three at least were to prove a disappointment to liberals. The new tariff of the 1960 legislation was still markedly protectionist, not until July 1963 was a feeble anti-monopoly law enacted, and the tax reforms proposed in 1959 did not come into effect until June 1964.

There is general agreement that the 1959 Stabilization and Liberalization Plan, despite short-term costs (measured by rising unemployment and falling real wages), was to bring long-term economic benefits. Growth recovered rapidly between 1961 and 1966 and remained high until the oil crisis of 1973. The Spanish authorities, moreover, were assisted in their task by a fortuitous set of trends which affected Western economies as a whole during the 1960s. Above all, Spain was able to finance massive increases in imports that made possible her rapid industrial growth due to three main factors – a huge increase in earnings from foreign tourism, emigrant remittances and an upsurge of foreign investment in the Spanish economy.

Notes

1 Grupo de Estudios de Historia Rural, 1983, 'Notas sobre la producción agraria española, 1891–1931', *Revista de Historia Económica*, 1 (2): 185–252; Tortella, G., 1984, 'La agricultura en la economía de la España contemporánea, 1830–1930', *Papeles de Economía Española*, 20: 62–75.

2 See especially García Delgado, J.L., 1984, 'La industrialización española en el primer tercio del siglo xx', in Jover, J.M. (ed.), 'Los comienzos del siglo xx', vol. 37 of *Historia de España Menéndez Pidal*, Espasa Calpe, Madrid: 1–171.

3 Perpiñá, R., 1936, *De economía hispana: contribucción al estudio de la constitución económica especialmente la comercial exterior*, Labor, Barcelona: 7.

4 Carreras, A., 1989, 'Depresión económica y cambio estructural durante el decenio bélico, 1936–45', in García Delgado, J.L. (ed.), *El primer franquismo: España durante la segunda guerra mundial: V Coloquio de Historia Contemporánea de España*, Siglo xxi, Madrid: 8; and by the same author, 1984, 'La producción industrial española, 1842–1981: construcción de un índice anual', *Revista de Historia Económica*, 2 (1): 144–7. See also García Delgado, J.L., 1987, 'La industrialización y el desarrollo económico de España durante el franquismo', in Nadal, J. Carreras, A., and Sudrià, C. (eds), *La economía española en el siglo xx: una perspectiva histórica*, Ariel, Barcelona: 166–7.

5 See for example Arburúa, M., 1956, *Cinco años al frente del Ministerio de Comercio: discursos y declaraciones*, Madrid: 17; and Suanzes, J.A., 1963, 'Franco y la economía,' in *Ocho discursos*, INI, Madrid: 143–8.

6 For a critique of official explanations see Clavera, J., Esteban, J.M., Monés, M.A., Montserrat, A. and Ros Hombravella, J., 1978, *Capitalismo español: de la autarquía a la estabilización, 1939–59*, Cuadernos para el Diágolo, Madrid: 52–6 and 139–48; González, M.J., 1979, *La economía política del franquismo, 1940–70: dirigismo, mercado y planificación*, Tecnos, Madrid: 46; and Catalán, J., 1989, 'Reconstrucción y desarrollo industrial: tres economías del sur de Europa, 1944–53', *IV Congreso de la Asociación de Historia Económica, Universidad de Alicante, 18–20 diciembre de 1989*: 213–32.

7 For a variety of critical accounts see Velasco, C., 1984, 'El "ingenerismo" como directriz básica de la política económica durante la autarquía, 1936–51', *Información Comercial Española*, 606: 103; Fuentes Quintana, E., 1984, 'El plan de Estabilización económica, veinticinco años después', *Información Comercial Española*, 612–3: 29; Viñas, A., 1984, *Guerra, dinero, dictadura: ayuda fascista y autarquía en la España de Franco*, Critica, Barcelona: 208; and Tedde, P., 1986, 'Economía y franquismo: a propósito de una biografía', *Revista de Historia Económica*, 4: 628–9.

8 See especially Barciela, C., 1986, introduction to 'Los costes del franquismo' in Garrabou, R., Barciela, C., and Jiménez Blanco, J.I. (eds), *Historia agraria de la España contemporánea, 3, El fin de la agricultura tradicional, 1900–60*, Critica, Barcelona: 383–454.

9 Schwartz, P., and González, M.J., 1978, *Una historia del Instituto Nacional de Industria, 1941–76*, Tecnos, Madrid.

10 Melguizo, A., 1973, El papel de la empresa pública en la economía española, in Velarde, J. (ed.), *La España de los años 70*, 2, Editorial Moneda y Crédito, Madrid: 600; Braña, F.J., Buesa, M., and Molero, J., 1979, 'El fin de la etapa nacionalista:

114   *Joseph Harrison*

industrialización y dependencia en España, 1951–59', *Investigaciones Económicas*, 9: 151–217.
11 See Donges, J., 1976, *La industrialización en España: políticas, logros, perspectivas*, Oikos Tau, Valassar de Mar: 40–44.
12 Catalán, *Reconstrucción*: 225.
13 See Donges, J., 1971, 'From an autarkic towards a cautiously outward-looking industrialization policy: the case of Spain', *Weltwirtschaftliches Archiv*, 107: 30–40.
14 Catalán, J., 1989, 'Autarquía y desarrollo de la industria de fábrica durante la segunda guerra mundial: en enfoque comparativo', in García Delgado, J.L. (ed.), *El primer franquismo:* 35–88.
15 Walker, J., 1949, *Economic and commercial conditions in Spain*, HMSO, London: 1.
16 Ibid.: 3.
17 Viñas, A., 1982, 'La primera ayuda norteamericana a España', in *Lecturas de economía española: 50 aniversario del Cuerpo de Técnicos Oficiales del Estado*, Ministerio de Economia y Commercio, Madrid: 89; González, op. cit.: 88–90; Schneidman J.L., 1973, *Spain and Franco, 1949–59*, Praeger, New York: 49.
18 Walker, op. cit., 3.
19 Catalán, *Reconstrucción:* 225.
20 Pelham, G.C., 1952, *Economic and commercial conditions in Spain*, HMSO, London: 1–6.
21 Alcaide, J. 1976, 'Una revisión urgente de la serie Renta Nacional española en el siglo xx', in Instituto de Estudios Fiscales, *Datos básicos para la historia financierà de España, 1850–1975*, 2 vols. Instituto de Estudios Fiscales, Madrid: 1, 1136 and 1142.
22 Carreras, *La producción industrial:* 127–57; García Delgado, *La industrialización:* 171; *Información Comercial Española*, 1962, 'Como y cuanto ha crecido la economía española en la década 50–60', 341: 58–9.
23 Donges, *From an autarkic (policy):* 45–9; Rogers, T.E., 1957, *Economic and commercial conditions in Spain*, HMSO, London: 4.
24 See especially the balanced evaluation of Barciela, op. cit.: 416–23.
25 Torres, M., 1975, 'La economía española en 1958', in Ros Hombravella, J., *Trece economistas españoles ante la economía española*, Oikos Tau, Vilassar de Mar: 20.
26 The leading pro-Arburúa account in Viñas, A., Viñuela, J., Eguidazu, F., Pulgar, C.F. and Florensa, S., 1979, *Política commercial exterior de España, 1931–75*, 2 vols, Banco Exterior de España, Madrid: see especially 1: 864.
27 Most critical of Arburúa is González, op. cit: 103; but see also Clavera *et al*, op. cit., 261–9.
28 Most revealing on this matter is Franco Salgado Araujo, F., 1976, *Mis conversaciones privadas con Franco*, Barcelona: 182. An early hint was dropped by Anderson, C.W., 1970, *The political economy of Spain: policy making in an authoritarian system*, University of Wisconsin Press, Madison: 107. Stanley Payne also takes up the point in his recent account of the Franco regime. See Payne, S., 1987, *El régimen de Franco 1936–75*, Alianza, Madrid: 480.
29 Banco Urquijo, 1954, *La economía española, 1952–3*, Madrid: 14.
30 Rogers, op. cit.: 3.
31 Torres, M.de, 1956, *Juicio de la actual política económica española*, Aguilar, Madrid: 82; Alcaide, J., 1957, 'Problemas del comercio exterior', *Balance*, 15 October: 16–17; Rogers, op. cit.: 3.
32 Thus, for example, argues González, op. cit.: 10 and Viñas *et al*, op. cit.: 2: 795.
33 Instituto Nacional de Industria, 1959, *Memoria*, INI, Madrid: 275–6, cited in Braña *et al*, op. cit.: 192–3.

34 This point was repeatedly stressed by Manuel de Torres, see *Juicio*: 107.
35 See especially Sause, O.L., 1957, 'Algunos aspectos de los programas de cooperación económica hispano-americanos', *Revista de Economía Política*, 8: 35-45, and Shearer, E.B., 1959. 'Significado para España de la ayuda económica norteamericana', *Revista de Economía Política*, 10: 989-1006.
36 Plaza Prieto, J., 1954, *Tourism and the balance of payments*, J. Plaza Prieto Madrid: *passim; Balance*, 4 August 1954: 29.
37 Huguet, F., 1957, 'El desarrollo del turismo en España', *Balance*, 1 September: 16-17; 'El turismo, factor de bienestar', *Balance*, 15 October 1957: 3.
38 Navarro Rubio, M., 1976, 'La batalla de la estabilización', *Anales de la Real Academia de Ciencias Morales y Políticas*, 53: 176.
39 Nueva orientación de la política económica, 1956, *España Económica*, 7 July: 3.
40 Easily the most readable account, written by an active participant, is Enrique Fuentes, *El Plan de Estabilización, passim*. See also Merigó, E., 1982, 'Spain', in Boltho, A., (ed.), *The European Economy: Growth and Crisis*, OUP, Oxford: 554-80.
41 Fuentes, *El Plan de Estabilización*: 29.
42 See especially Merigó, op. cit.: 564-5.

7 A note on the structure of the world economy, 1850–1987

Jürgen Kuczynski
formerly of Humboldt University, Berlin

The rise of the tertiary sector in the economically most modern and most productive countries is a subject which has only comparatively recently come to the attention of economic and social historians. Not surprisingly, one of the first to comment upon this trend was Sidney Pollard, in a conference organized by Bo Gustafsson.[1] In this paper, Pollard drew attention to the rise of the service industries and white collar employment, a movement which has been so pervasive that it is curious that we refer to the richest countries as industrial states for, when measuring the comparative shares of the social product of agriculture, industry and the services during the nineteenth and twentieth centuries, we do not often find industry occupying the leading position.

Thus, in the case of the USA, for instance, the share of services fluctuated during the period from 1869 to 1987 between 55 and 70 per cent, so that the overwhelmingly large portion always fell to this sector, whereas the share of agriculture dropped from little over 20 per cent in 1869 to two per cent, and that of industry rose from about 20 per cent in 1869 to 36 per cent in the 1950s, only to decline again to about 25 per cent in 1987.

The figures for Western Europe are given in Table 7.1. Of course these are merely rough calculations. Nevertheless they may allow us to say that, according to these statistics, only in the French case did industry dominate the service sector for a long period of time but, in turn, industry also lagged behind agriculture for a lengthy period. In Germany and Great Britain the service sector dominated in all but a short spell in the inter-war period, while in Italy services were always in front of industry but lagged behind agriculture until the First World War.

How rough these figures are may be judged by the following. Table 7.1 is derived from the work of Kuznets who included handicrafts within the service sector in the case of Germany. But such a procedure is justifiable only during the first decades after the First World War, and then only partially so. At that time, the handicrafts switched from production to repair work. But even then it seems to me to be doubtful whether one may consider them to be counted as part of the service sector. Moreover, there exist alternative calculations for Germany as can be seen in Table 7.2, derived from the work of Hoffman. According to this table, it was industry which always occupied first place from

Table 7.1 Social product by economic sectors (in percentages)

Year	Agriculture	Industry	Services
FRANCE			
1789	49	18	33
1847	44	29	27
1892	37	32	30
1834/8	22	40	38
1986	3.7	30.9	65.4
GERMANY			
1860/9	32.3	24.0	43.7
1875/84	24.3	26.7	49.0
1905/14	18.0	38.8	43.2
1930/8	13.7	44.0	42.3
1986	1.8	47.7	50.5
GREAT BRITAIN			
1895	9.7	36.9	53.4
1911	8.0	39.3	52.7
1930	3.8	45.4	50.8
1934	4.1	49.3	46.6
1986	1.8	37.9	60.3
ITALY			
1862/5	57.1	20.0	22.9
1876/80	55.7	19.6	24.7
1891/5	46.7	21.0	32.3
1931/5	27.7	28.9	43.4
1986	4.3	34.4	61.3

Sources: S. Kuznets, *Economic Development and Cultural Change*, Supplement to Vol. 5 (1957), pp. 68f; *Statistisches Jahrbuch 1988 für die Bundesrepublik Deutschland*, Stuttgart und Mainz, 1988, p. 728f.

1875–1884 onward. We see a slightly smaller change when comparing the figures for Britain in Table 7.1 with those given by Phyllis Deane, in Table 7.3. In two of the five years considered here the figures for the service sector were outstandingly high as compared with those for industry and in two further years, they hardly lagged behind the share of national output produced by the secondary sector.

Nevertheless, the question why we speak of *industrial* states remains to be answered, especially when we focus our attention on the twentieth century. In all likelihood the answer lies in the fact that since about 1850 the fluctuations in industry have always been the decisive factor influencing the development of the economy as a whole. General economic crises were brought about by crises starting in industry, a causation and a sequence which early bourgeois economists also recognized. But it was Marx who established that this sequence was, by its nature, an economic law. In the years under review,

Table 7.2 Net domestic product grouped by economic sectors

Year	Agriculture	Industry	Services
1860/9	44	28	28
1875/84	36	37	27
1905/13	25	48	27
1930/4	21	47	32

Source: W.G. Hoffman, *Das Wachstum der deutschen Wirtschaft seit der Mitte des 19 Jahrhunderts*, Berlin Heidelberg, New York, 1965, p. 33.

Table 7.3 National income*, Great Britain

Year	Agriculture	Industry	Services
1801	33	29	39
1851	20	42	37
1901	6	48	45
1935	4	38	58
1955	5	48	47

*For 1935 and 1955 Gross Social Product
 All figures rounded.

Source: Phyllis Deane and W.A. Cole, *British Economic Growth, 1688–1959: Trends and Structure*, Cambridge, 1962, pp. 166 and 178.

industry was always the decisive element which carried along development in the other sectors, either forward or backward.

The situation is quite different in the socialist countries. The statistical Yearbook of the German Democratic Republic regularly publishes calculations giving the shares of industry and agriculture as related to the 'national income produced'. From this source, Table 7.4 shows the following proportions in the four most important industrial states. If we take into account that services also include the building industry, it becomes quite obvious that the share of the service sector in total national product is definitely lower in the socialist countries than in capitalist nations, a fact which must be attributed to their insufficient development.

Let us now investigate the development of productivity in the three main sectors of the economy of the major capitalist industrial states. We begin with the US comparing, to begin with, only industry and agriculture (Table 7.5). From 1843/48 to 1900 productivity increased more than twice as rapidly in industry as in agriculture, that is 194 per cent as compared with 92 per cent, and until 1933/41 it increased even three times as quickly. After that, productivity raced ahead in agriculture. If we assume 1933/41 to equal 100, the increase in agricultural productivity amounted to roughly 1050 by

Table 7.4 National income produced in the economic sectors (in percentages)

Year	Agriculture	Industry	Services
USSR			
1950	22	58	20
1970	22	51	27
1987	21	45	35
GDR			
1950	31	44	25
1970	17	56	26
1987	11	64	25
CSSR			
1950	17	63	21
1970	11	62	27
1987	7	61	32
HUNGARY			
1950	48	27	26
1970	23	43	35
1987	14	46	39

Figures are rounded and so do not always sum to 100.

Table 7.5 Index of productivity in the USA

Year	Agriculture	Industry
1843/8	100	100
1900	192	294
1933/41	271	697
1975/82	3115	3403

Source: J. Kuczynski, 'Die Entwicklung von Sozialstruktur und Productivität seit 1850', *Jahrbuch für Wirtschaftsgeschichte*, 1988, p. 9f.

1975/82, while in industry the figure was only 390. Today agriculture has possibly entirely caught up with industry, if we take the long view from 1843/48 to the 1980s.

For services our figures are too uncertain to permit us to calculate the corresponding increases in terms of index numbers. However, the following officially published data in Table 7.6 confront us with astonishing enigmas. Quite obviously the increase of productivity has been far lower in the service sector than in that of material production. In part, it may even have decreased.

As far as industry is concerned, we can construct a rough world index from the 1840s onwards (Table 7.7). The increases in productivity were very considerable, especially in the last quarter of the century. Possibly, though, the

Table 7.6 Services related to the social product and to the gainfully employed population in the USA (percentages)

Year	Gainfully Employed Population[1]	Year	Social Product[2]
1870	25	1869	58.5
1910	37	1904/13	56.3
1980	67	1975/82	65.8

[1] The calculations are based on the *Historical Statistics of the United States* published by the US Department of Commerce, Washington D.C. 1960 and the regularly published *Statistical Abstract of the United States*. Forestry is included in agriculture, industry includes mining as well as the building trade, the remainder being considered to embrace the services.

[2] Kuczynski, 1988, op. cit. In the source quoted the calculations were carried beyond the decimal point, which was totally unnecessary since these figures as well as those contained in the preceding Table are far too inexact.

Table 7.7 Development of productivity in industry (1900 = 100)

Year	Index	Percentage increase
1840/9	40	
1850/9	45	10
1860/9	55	20
1870/9	70	30
1880/9	80	15
1890/9	90	10
1900/9	110	22
1910/9	133	21
1920/9	155	17
1930/9	197	27
1940/9	225	14
1950/9	274	22
1960/9	362	32
1970/9	503	39

Sources: J. Kuczynski, *Die Geschichte der Lage der Arbeiter unter dem Kapitalismus*, Berlin, 1967. In addition I used the series of the *United Nations Statistical Yearbook*. Since the calculations published are necessarily quite rough, the figures given here are rounded off.

figures up to 1900 may show an exaggerated increase because they relate only to the major industrial states – those states, however, have always made up about two thirds of the world's industry.

Table 7.8 Yearly increase of the productivity of labour (Gross social product per head of the gainfully employed)

Years	USA	FRG
1961/4	+3.0	+4.3
1965/9	+1.9	+4.7
1970/3	+1.4	+4.1
1974/9	+0.1	+3.1
1980/7	+1.1	+1.5

Source: For 1961–1979, *Monthly Reports of the German Federal Bank*, 1980. Further years are based on official data.

But if we investigate the development of productivity in the economy as a whole in the USA and the Federal Republic of Germany during the so-called scientific-technical revolution, we make an astounding discovery (Table 7.8). We witness a total disintegration of the rate of increase in the American economy as a whole from the middle of the 1960s and in the Federal Republic from the 1980s onwards.

For socialist countries there are no comparable figures but it was estimated that even in the technically most advanced nation, the German Democratic Republic, productivity levels were at least 30 per cent below those in the FRG.

I venture to hope that my remarks have shown how much work remains to be done, both statistically and analytically, before we can arrive at reliable conclusions about the balance and driving motors of economic development in the most modern and most productive economies.

Part II: The social consequences

8 Artisans, workers, and the state: Towards a social history of the early German labour movement*

Jürgen Kocka
Free University, Berlin

8.1 The broad pattern of development

It has become common to date the formative phase of the German labour movement within the period from the 1840s to 1875.[1] For the pre-1848 period we can distinguish three types of organizations from which the German labour movement emerged.

1. There were hundreds of local friendly and mutual aid societies under various labels. Though usually only organizing particular occupations, they sometimes encompassed all the labourers within a particular factory, or at least within a number of occupational groups. The journeymen's associations were among such friendly societies. Their major tasks were to pay sickness, accident, and death benefits and support itinerant journeymen. Because of such functions, government officials tolerated and even supported the societies. Yet these mutual aid societies did not merely insure and care for their members. They also served as social and educational societies whose programmes and discussions were concerned with general social and political themes, and, particularly in the pre-revolutionary forties, they were sometimes closely linked to democratic or socialist aspirations.[2]
2. Before the revolution of 1848–9 thousands of journeymen were members of general artisanal associations and workingmen's educational associations that neither limited membership to a specific occupation nor excluded masters. Their most important goal was to transmit education to workingmen. They conformed to the contemporary enthusiasm for voluntary associations (*Assoziationen*), holding that, according to liberal principles, they should replace the dwindling role of compulsory corporations and thereby prevent atomization in an unrestrained society. These associations were simultaneously an expression of the liberal belief in the power of education as the most important means of self-help and social progress. Most of them were founded from the 1820s onwards by socially committed members of the liberal bourgeoisie, and they also fulfilled functions of

*Translated from German by Jonathan B Knudsen, Wellesley, Mass.

sociability alongside their educational ones. The spectrum of these associations went from anti-socialist bulwarks controlled by members of the bourgeoisie to the radical democratic and socialist societies in, for example, Berlin and Hamburg. Left-Hegelian intellectuals, democrats, and socialists of varying kinds used a few of these associations as platforms. A radicalization took place in the 1840s: Stephan Born, Wilhelm Liebknecht, and August Bebel were first politicized in such workingmen's educational societies.[3]

3. Under the more liberal constitutional conditions of France, Switzerland, England, and Belgium, travelling journeymen, workingmen, and émigré intellectuals formed associations in the 1830s and 40s that usually followed socialist and communist programmes. Marx and Engels were leading members of the 'Communist League' which had branches in Paris, Zurich, and London and had evolved in 1846–7 from the 'League of the Just'. These émigré associations, or *Auslandsvereine*, were small gatherings that never had more than a couple of hundred members at any one time. Radical democratic and socialist ideas from western Europe found great resonance within them, but so too did left-Hegelian views and the religiously tinged strands of artisanal socialism that, for instance, shaped Wilhelm Weitling. At first the emigré associations exerted a clandestine influence on the artisanal and workingmen's associations within Germany but in 1848–9 the ties became public.[4]

The revolution of 1848–9 constituted a leap forward in the development of the German labour movement. Once again we can observe three different patterns.[5]

1. Especially in the larger cities there were waves of strikes led by journeymen, labourers, and domestic outworkers who were protesting against masters, contracting middlemen, and entrepreneurs. Trade-union-like organizations crystallized mostly at the level of individual occupations. These local organizations rapidly contacted each other and regional meetings took place. Two occupations formed all-German trade unions: the printers and typesetters, on the one hand, and the cigarmakers, on the other.

2. In Frankfurt in July of 1848 masters and journeymen gathered together at a German Artisans' Congress after numerous local and regional meetings had prepared the way. They opposed unlimited freedom of trade and sought to present before the Frankfurt National Assembly a quasi-corporatist economic and social programme. Yet they quickly split along class lines: the journeymen, who were in the minority, left the congress, feeling the masters discriminated against them and failed to treat them in the debates as equal partners with equal rights. The masters continued on alone and finally sent to the National Assembly a draft of industrial legislation that was critical of capitalism and recommended re-establishing guild controls with substantial administrative authority. The journeymen formed another assembly and named it the *Allgemeiner deutscher Arbeiterkongreß* (General German Workingmen's Congress). Their debates consisted of a mixture of radical political demands, sympathy for the guilds, socialist perspectives, and plans

for co-operatives. Later they attached themselves to the *Allgemeine deutsche Arbeiterverbrüderung* (General German Brotherhood of Workingmen).
3. The *Allgemeine deutsche Arbeiterverbrüderung* was founded in Berlin in August of 1848 and thereafter directed from Leipzig. It was a loose federation of diverse workingmen's and artisanal associations, trade unions, and other loosely-knit groupings. Its rapid expansion reflected and intensified widely-held feelings that journeymen and labourers had enough in common, in spite of diverse occupations and qualifications, to warrant an association separate from the bourgeois classes. If the Brotherhood of Workingmen did not break all ties to the bourgeois-democratic and left-liberal groupings, it still developed its own independent political goals. Certain ideas came together within this movement: co-operative self-help with an emphasis on education as a mode of emancipation, and a co-operative-socialist reform vision with a commitment to democratic and liberal constitutional changes – these, if necessary, by revolutionary means. The Brotherhood of Workingmen supported strikes. Its members were open to ideological influences from numerous quarters, among them, Marxist and other communist notions. Under the leadership of the typesetter Stephan Born, a pragmatic socialist, the Brotherhood constituted the first mass movement of workers in Germany – there were approximately 170 branches in 1849 and about 18,000 members in 1850.

Just as the development of an independent labour movement indirectly contributed to the failure of the revolution, so too did the extensive failure of the revolution disrupt the development of the labour movement. Most of the organizations were dissolved in the period of reaction (1850s), radical labour leaders were persecuted, and the founding of new societies was made difficult. But the friendly and co-operative societies continued to survive alongside workingmen's educational societies and reading clubs. To a certain extent the labour movement retreated to the pre-1848 organizational patterns. The Kolping associations, the Catholic journeymen's movement that had begun in 1845, were also hardly affected. Many activists and many of the revolutionary aspirations survived in local discussion groups; figures such as Lasalle, Marx, and Liebknecht re-emerged once again after 1858 when the so-called 'New Era' began – the most liberal fifteen years in the history of nineteenth century Germany. The labour movement finally established itself in the eighteen-sixties and early seventies. Once again we can distinguish three different phenomena.

1. In the revolution of 1848–9, between fifty and one hundred producers' co-operatives were founded in close connection with the *Arbeiterverbrüderung*. In the fifties and sixties their numbers grew to at least three hundred. These were mostly short-lived, local associations of small, partly dependent masters, contracting domestic labourers, and even journeymen and factory labourers. They were formed especially in textiles, tailoring, woodworking, metalworking, cigarmaking, construction and printing. The well-established master artisans usually did not support such local bodies, but in the sixties they began to be supported by the emerging trade unions and labour parties. From the early seventies onwards their significance began to

decline. They suffered from internal difficulties: they could not easily accumulate enough capital; their commitment to internal democracy could not always be easily united with a need to be economically competitive; and they were hampered by legislation. Soon the trade unions and the social democratic parties turned away from them as well. Credit, consumer, and retail co-operatives came to dominate the co-operative movement in the next decades, whereas workers' and producers' associations became increasingly marginal.[7]

2. It was otherwise with the trade unions. After 1858 every type of association acquired a new lease of life, and once the right of combination was gradually admitted in the years between 1861 and 1869, the trade unions began to stir themselves again. Again, as in 1848, they partly developed from pre-existing organizations – friendly societies and workingmen's associations – but often they were newly founded or emerged from the experience of a particular strike. Between 1869 and 1873 Germany experienced the most extensive wave of strikes that had yet occurred in its history.

Aside from the weapon of the strike, collective self-help and self-organization in the form of trade unions appeared to many workers as the natural answer to the insecurities of the market economy and the superiority of the employers. Trade unions offered their members insurance payments of the most diverse sort and frequently, in addition, legal aid. Some of them had a limited success in controlling the distribution of work. They sought to improve wages and working conditions, and they fulfilled social and cultural needs. They gave to their members collective acceptance and a recognition denied to them in bourgeois associations and bourgeois social relations in general. In 1865-6, the printers and the typesetters on the one hand, and the cigarmakers, on the other, were again the first to establish all-German trade unions. Other occupations followed. These organizations, however, were extremely unstable, decentralized, and fluid.

From 1868 onward the political parties had a diverse impact on trade union development, partly promoting and partly weakening them. Within one and the same occupation there were often three competing trade unions with differing political tendencies: those sympathizing with the ADAV originally founded by Lasalle; those closely allied to the SDAP of Bebel and Liebknecht; and those linked to the liberal trade unions or *Gwerkvereine*. In the seventies trade-union-like organizations also emerged within the Catholic labour movement, especially in the Rhineland, the Ruhr region and Silesia. A few especially powerful trade unions, such as the printers and typesetters, and many local associations refused to join any of these movements and sought to remain outside of party politics.

In the middle of the seventies some 50,000 labourers were members of trade unions with a socialist or social democratic orientation. The largest contingents were among the cigarmakers, the printers and typesetters, the shipwrights, the tailors, and the masons. In addition, there were approximately 20-25,000 members of liberal trade unions, who were especially found among the machinists and metalworkers. There were also about 10,000 members of Catholic workingmen's associations, located particularly in the Rhineland and Westphalia. On the whole, only two to three per cent of all industrial workers may have been organized – at the most four per cent – if we do not include the small shops with five and fewer labourers. The cigarmakers and the printers/typesetters, however, had already reached organizational quotas of approximately twenty per cent.[8]

3. Finally, there were those parties that put the term 'Arbeiter' in their name, that sought especially to represent the interests of workers, and that, more than the other parties, were able to gather workers among their membership and electors. These were Lasalle's *Allgemeiner Deutscher Arbeiterverein* (ADAV) [General German Workingman's Association], founded in 1863, and the *Sozialdemokratische Arbeiterpartei* (SDAP) (Social Democratic Labour Party), founded in 1869 under the leadership of Bebel and Liebknecht. As small as these two parties were, their integration in Gotha (1875) as the *Sozialistische Arbeiterpartei Deutschlands* (SDP) (German Socialist Labour Party) can be viewed as marking a certain end to the developmental phase of the German labour movement. At that point they numbered approximately 74,000 members, and in the elections of 1874, where they both were listed separately, they received together 325,000 votes – 6.8 per cent of all votes cast. Still they were distributed very unevenly. In Catholic Germany the Social Democrats remained a tiny minority with less than four per cent of the electorate, whereas in largely Protestant areas they gained shares of more than 14 per cent, in Berlin 28 per cent, and in Hamburg 41 per cent.[9]

8.2 Continuities between artisan traditions and the labour movement

Historians have traditionally asserted a deep division between an older craft history that went back into the late Middle Ages and the new labour movement of the industrial age. One has to distinguish between:

1. Masters.
2. Contracted artisans or cottage workers.
3. Journeymen.

The conviction about the deep gap between the older craft history and the new labour movement was particularly pronounced with respect to the master artisans (1). They were independent owners of the means of production and often even employers, whereas the labour movement was most concerned with dependent, wage-earning workers (2). One always knew, however, that many small master craftsmen in those decades were only formally independent – they may have had their own tools and worked in their own shops, but they were often completely dependent on a certain contractor who distributed the raw materials or half-finished goods and demanded that the artisan labour for him exclusively according to his instructions. We speak in this sense of contracted artisans or outworkers as cottage or domestic labourers, and have in mind spinners, weavers, and knitters; toymakers, watchmakers, needleworkers and nailsmiths; file cutters and knife grinders; and tailors, cobblers, and cabinet-makers – all of whom may have worked for warehouses of various kinds. But according to the traditional view, domestic or cottage outworkers were economically weak, isolated from one another, and usually possessed of so little class consciousness that they could hardly be affected by the labour movement.

As to the journeymen (3), it was well-known that they had a long tradition of collective action. It was also well-known that journeymen were strongly represented in the early trades unions of the 1860s and 1870s. In spite of this evidence, however, historians were still most likely to emphasize the cleavages – the qualitative difference between the journeymen's movement and the newer labour movement, and the different life within artisanal culture and within the emerging working class. Were not journeymen artisans, in so far as they still had guild memories or experiences? Were they not strongly oriented toward their specific occupations, concerned with corporate exclusivity, and focused on co-operation with the masters? Were they not preoccupied with disintegrating working conditions from a pre-industrial era? And thus, were they not backward looking? In contrast, the labour movement appeared to constitute a class movement transcending particular occupations, was prepared to engage in conflict, and was radical and orientated toward the future. It was new, a product of industrialization itself, with the factory proletariat as its core. Had not the leaders of the early social democratic labour movement distanced themselves disparagingly from the guild cliquishness or *Zünftelei* of the artisans? And had they not even avoided the word *Gewerkschaft* or trade union, because it was too focused on occupations and sounded too particularistic? In spite of all of its criticism of capitalism and private property, had not the social democratic labour movement refrained from criticizing industry, technology, and industrialization as such? Were not the fifties and sixties simply the beginning of a movement that culminated in the late nineteenth and early twentieth centuries as large-scale industry, and with it the labouring classes in the factories had long since driven the handicrafts and domestic industries far into the background? Such was the view of scholarly literature until recently.[10]

In recent years this perspective has changed somewhat under the impact of new questions and new research. First it has been discovered that a far closer relationship existed between independent or semi-independent artisans, small masters, and domestic industrial outworkers, on the one side, and the early labour movement, on the other. Second, we have come to emphasize much more strongly the continuity between the traditions of artisanal journeymen and the labour movement. As a consequence, the interpretation of the early labour movement appears to be altering fundamentally.[11]

With regard to the first point: domestic labourers, industrial outworkers, contracted artisans – I use the terms synonymously – differed from artisans in the full sense of the term in that they were dependent on *one* buyer, either as a merchant contractor, a clothing goods warehouse, a depot, or the like. The labourers received the raw materials and the directives from the buyer, and they delivered their goods to him, and only to him. In contrast, a true artisan was able to sell his wares to customers or to several buyers, could choose between them, and usually also bought the raw materials himself. In this sense, he was independent. In contradistinction, the independence of the contracted artisan was largely formal and illusory.

In 1850 there were still twice as many contracted domestic labourers as workers in factories and other centralized plants in Germany. Domestic industry and handicrafts were almost equal in their number. In the next two and one-half decades of rapid industrialization, the number of factory labourers indeed sped past that of domestic labourers. However, in the middle of the seventies there were still more domestic labourers in Germany than in 1800 – 1.1 million in comparison with 1.8 million factory and mine workers and with 2.5 million craft workers. It was only in the second phase of industrialization, during the last quarter of the century, that domestic industries largely collapsed – though even then they did not completely disappear. Often the sources label as artisans, individuals who were, in truth, contracted artisans or domestic labourers.

We can distinguish among three quite general subgroups within the domestic labour force.

1. In historical terms the oldest and numerically most significant were rural labourers who were still substantially integrated into rural patterns of life, often working a small plot of land as a subsidiary occupation. These were the rural spinners, weavers and knitters, the needlemakers, cutters, and thatchers. They were sharply affected by industrialization. They lapsed into poverty and isolation, were forced to migrate, to enter the new factories, and to learn new occupations and specializations. Some were virtually eliminated as economic categories, as for instance the rural spinners in the first half of the century; others were severely decimated, as in the case of weavers after mid-century.
2. The second subgroup comprised former artisans, especially those in the cities and villages close to urban centres. They were former independent guild masters, stockingers; qualified weavers of wool, silk, and cotton; laceworkers; filesmiths; toymakers; knife grinders; cutters; and other craftworkers in the small-scale iron industry. After mid-century other occupations such as the tailors, cabinetmakers, and cobblers also became increasingly affected.
3. A third group of domestic workers, who produced for the decentralized clothing industry in cities such as Berlin or Vienna, came into existence in the late nineteenth century. They were usually women, often young, and without artisanal training or traditions. They were also economically weak because they could be easily replaced; and they were thoroughly urban.

Rural domestic labourers – the first type – lacked the support of a strong artisanal tradition. They were often still narrowly tied to peasant and subpeasant ways of life. They were not easy recruits for the emerging labour movement. The same might be also said of the third type: they were too weak, easily replaced, without artisanal qualifications, and often did not remain throughout their working life within one occupation. Those female outworkers who found their way into the labour movement, shaped as it was by men, proved to be exceptions. It was otherwise with the second type, those once independent artisans who had often been in a guild for many years and who had only gradually fallen into contractual dependency on middlemen. Among such domestic workers were, for instance, the metal craftsmen of Solingen and Remscheid, the highly qualified textile craftsmen in Saxony, and the *de facto* dependent but formally independent cobblers and tailors in the large cities during the second half of the nineteenth century. They often reacted with bitterness and protest – at first during the transition to the dependency of the contract system, and then later during the struggle against a superior machine technology which forced them to migrate or enter the factories. They held on to artisanal values as long as possible, sought to remain independent, sustained a belief in a just and adequate wage, and tried to retain their occupational integrity. All of this apparently did not prevent them from attaching themselves to the early labour movement. They were, it is true, not prepared to join trades unions based on principles of wage labour. But the producers' associations found great interest among them. And the emerging labour parties in their first years found support in those older, and then endangered, areas of domestic industry – the ADAV in the region of Berg and the Rhineland, and the SDAP in the Saxon textile regions. The early labour movement was far more strongly a movement of domestic labourers, especially among the co-operatives and the political activists, than normally has been portrayed.[12]

Let us move from the formally self-employed domestic workers to the journeymen. Their significance to the early labour movement is most clear with respect to the trades unions. Recent research has argued that the trades unions were far less creations of the labour parties than has been long assumed. This research has shown that, in a few cases, occupational trades unions from the sixties emerged directly from surviving journeymen's organizations. Journeymen's travel and sickness funds in these cases were transformed into the friendly societies and strike funds of the trades unions. Their hostels became the sites of trade union branches. Their flags and badges were absorbed into the trades unions as part of the pattern of sociability. These examples reveal a completely fluid pattern of transition – one that has been particularly demonstrated for Hamburg, a city where the guilds and journeymen's brotherhoods were legally protected until 1864.

But even where the trades unions could not adapt journeymen's brotherhoods – perhaps because they no longer existed or because they were controlled by masters and local authorities – artisanal traditions may have been significant for the emergence of the labour movement. Even without formal organization, basic experiences and values of the journeymen were constantly reaffirmed in common work situations, travel, and life in the hostels. This was clearly the case among the carpenters and masons, the tailors and the cobblers. They shared values of honourable labour – a just wage, as little division of labour as possible, and traditional rights. These were values, in other words, that increasingly came into conflict with the realities and demands of an ever-expanding market economy and industrialization process. Such conflicts revealed themselves, for instance, in the well-known defence of 'Saint Monday' against intensified efforts to be bound to the clock, or in the well-documented refusal of journeymen to accept the division of labour by working alongside unskilled labourers and women and by adapting themselves to the new wage patterns.[13]

I want to stress two general conclusions that follow if we accept seriously the substantial shaping of the early labour movement by domestic labourers and journeymen. First, it appears that the early labour movement – in contra-distinction to its own self-understanding and buried beneath its own radical and often revolutionary rhetoric – was partly nourished by defensive groups, who were filled with the bitterness that developed from the clash between their traditional values and ways of life and modern capitalism and industrializ-ation. The friction and potential for protest released from the collision of these traditions with the process of modernization may have contributed as much to the genesis of the early labour movement as the opposition of capital and labour that came to be at the centre of the increasingly Marxian self-under-standing of the labour movement. Second, it affects our view of the inter-connections between the earlier and the later stages of the labour movement. There is no doubt that from the seventies onwards the trades unions and the labour party moved away from supporting producers' co-operatives. This is a signal that they increasingly detached themselves from their clientele of domestic labourers to focus more exclusively on workers in factories and other centralized work situations. There is no doubt that skilled *factory* workers were the backbone of the labour movement in the late nineteenth and early twentieth centuries. The significance of domestic outworkers and journeymen in the labour movement declined, and this must have meant that organized labour lost the progressive energies that could be released in the defence of traditional cultures against modern challenges. The rapid growth of the labour movement after 1890 must therefore have a different explanation than for the period I am presently considering. Should we not consider that there were two labour movements, an early and a later one, and that these were sharply distinct in social-historical terms?

8.3 Discontinuities

I do not want to pursue this somewhat speculative thought in greater detail. Rather, I want to change perspective. So far I have stressed the continuity between artisan traditions and the labour movement. But this is just one side of the question. It is equally important to emphasize that the labour movement was limited in its ability to link itself to the artisan tradition. There were significant discontinuities as well. It was, and is not, completely false to stress the new, the anti-traditional, and the forward-looking aspects of the early labour movement.

In order to prove this point it would be necessary to explore the important role of critical intellectuals and their ideas in the early labour movement, and examine how this alliance between workers and intellectuals differed from the earlier movements of the journeymen and labouring poor. In many respects the early labour movement inherited the emancipatory demands of the Enlighten-ment and, with them, went beyond being a movement defensively critical of modernization. The labour movement was born in a revolutionary era when political relations, as well as human expectations, altered. There was far less willingness to accept want and inequality with resignation. More and more members of the labouring poor came to see the world as alterable. The fundamental changes that had occurred from the end of the eighteenth century onwards spoke in their favour – the process of secularization, the far-reaching reforms, the upward and downward mobility, and finally the process of industrialization itself, which did much more than simply alter the landscape with smoking chimneys and railways that shrank distances. Such experiences of prior change authenticated the expectations of future emancipation. These hopes and experiences concentrated themselves in the early labour movement – this was clearly something new.

It would also be necessary to consider the historically new political constellation in which the labour movement developed: for instance, the role of the liberals as often unwilling allies, the labour movement's connections to the struggle for constitutional reforms in 1848–9, the mobilization of bourgeois public opinion from 1859 onwards, and finally the achievement of the right of combination and the expansion of universal norms that proved to be of substantial indirect help to the growing labour movement. Last, one would need to discuss in detail in what ways the early labour movement already possessed attitudes that transcended particular occupations; how it reached out to labourers in a completely different manner; and how, by tending to represent an entire class, it helped to eradicate the surviving corporate divisions of the society. All of these elements stood in sharp distinction to those characterizing the journeymen's movement of earlier centuries.[14]

This tendency of organized labour to constitute itself as a class movement derived from a large number of circumstances. Any detailed analysis would need in particular to emphasize the power of capitalism to transform the basic structure of the nineteenth century economy, the opposition between wage labour and capital, and the experiences of proletarian insecurity and dependency – all contributed to creating something like class consciousness. Rather than exploring these matters, however, I want to consider in greater detail a single related thesis – namely that the impact of the *state* in Germany contributed to the labour movement constituting itself as a distinctly proletarian class movement. It was due to the impact of the state that the labour movement in Germany maintained a lesser continuity with older artisanal traditions than was the case in other countries such as England. I want to develop this in four points.

8.3.1 Regulation and the journeyman

From the mid-eighteenth century onwards, journeymen and their brotherhoods were particularly affected by the efforts of the monarchical-bureaucratic states to extend their power through regulation. Administrative measures to discipline them intensified other effects that threatened the very existence of the journeymen's organizations – the rapid population growth, increasing underemployment, and the dislocations from an expanding market economy. In the nineteenth century, liberal economic attitudes and political fears became additional factors – they led to the suppression of, or to the tightest of controls being placed over, those societies which had managed to survive. As much as possible, the societies were reduced to their function as mutual aid funds. Administrative supervision affected the journeymen's organizations much more effectively than it did individual journeymen, but even so these individuals were forced to suffer supervision and chicanery (such as visitations and journeymen's passes) to a degree unthinkable in England. The situation intensified between the 1840s and the 1860s with the anti-combination laws. The authoritarian state contributed more than its share to break the collective back of the journeymen.

There is no doubt that conditions varied from state to state and occupation to occupation. Laws in Hamburg allowed more continuity than those in Prussia. Journeymen's organizations apparently played a greater role among printers, who had traditionally considered themselves as independent 'artists', than they did among those classical guild occupations such as the tailors. Future research may clarify these patterns even more. Certainly, administrative prohibitions were often very ineffective. Still it is certain that most of the journeymen's brotherhoods from the eighteenth century no longer existed in the second third of the nineteenth century when the labour movement constituted itself. Even where they still existed or were re-established, they were usually extremely weak, externally controlled organizations with little power. They lacked central means to control the labour market, such as the ability to gather information concerning the labour market, the authority to oversee the training of apprentices, or the capacity to set wages. Thanks to the consequences of intervention by the authoritarian state, there was not much left for the new trade unions to maintain or build upon.[15]

8.3.2 Regulation and the masters

Administrative efforts to control and discipline the workforce affected the journeymen's organizations much more severely than those of the masters. Under the name of *Innungen*, the masters' guilds either survived the reforms of the early nineteenth century or were restored at the end of the Napoleonic period. It is true, their competence was often modified and limited as well. But even when we allow for the many variations from state to state in the artisan codes, we can still conclude that these codes generally gave the masters decisive advantages and power over the journeymen – with respect to giving notice, for instance. The artisan codes transferred to the masters the organization and control over the labour market and the education of apprentices. The codes gave to them other important rights of supervision and control – to individual masters over those apprentices and journeymen living in their households, and also to the masters' guilds and corporate bodies over the mutual aid funds and hostels of the journeymen. The guilds basically owed their survival to the supervisory and policing powers which the authorities felt could not be abolished in the tense decades before and after the revolution of 1848-9.

Under such conditions it is understandable that journeymen often had quite a limited desire to see corporatist guild rules strengthened or re-established. It is true that they were not glowing admirers of the expanding liberal capitalist market economy, but they were also not decisive defenders of the old precapitalist, preindustrial system. We suspect that most of them were quite far from a nostalgic glorification of the good old days. To most, the 'loss' of corporate controls was most likely to be perceived as an emancipation, rather than as a loss.

In sum: the corporatist-guild tradition survived in Germany longer than in France and England but, in addition, it was controlled more strongly by the masters and shaped more hierarchically east of the Rhine than in western Europe. The masters strongly defended it because they were concerned to maintain, or extend, their own control. The early labour movement could attach itself much less to these traditions, since to a certain extent they were controlled by the other side. Its anti-guild, and anti-estatist attitudes prove, in social historical terms, to have been completely logical.[16]

8.3.3 Legally codified class distinctions

It was a characteristic feature of corporatist society to fix social differences juridically. The detailed legal codification of social, economic, and cultural distinctions between artisanal masters and journeymen was a case in point. The artisan codes, stamped as they were by the lengthy historical experience of the guilds, survived, if in a modified form, the ancien régime in Germany. In the nineteenth century the differences between masters and journeymen continued to be sanctioned by law. Consequently, such differences were far more sharply delineated than in France or England, and far more sharply delineated than should have been the case simply on the basis of diverse economic interests and varying social expectations. Administrations sought to prevent too narrow a co-operation between masters and journeymen. 'It is not feasible,' wrote the Berlin magistracy in an admonition to the city's guild of tailors in 1854, 'that the difference between masters and journeymen [be] set aside . . . [,] only the worker himself emerge, [and] masters and workers no longer exist as separate groups. Such a social aspiration is not reconcilable with the legal provisions . . . '.[17] The estatist traditions, as reconstituted and legally codified by the authoritarian state, thus contributed both to cementing the difference between formally independent and formally dependent artisans and to sharpening the class lines that crystallized thereby.

From this perspective we can understand why an observer in the 1850s stated that class tensions developed especially in those 'areas with previous guild regulations'.[18] From this perspective we can understand why journeymen and masters tended, by 1848 at the latest, to belong to separate organizations – the 'itio in partes' at the Frankfurt Artisans' Congress in the summer of 1848 proved to be the most spectacular and best known single case.[19] These relations also became to be historically manifested in linguistic distinctions. In English, for instance, the pairing of 'master and men' came to describe the division between large-scale masters and entrepreneurs as employers on the one side, and journeymen plus small-scale, formally self-employed members of the workforce on the other. In comparison, as a rule in Germany the linguistic and conceptual distinction, as revealed in the decrees, statistics, and surveys, placed all masters together with factory owners and merchants on one side – without regard to whether they were small employers or individual masters without journeymen or helpers. Journeymen, however, were placed on the other side with *Gehülfen* or helpers and factory labourers. Surely the social concepts mirrored the perceptions and interpretive patterns of the age. They help us to understand how the social world was registered in the minds of contemporaries. They confirm the other evidence gathered here – that many of the numerous small masters thought of themselves as distinct from the formally dependent journeymen, by whom this distinction was equally felt.

Certainly, small masters and journeymen lived in similar conditions. Their incomes were approximately equally meagre, and their living standards were similarly precarious; they lived in the same neighbourhoods in similar conditions; and they shared similar work experiences, family traditions, and modes of life. They had certain common interests and sometimes joined together in protest. Nevertheless, the small masters seldom joined the early trades unions, even though they were allowed to by statute. This was due to a consciousness that saw the primary boundary as being between journeymen and masters, not between capitalist employers on the one side, and journeymen plus small masters on the other. Such a distinction survived as a remnant of legally anchored estatist values. A Berlin trade-union activist and shoemaker, concerned with the relations between small masters and journeymen in his branch and with the wage reducing dependency of the artisans on 'bazaars' and 'factories', wrote in 1875: '. . ., it would be impossible for the large factory owners to employ so many journeymen if the Mr Small Masters were to go hand in hand with the journeymen. But the small masters take so much pride in the title "master"; it would be disgraceful if they were to stoop so low as to discuss conditions in the industry with the journeymen.' [20] The German trades unions, as a consequence, rather quickly and quite early became transformed into pure employee organizations – they excluded the self-employed and tended to co-operate beyond the specific occupation. To summarize once again, the manner in which the guild traditions survived in Germany and were structured by the authoritarian legislation of the state hampered the early labour movement in attaching itself to artisan traditions and forced it into a direction that stressed class.

8.3.4 Class consciousness and solidarity

Administrative intervention also contributed to the sense that, though of differing occupations, labourers were all in the same boat. Early – already in the pre-1848 period – the Prussian legislation regulating friendly societies caused artisanal societies to be established that were not simply limited to a particular occupation but, in order to survive financially, encompassed a number of industries or the workers in a number of factories. The state social insurance programme from the 1880s onwards also did not make distinctions between branches of industry or occupation but distinguished fundamentally between workers and employers. The collective sense of solidarity among

workers, with the corresponding sense of separation from other classes, may
have been strengthened, in addition, by the myriad modes of exclusion and
discrimination with which bourgeois society and the state distanced themselves
from the classes who worked with their hands and from their politically active
representatives. In this sense, the worker as such was rejected and not any
particular occupation. The inegalitarian electoral laws, the missing parliamentary system, the restrictions on mobility, marriage, and residency that
survived until the 1860s, the laws against associations and combinations, later
also the anti-socialist law – all of these gave the working population occasion
to acquire experiences that transcended occupation but remained class
specific.[21]

8.4 Conclusion

We can state in conclusion, first, that the early labour movement was more
powerfully shaped by artisanal and domestic labourers and their traditions
than was perceived by the labour movement itself or than customarily has
been portrayed by later historians. If we take this point seriously, then we
can see that the early labour movement was not simply a reformist or revolutionary movement of emancipation but that it was also the expression of a
traditionally rooted, defensive protest against the process of modernization. Second, I have tried to demonstrate that this interpretation should
not be over-emphasized. In many respects the labour movement was genui-
nely and fundamentally new – in its perspective on the future and in its
capacity to constitute itself as a class movement transcending particular
occupations. From the eighteenth century onwards the interventionist
policies of the authoritarian state were not the only, but a principal contributor in this process. And the state had been far more invasive in its
shaping of social relationships in Germany than in other countries. The
constellation of forces bounded by artisanal-corporatist traditions and the
influence of the authoritarian state shaped important features of the German
labour movement and form the particularity of the German case in international comparison.

Notes

1 Cf. Sheehan, J.J., 1989, *German History 1770–1886*, O.U.P., Oxford 1989, pp. 648–
652, 884–887; Breuilly, J., 1985, 'Liberalism or Social Democracy: A Comparison of
British and German Labour Politics, c. 1850–1875', in *European History Quarterly*
15/1: 3–42; Kocka, J., 1986, 'Problems of Working-Class Formation in Germany:
The Early Years, 1800–1875', in Katznelson I. and A.R. Zolberg, A.R. (eds),
*Working-Class Formation. Nineteenth-Century Patterns in Western Europe and
the United States*, Princeton University Press, Princeton, pp. 279–351.
2 Cf. Tennstedt, F., 1981, *Sozialgeschichte der Sozialpolitik in Deutschland. Vom 18.
Jahrhundert bis zum Ersten Weltkrieg*, Vandenhoeck and Ruprecht, Göttingen, pp.
110–113; Frevert, U., 1984, *Krankheit als politisches Problem 1770–1880. Soziale
Unterschichten in Preußen zwischen medizinischer Polizei und staatlicher*

Sozialversicherung, Vandenhocek and Ruprecht, Göttingen ch. 4; Ritter, G.A., 1989, *Der Sozialstaat. Entstehung und Entwicklung im internationalen Vergleich*, Oldenbourg München, S. 45–59.

3 Cf. Birker, K., 1973, *Die deutschen Arbeiterbildungsvereine 1840–1870*, Colloquium Verlag, Berlin; Schraepler, E. 1972, *Handwerkerbünde und Arbeitervereine 1830–1853. Die politische Tätigkeit deutscher Sozialisten von Wilhelm Weitling bis Karl Marx*, de Gruyter, Berlin.

4 Cf. Schieder, W., 1963, *Anfänge der deutschen Arbeiterbewegung. Die Auslandsvereine im Jahrzehnt nach der Juli-Revolution von 1830*, Klett-Cotta, Stuttgart; Büsch, O. and Herzfeld, H. (eds), 1975, *Die frühsozialistischen Bünde in der Geschichte der deutschen Arbeiterbewegung. Vom 'Bund der Gerechten' zum 'Bund der Kommunisten' 1836–1846*, Colloquium Verlag, Berlin.

5 With respect to the following paragraphs: Noyes, P.H., 1966, *Organization and Revolution. Working-Class Associations in the German Revolutions of 1848–1849*, Princeton University Press, Princeton; Moore, B. Jr., 1978, *Injustice, The Social Bases of Obedience and Revolt*, Macmillan, London; Balser, F., 1962, *Sozial-Demokratie, 1848 bis 1863. Die erste Arbeiterorganisation 'Allgemeine Deutsche Arbeiterverbrüderung' nach der Revolution*, Klett, Stuttgart; Schieder, W., 1974, 'Die Rolle der deutschen Arbeiter in der Revolution von 1848–49', *Archiv für Frankfurts Geschichte und Kunst* 54, Frankfurt, pp. 43–56.

6 On the 1850s: Offermann, T., 1979, *Arbeiterbewegung und liberales Bürgertum in Deutschland 1850–1863*, Neue Gesellschaft, Bonn.

7 Eisenberg, Ch. C., 1985, *Frühe Arbeiterbewegung und Genossenschaften. Theorie und Praxis der Produktivgenossenschaften in der deutschen Sozialdemokratie und den Gewerkschaften der 1860er/70er Jahre*, Neue Gesellschaft, Bonn.

8 Cf. Engelhardt, V., 1977, *'Nur vereinigt sind wir stark'. Die Anfänge der deutschen Gewerkschaftsbewegung 1862–63 bis 1869/70*, 2 vols., Klett-Cotta, Stuttgart; Albrecht, W., 1982, *Fachverein – Berufsgewerkschaft – Zentralverband. Organisationsprobleme der deutschen Gwerkschaften 1870–1890*, Neue Gesellschaft, Bonn; Engelhardt, V., 'Gwerkschaftliches Organisationsverhalten in der ersten Industrialisierungsphase' in, Conze, W. and Engelhardt U. (eds), 1979, *Arbeiter im Industrialisierungsprozeß. Herkunft, Lage und Verhalten*, Klett-Cotta, Stuttgart, pp. 372–402; Tenfelde, K. 'Die Entstehung der deutschen Gewerkschaftsbewegung. Vom Vormärz bis zum Ende des 'Sozialistengesetzes' Borsdorf, U. (ed.), 1987, *Geschichte der deutschen Gewerkschaften von den Anfängen bis 1945*, Bund Verlag, Köln, pp. 15–165.

9 Cf. Herzig, A., 1979, *Der Allgemeine Deutsche Arbeiter verein in der deutschen Sozialdemokratie. Dargestellt an der Biographie des Funktionärs Carl Wilhelm Tölcke (1817–1893)*, Colloquium Verlag, Berlin; S. Na'aman, 'Arbeitervereine, Arbeitertage und Arbeiterverband – drei Etappen auf dem Weg zur Arbeiterpartei', in Dowe, D. (ed.), 1980, *Berichte über die Verhandlungen der Vereinstage deutscher Arbeitervereine 1863–1869*, Dietz, Berlin, pp. IX–LI; Grebing, H., 1985, *Arbeiterbewegung. Sozialer Protest und kollektive Interessenvertretung bis 1914*, Deutscher Taschenbuch Verlag, München.

10 For example: Mommsen, H., 1966, 'Arbeiterbewegung', in, *Sowjetsystem und Demokratische Gesellschaft*, vol. 1, Herder, Freiburg, p. 273; Bernstein, E., 1913, *Die Schneiderbewegung in Deutschland. Ihre Organisation und Kämpfe*, vol. 1, Berlin, pp. VI, 86.

11 Lenger, F., 1987, 'Die handwerkliche Phase der Arbeiterbewegung in England, Frankreich, Deutschland und den USA. Plädoyer für einen Vergleich', in, *Geschichte und Gesellschaft* 13, 232–243.

12 On domestic labour, cottage workers and contracted artisans: Kocka, J., 1990,

Arbeitsverhältnisse und Arbeiterexistenzen. Grundlagen der Klassenbildung im 19. Jahrhundert, J.H.W. Dietz, Bonn, pp. 221–293; Boch, R., 1985, *Handwerker-Sozialisten gegen Fabrikgesellschaft. Lokale Fachvereine, Massengewerkschaft und industrielle Rationalisierung in Solingen 1870 bis 1914*, Vandenhoeck and Ruprecht, Göttingen; Zwahr, H., 1987, 'Die deutsche Arbeiterbewegung im Länder- und Territorienvergleich 1875', in, *Geschichte und Gesellschaft* 13: 448–507; Lenger, F., 1984, 'Polarisierung und Verlag: Schumacher, Schneider und Schreiner in Düsseldorf 1816–1861', in, Engelhardt, U. (ed.), 1984, *Handwerker in der Industrialisierung. Lage, Kultur und Politik vom späten 18. bis ins frühe 20. Jahrhundert*, Klett-Cotta, Stuttgart, pp. 127–145.

13 On journeymen: Kocka, *Arbeitsverhältnisse*, pp. 329–358; Lenger, F., 1988, *Sozialgeschichte der deutschen Handwerker seit 1800*, Suhrkamp, Frankfurt; Neufeld, M.J., 1985/86, 'German Artisans and Political Repression' in, *Journal of Social History* 19: 491–502. Excellent English-German comparisons in: Eisenberg, C., 1986, *Deutsche und englische Gewerkschaften. Entstehung und Entwicklung bis 1878 im Vergleich*, Vandenhoeck and Ruprecht, Göttingen.

14 Cf. Kocka, J., 1986, 'Traditionsbindung und Klassenbildung. Zum sozialhistorischen Ort der frühen deutschen Arbeiterbewegung', in, *Historische Zeitschrift* 241: 333–376.

15 Cf. Breuilly, J. and Sachse, W., 1983, *Joachim Friedrich Martens (1806–1877) und die deutsche Arbeiterbewegung in Deutschland 1800–1875*, Schwartz, Berlin; Jessen, R., 'Handwerksmeister und Gesellen. Die Entwicklung der Beziehungen beider Gruppen in den deutschen Staaten zwischen 1806 und 1871 unter besonderer Berücksichtigung rechtlicher Aspekte'. Staatsexa-mensarbeit Bielefeld 1984; Bopp, H., 1932, *Die Entwicklung des deutschen Handwersgesellentums im 19. Jahrhundert*, Schöningh, Paderborn.

16 Cf. Kocka, *Arbeitsverhältnisse*, op. cit., pp. 335–358.

17 Eisenberg, *Deutsche und englische Gewerkschaften*, op. cit., pp. 70–71.

18 Böhmert, V., 1858, *Freiheit der Arbeit! Beiträge zur Reform des Gewerbewesens*, Bremen, p. 169.

19 Cf. Dowe, D. and Offermann, T. (eds), 1983, *Deutsche Handwerker- und Arbeiterkongresse 1848–1852. Protokolle und Materialien*, J.H.W. Dietz, Berlin, p. 58; Simon, N., 1983, *Handwerk in Krise und Umbruch. Wirtschaftliche Forderungen und sozialpolitische Vorstellungen der Handwerksmeister im Revolutionsjahr 1848–49*, Böhlau, Köln.

20 *Der Wecker. Organ für die Schumacher Deutschlands*, vol. 1, no. 13, Oct. 1, 1875 – Cf. Lenger, F., 1986, *Zwischen Kleinbürgertum und Proletariat. Studien zur Sozialgeschichte der Düsseldorfer Handwerker 1816–1878*, Vandenhoeck and Ruprecht, Göttingen; Rentzsch, W., 1980, *Handwerker und Lohnarbeiter in der frühen Arbeiterbewegung. Zur sozialen Basis von Gewerkschaften und Sozialdemokratie im Reichsgründungsjahrzehnt*, Vandenhoeck and Ruprecht, Göttingen.

21 Cf. Ritter, G.A., 1980, *Staat, Arbeiterschaft und Arbeiterbewegung in Deutschland. Vom Vormärz bis zum Ende der Weimarer Republik*, J.H.W. Dietz, Berlin.

9 Aspects of the social economy of working class women in nineteenth century Britain

John Saville
University of Hull

The lives of working-class women in advanced industrial societies in these past two centuries or so have exhibited in general terms broad similarities, although inevitably the particular character and nature of industrial capitalism in different countries have influenced custom, tradition and everyday practice. In Britain – Ireland being excluded from the analysis which follows –[1] the social formation which had evolved by 1800 was unique in Europe in a number of respects. The land of Britain, for example, was owned by a small minority of aristocratic and gentry families producing a degree of landed monopoly unknown elsewhere. When the first reasonably reliable census of landholding was made in the 1880s one quarter of the land of England and Wales, outside London, was owned by 1,200 families; one half of the land by just over 7,000.[2] At the other end of the rural scale, there were almost no peasants by the beginning of the nineteenth century, Britain being alone among the countries that industrialized out of a feudal background in having eliminated its peasantry before industrialization proper got under way. It followed, therefore, that the increasing number of children born in the countryside in the second half of the eighteenth century were entering landless families whose subsistence came only, or very largely, from wage labour. As will be discussed later, this particular social structure affected young women in the rural areas in certain important ways.

The growth of population in the closing decades of the eighteenth century was central to the economic changes that were taking place, with urbanization developing at a much faster rate than population growth. In the first half of the nineteenth century, the population of England and Wales doubled between 1801 and 1851, but the growth of towns was expanding at a much more accelerated rate. In the single decade of 1821 to 1831 all the large towns of England, with the exception of London which was already huge (and with Glasgow in Scotland), grew in population by more than forty per cent.[3] Ruskin's 'ferrugineous temper', which was changing Britain into 'the Man in the Iron Mask', became more marked in the middle decades of the century after the coming of the railway, and the economic and social balances within society altered accordingly. In 1801 32 per cent of gross national income derived from agriculture, forestry and fishing; it was 20 per cent in 1851, and 14

per cent in 1871. The comparable figures for mining, building and manufacturing – combined together as one group – were 23, 34 and 38 per cent.[4]

One peculiar feature of the demographic structure of nineteenth century
Britain was the very large surplus of women in the working, marrying and
child-bearing age groups of 15 to 49. Within this age grouping there was a
seven to eight per cent surplus of women compared with men, and the
proportion tended to increase in the decades towards 1914. This surplus was a
biologically abnormal situation since, like all or most mammals, humans
produce more male than female offspring, and the higher mortality rate of
young males was not sufficient to eliminate the male surplus – although it was
reduced. The male surplus at birth in the second half of the nineteenth century
was around four per cent. The reasons for the emergence of the very high
female surplus from the 15 to 19 age group was not war, since between 1815
and 1914 there were no wars with large scale casualties, but emigration from
Britain in very large numbers. Most emigrants were men, and it has been the
decline of male emigration in any significant volume since 1931 that has
produced, in the second half of the twentieth century, a sex-ratio in the middle
age groups opposite to that which obtained in Victorian Britain – although the
male surplus before the age of 50 is now a matter of only a few percentage
points. This phenomenon of a very large female surplus before 1914 has been
less widely remarked upon in the discussion of the social history of the period
than it deserves.[5]

Most women who worked were the mothers, wives or daughters of manual
workers for whom the sexual division of labour, low pay and exploited
conditions, constituted the norm in the Victorian labour market. The largest
occupation was domestic service, which employed about two million women in
1901 (Domestic Service and Personal Services), and as soon as alternative
opportunities became available, young women began to turn away from what
was often matriarchal tyranny and male sexual harassment. The 1901 Census
of Population commented on the ageing distribution of the domestic labour
force, and the reluctance of young women to enter it continued thereafter. The
same Census found another two and a half million women in full-time
employment, and not only in what is often thought of as Victorian women's
work – what today we call the rag trade, e.g. dressmaking, millinery and so on
– but women were also employed throughout the century in heavy manual
work in larger numbers than is sometimes appreciated. Such were the pit brow
girls of whom Angela John has written;[6] but all round the country there were
pockets of heavy manual labour in which women were to be found. In the
Cornish china clay industry, technically unrevolutionized in the processes of
clay getting, men, women and boys extracted the clay and cleaned it. The final
process of cleaning was performed by women known as 'Balmaidens', whose
job it was to remove the last impurities from the clay before it was shipped to
the Staffordshire Potteries. The women used a small iron scraper, rather like a
Dutch hoe, and in the 1860s they were expected to clean between two and three
tons a day, for which they were paid one shilling. But it was in the service
sector, in addition to domestic service, that many women found employment.
The 1901 Census recorded 180,000 female laundry workers, with rates of pay

between one shilling and sixpence to two shillings a day. There was, of course, large scale charring, either on a part-time or full-time basis.[7]

Part-time work, which has left few official records, was widespread. It is an error to think of industrialization as a linear process of change from small-scale organization, in the workshop or the home, to the large factory. That certainly was the central path of industrialization in most industries, although the time period of complete transformation could often be stretched over many decades, and in a range of industries the conversion was never absolute. Alongside the steady shift towards an increasing centralization of production, small-scale structures of industrial and service organizations which drew upon the considerable reservoirs of cheap labour, especially of female labour, continued to be created. These small groupings were often in the sector of consumer goods or services and were located either in small workshops or in the home. The workshops would often be in rented rooms in tenement buildings in the larger towns or cities. The work was usually seasonal in demand, and it could easily be adapted to the working life of married women with children. It was mostly sweated labour of an extreme kind. By the end of the century there was an extraordinary variety of work being done in the home: a sample of such activity would include paper box making, leather work, brush making, many different sorts of machining and sewing, and the making of artificial flowers. Piece work was the rule; demand for work was irregular, and to earn a miserable total involved very long hours. The *Daily News* organized in 1906 a Sweated Industries Exhibition which attracted much attention, much outrage, and very little practical remedy. There was on show the earnings book of a widow with five children – she worked on underwear, and her fortnightly recorded earnings (in old money) were 6/8 ¾; 9/2¼; 3/7½; 5/2; 8/1; and 3/11½. When there was work to do, she sat up through the night. For all homeworkers, work was always more difficult to obtain as they became older.[8]

Throughout industry and the service sector the sexual division of labour operated rigidly, with only few exceptions. Women could normally never earn more than one third to one half of the men's wages for more or less equivalent work. It is possible, however, to find exceptions. The textile industries were the first major sector of the economy to move into the factory, although as always the rate of technological change, and of industrial organization, were as variable as the geology of England or the fluctuations in its weather. Spinning was the earliest branch to become mechanized, and cotton in Lancashire generally was more advanced in both technology and structure than West Yorkshire. In the cotton industry, women provided a major part in the labour force. In the 1851 Census, in cotton work of all kinds, there were about a quarter of a million males and rather more women; and in Lancashire as a whole, by the end of the nineteenth century women made up two-thirds of the cotton industry's workforce. Most of these women were young and single, but in Lancashire it was quite usual for women to keep on working after marriage, and after the birth of children. In the weaving sector in particular, in the towns of North-East Lancashire – Burnley, Blackburn and Preston – three out of four single women worked in the weaving mills and about half continued after marriage.[9] By the closing decades of the century, women weavers could earn up to 25 shillings per week – as much as many men – and about five to six shillings more than the better paid female occupations in the rest of the country. They were strongly unionized, although almost all of their officials were male. But what is interesting is the way in which these Lancashire weavers at least partly domesticated their men: the 'Mary Ann' night, when joint domestic duties were undertaken, was an accepted part of domestic life in the weaving areas, and certain other parts of Lancashire. Moreover, the fertility levels of the weaving communities were significantly lower than in most manual occupations, although it must be noted that infant mortality was high, at least in part due to the extensive use of child care outside the family. In the earlier decades of the century the scandal of these child minders was widely discussed – 'angel-makers' was the expressive term applied to them.

Across the Pennines, in the woollen industry of West Yorkshire equal pay did not obtain for the same work. Wages in general were lower than in Lancashire, and women's work in worsted and wool would normally be paid at a fixed rate below that for men. There were historical reasons for these arrangements – among them, the slower rate of mechanization in Yorkshire, and the lower levels of unionization. Most women did not live in the relatively privileged sectors of Lancashire textiles – the statement is strictly relative – although there were other small pockets of work and living where women were able to offset, to a varying degree, the exploitation involved in the sexual division of labour and the consequences of a patriarchal society – a patriarchy, it should be emphasized, which became more firmly delineated as the century moved along, with the male breadwinner image becoming the norm in working class communities. In other words, the overwhelming majority of working women remained locked in their unfreedom.[10]

There are some aspects of the industrializing process, and its effects upon the lives of women, that have been ignored or much neglected. Shift work is an example. It was not only in mining areas that clothes had to be dried between shifts, so that the kitchen was never free of hanging clothes, but it is from mining that we have some of the most evocative descriptions of the impact of shift work on the lives of wives at home. Not all mining regions worked in shifts, but many did, and shift work grew steadily from the 1850s on. In Durham, where we seem to have most evidence, multiple shift work began to be worked increasingly in the second half of the nineteenth century. There was an illuminating statement from a miner's wife to the Sankey Commission of 1919, of which Sidney Webb was a member. It was always said of Webb that he never forgot anything, so his membership of the Commission may well have encouraged him to include the paragraph given below. It was published in 1921 in his *Story of the Durham Miners*:

> But to the wives of the miners, it is to be feared, the multiple shifts of the County of Durham have proved less of a boon. It was not found convenient – though no one seems actually to have made the attempt – to arrange so that all the men resident in one house, or at any rate all those of one grade, should always be working in the same shift, changing simultaneously from fore-shift to back-shift and from back-shift to night-shift. The consequence has been that, where there is more than one man in the household, the labour of preparing meals and drying the pit clothes has to

be undertaken every few hours during the whole day and night. With the progressive over-crowding of the colliery houses that, owing to the increase in population and slackening of building in the past decade, has nearly everywhere occurred, the pressure of work on the women has been intensified. 'I go to bed only on Saturday night' said a miner's wife, 'my husband and our three sons are all on different shifts, and one or other of them is leaving or entering the house and requiring a meal every three hours in the 24' . . . the effect of the multiple shifts on the miner's home life, and on the social environment in which the children are reared, does not seem to have been foreseen, or to have been as yet adequately considered . . .'[11]

There is still a great deal to be uncovered about the lives of working women in their role as helpmate to the working males of their families; and there is much evidence so far not researched. More clouded are those areas of life summed up by T.S. Eliot as 'birth, and copulation, and death'. The personal spaces of life are always going to be less easy of access to the historian, as indeed they often are to the contemporary enquirer, even in these days of joyful revelation, or reluctant but well paid, confession. Family structures have always varied quite widely, and while the domination of the male was everywhere in nineteenth century Britain, it manifested itself differently in different types of family. One such manifestation was physical violence against the wife and children of the family. We are beginning, but only beginning, to learn something about domestic violence within the working class family, and we know almost nothing about the middle class family in this regard. For the working class family there developed a national debate in the middle-class press in the 1870s, and it became clear that violence was very often associated with heavy drinking, and heavy drinking with arduous manual occupations. But the correlations are not to be found everywhere. What did become apparent was the complex of custom and tradition whereby neighbours would often not interfere unless the levels of violence became extreme.[12] It needs to be remarked that Victorian society was, in many of its public aspects, an unpleasantly violent society. Public executions did not cease until the Commission of 1866 recommended their ending; flogging in the army continued until the last quarter of the century; flogging in prison was widespread for often quite minor offences until the Act of 1895 limited its usage; for male children by 1900 the rules had been codified – one can hardly use the word civilized – so that boys over seven and under twelve could only receive six strokes of the birch-rod, and boys of twelve but under fourteen were limited to no more than twelve strokes. Most of the violence in the street was contained within working class neighbourhoods, as documentary fiction such as *A Child of the Jago* makes clear, but given the propensity of the upper classes to approve the flogging of their own sons at their private academies, their semi-barbarous way of enforcing discipline in the Armed Forces which they officered, and their private enjoyment in the large-scale slaughtering of wild life, historical perspective offers the image of a society in which considerable numbers of its male population wanted to inflict physical hurt upon the remainder.

Women, without the threat of violence from their husbands, confronted other terrors of which the damage to health from repeated conception was the most serious. In working class families, and the generalization becomes more true the further you go down the income scale, child bearing often lasted until the late thirties of a woman's life – and not seldom until the menopause. Richard Titmuss calculated that the average working class woman marrying in her teens or early twenties during the 1890s would experience ten pregnancies, and spend fifteen years in pregnancy and nursing. The ravages to health were formidable. When Marie Stopes published her Preliminary Notes in 1930 on the first 10,000 women she had examined in the course of her birth control work she reported that 1,321 had slit cervixes, 335 serious prolapses and 1,508 some kind of internal deformation. We do not know the proportion of women disabled by the experience of child birth in the nineteenth century. And it is not only the slow growth of medical knowledge that must be noted, but more, that the majority of births in working class families were assisted by neighbours or midwives – and the title 'midwife' embraced a very wide variety of experience. Custom and tradition have always played a quite crucial part, in all societies, in the way that women's bodies have been understood and in particular in the way that child birth has been approached – literally, old wives' tales have in most periods of history and in quite different cultures, enjoyed a remarkable influence. The Co-operative Women's Guild famous symposium, *Letters on Maternity* first published in 1915, included some horrifying details of how child birth was organized – and remember that these testimonies came from women in the better-off groupings within the working class community, and that they relate to the years, roughly, 1890–1914:

> Never once can I remember – a woman wrote – having anything but face, neck, and hands washed until I could do things for myself and it was thought certain death to change underclothes under a week. For a whole week we were obliged to be in clothes stiff and stained, and the stench under the clothes was abominable and added to this we were commanded to keep the babies under the clothes.

The response of women to repeated pregnancies was, inevitably, defensive. The extent of induced miscarriages, abortion and infanticide can be inferred only from the shadowy evidence available to us. It is likely that abortion or attempted abortion was the most commonly used female initiative. Induced abortions within the first three months were widely, but wrongly, assumed to be legal and only after that period was the intervention of a professional, back street abortionist required, and that was understood to be illegal. The assumed legitimacy of abortions within the first three months was part of what might be called the moral economy of working class women. There were, as is again well known, large numbers of neighbours' tales about home-made mixtures that were capable of effecting abortions, in addition to the growing number of commercially patented medicines advertised under thinly disguised wording. The commercial products were themselves in a range from the harmless confidence trick to seriously damaging medicines, especially those made with lead plaster as an ingredient. The *British Medical Journal*, from the 1890s, began to carry articles on the widespread use of lead plaster as an abortifacient and it noted that it was common particularly in the Midlands and the industrial North.

The use of birth control methods in the nineteenth century was probably more common than the immediate evidence would suggest. We know of Greek philosophers and their writings, and the Bradlaugh-Besant trial of 1877 did a great deal to spread the news – but how much it was working class news is difficult to determine; probably not very much. Demographers are acutely aware of differing levels of fertility before birth control techniques became widely used and there is much debate about their motivation. Elizabeth Roberts, in her study of the industrial working class of the North – her period was the thirty years or so before the First World War – demonstrated that although the fertility levels of female textile workers were low in most of the cotton districts of Lancashire, notably in the weaving areas, this was not the case in Preston where women textile operatives tended to marry out of the trade. The implications of the higher fertility rates in Preston were that social attitudes towards sex, and family, were different from other parts of Lancashire and that it was the male attitudes which were dominant.[13] When birth control techniques became more widely available in the twentieth century, especially the sheath, it was the hostility and obduracy of the men which often restricted their usage. The tradition of old men's tales also exerted its influence, as this comment which related to the second decade of the twentieth century makes clear: 'He said it was his rights, and he'd have consumption if we took any precautions. He said that's what always gives men consumption. And now I'm like this'.[14]

Of the other controlling factors, infanticide has always been important, or certainly more important, than is usually appreciated – but again, by its nature, the full extent of the elimination of babies by design will always be difficult to assess. It had been a European problem for many centuries before the industrial era. Up to the sixteenth century, and in some places much later, it was dealt with by the Church. The method most commonly used was the 'overlaying' or 'overlying' of an infant by its parents while in bed, the parents being mostly drunk – allegedly or actually. In the case of married women the Church or lay authority, in proven cases, imposed penance for at least a year of bread and water; but for the unmarried, or those presumed witches, penalties were barbarous – in some parts of central Europe before 1500, burial alive.[15] Infanticide was much discussed in both France and England in the eighteenth and nineteenth centuries, and by the mid-nineteenth century it had become a matter of national concern in Britain. Disraeli, in his novel *Sybil* published in 1846, was no doubt exaggerating that infanticide was no less prevalent in England than on the banks of the Ganges; but the English press in the 1850s and 1860s certainly reported the frequent discovery of the bodies of infant babies under bridges, in parks and ditches, and even in cess pools.[16] These would mainly be the babies of unmarried mothers. For the married, we can hardly begin to quantify the problems, bearing in mind that the infant mortality rate was at a national average of 150 per thousand right down to the end of the century, with considerably higher rates for the lowest paid, as well as for particular towns with especially bad sanitary conditions. Some years ago the present writer heard a tape-recording of a man of ninety giving his reminiscences. He was, at the time, just ninety so he had been born around 1885/6. The recording was part of an enquiry into that splendid social phenomenon, the brass band movement of West Yorkshire and Lancashire, and this respondent in his day had been a well-known conductor – as prestigious a position in working class communities then as today's manager or coach of Wigan Rugby League Club. The man being interviewed was telling a story that his mother had told him: of how weakly an infant he had been when first born; and of how the midwife had come into the bedroom soon after he was born and had said to his mother, 'That little bugger u'll come to nowt. Tha had better lee(lie) on him.'

The miserable and grisly story of conception, pregnancy, child birth and the physical consequences of reproduction, underwrite the feminist's assertion that control over her body is central to the life of a woman. Illness was one major consequence, although there were many other factors which combined to produce the extent and intensity of sickness in Victorian England: not least that in most towns, for most of the century, once you stepped outside your own home you were in a permanently infected atmosphere. It was this, and the much less polluted water supplies in rural areas that helped to account for the differential mortality and incidence of illness between town and country. It was not that the labourers in the countryside ate better than labourers in towns, although they may well have eaten less adulterated food, or that their housing was superior since they too lived in damp, overcrowded cottages, but that the air they breathed was pure and the water they drank was usually clean. Working class women would have to treat themselves if they were ill, or just sit it out. Their menfolk might be in friendly societies or have access to trade union benefits – the latter if they were skilled of course – but these advantages were not available to women – and if they were one parent families or widows their only recourse was the Poor Law. Dispensaries were few, the medical profession expensive, and charitable institutions scarce in many towns. It was this absence of medical help for large sections of working people that led to the development of the patent medicine industry that grew so rapidly in the second half of the nineteenth century. Brand names appeared early and, by 1900, there was a veritable torrent of self-help medicines which ranged in effectiveness from the utterly useless to the positively dangerous. A Select Committee on Patent Medicines in 1913 uncovered a mountain of horror stories. One of the most commonly consumed bottles was *Mother Segal's Syrup* which sold in many thousands each year in two sizes, at one shilling and two shillings and sixpence. It was advertised, among its other virtues, as a cure for dyspepsia, anaemia and all liver complaints, and was described on its label as a highly concentrated vegetable compound. The origin of Mother Segal and her Syrup was way back in past centuries when an old peasant woman, close to death, suddenly began chewing a wild herb she had picked randomly from the hedgerow, and miraculously recovered – and this was the basis of Mother Segal's elixir. When the Government analyst presented his report, it showed that the medicine was made up of 50 per cent water, 40 per cent treacle, and ten per cent vegetable extracts – most of which could not be identified. The Committee did their best: they put the managing director on the stand and asked him a total of 1,607 questions; and to the end he refused to give the make-up of the secret formula which he claimed incorporated the enhancing qualities so widely advertised. Two shillings and sixpence for three fluid ounces of water and treacle – a remarkable tribute to the untrammelled workings of the free market.[17]

The long years of child bearing, the burdens of housework, inadequate diet, and often the additional miserably paid sweated labour in the home for outside contractors, not only meant that women aged prematurely – something that all commentators noted – but that the lives of women were physically restricted to home and its immediate neighbourhood. The cultural and social mechanisms developed by men in the second half of the nineteenth century were almost wholly not available to women. The pub, the trade union, the friendly society, the Working Men's Clubs and Institutes, and a whole range of leisure activities limited to men – whippet racing, pigeon fancying, fishing (a major activity), debating forums, the famous leek competitions of gardeners and allotment holders in Durham, and so on. When libraries began to be collected around the mining lodges of South Wales they were not open to women. The typical working class auto-didact of the nineteenth century was male. And were there any women in the first WEA classes run by RH Tawney at Rochdale and Longton?[18]

For working class women there was nothing at all comparable. Like their men they had the church or chapel, and depending on the traditions of the latter they might be offered some role in the organisation of the chapel, and even in preaching. Against this, one must put the passivity encouraged by the Pauline teaching of the subordination of women to men, an influential factor in the rampaging sexism of Victorian Britain, although sexism cannot be blamed, wholly or even mainly, on religion. Large sections of the working class populations in the bigger towns and notably in London were what the 1851 Census on Religious Observance called 'unconscious secularist'. Contrary to what is often stated about the Victorian years, there was a considerable dispersion of irreligiosity throughout society, although only in minority groups did it become anti-clericalism. The most important institution of religion, of any denomination, was the funeral. As living standards rose in the second half of the century, and as respectability spread, so did the importance of the funeral in working class life – and its importance went well beyond the boundaries of respectability. The celebration of this first stage of entry into the joys to come on the part of the miserable upon earth had social and psychological dimensions which remain largely unexplored.

Whether working class women had the consolations and sustenance of religion or not, there was gossiping with neighbours at the doors of their houses or in the communal laundries, or shopping, or, in the years between the wars, the cinema. Earlier, there had been the music hall in London and the larger cities. The cumulative effects of industrialization pushed many groups of working class women out of public life and into the very restricting round of housework, housekeeping, child producing and child rearing – a task made immeasurably more restricting by low and often uncertain income. An extreme example was recorded by an American who lived and worked for a short time in a mining community of Fife in Scotland. This was Kellog Durland whose book *Among the Fife Miners* was published in 1904. Durland was amazed how the women in his village – mothers and daughters as well as small children – were all separated from the men; how women automatically surrended their chair to a man; and how the mother of a family fetched and carried on demand. The crucial distinction in this kind of household, common in many kinds of mining communities, was between the wage earner and the dependants; and in the Fife coalfield as soon as a boy became 14 and went to work in the pits, he was given the privileges of his gender. It is necessary to recall how hard the working life of the miner was throughout the whole period. Even in geologically easy areas such as Nottingham it was exhausting work, and down to 1914 – and beyond – it remained for many, pick and shovel technology. It is equally necessary to remember that the solidarity of miners' wives with their men in times of dispute, strike or lockout was always forthcoming. But to return to the cultural impoverishment of so many working class women in the nineteenth century. There was some evidence of change to lighten the dark picture which has so far been painted. The very slow decline in fertility levels in the closing decades of the nineteenth century were the herald of the much smaller sized family of the last 70 years or so. There were also institutional developments: the Education Act of 1870 educated girls and boys; and the Co-operative Women's Guild, first established in 1883, was to exercise a very positive influence as were the beginnings, at this same period, of women's trades union organization.[19]

One of the unregarded revolutions of the twentieth century in the advanced industrial countries, given the near universal division of labour between the sexes in domestic matters in the home, has been the provision of piped water supplies to domestic living accommodation. It has been the most important single change in housework, for the transporting of water has been one of the most onerous of all the many burdens of housework. In rural areas, women of the labouring class would have access to private wells or to an outside source, and a Scottish enquiry of 1917 found that water for the home was commonly carried an average distance of 150 yards, sometimes up to a quarter of a mile, and occasionally much further. In the countries of the third world today, women carry on average three to three and a half gallons of water per journey, and it is estimated that this is about the weight a woman in the nineteenth century would carry where there was no private supply at her back door. In early industrial Britain the growing towns of increasing population, increasing filth and increasing pestilence had always inadequate supplies of water – and what there was arrived seriously polluted. In Liverpool, so the 1844 Enquiry into the State of Large Towns and Populous Districts reported, there were areas of the town where 200 hundred families shared one standpipe which was turned on every other day for three hours, Sundays excepted. And there were similar accounts all round the country, in all the large towns. It is seldom appreciated how recent is the provision of piped water for working class homes. The New Survey of London Life and Labour found that in the early 1930s, of the houses they investigated one half had to fetch their water from outside the house or tenement rooms – from a tap on the landing, outside in the yard, or up or down stairs. For much of the nineteenth century water was not free. In the 1840s Londoners living in Southwark paid the water carriers one shilling per week for their supplies, at a time when average earnings for women were about seven shillings per week, for male labourers 18 shillings, and for male skilled workers 32 shillings. And as always, with water as with food, the smaller the quantities purchased, the more expensive each unit. Penny capitalism, which most workers were involved with, was always more expensive per item consumed than the economy of the skilled worker or of the middle class.

The water the housewife obtained was heated on an open coal fire on which was balanced kettle, saucepan or frying pan. Side ovens began to appear in working class homes in the 1860s. Gas was not used for domestic purposes until the 1880s, and it was very slow to penetrate into the homes of working people. Lighting was by rushlight, tallow candles, fish oil lamps, with the paraffin lamp slowly coming into use in the last thirty years of the century. All these matters of technical detail are well enough known,[20] but what must be emphasized are the ways in which the success of the family – the quality of family life – depended upon the skills of the housewife. Accommodation can be assumed to be overcrowded and cramped, all the laundry was washed by hand; all water had to be heated over the same fire on which the food was cooked; and there would be children around for many years of a women's life. Life was unrelenting in its demands.

The overall female surplus in Victorian society had a considerable and diverse influence upon the position of women in society. The marriage rate was, in any case, lower than that of the second half of the twentieth century, and the additional surplus of women meant very large numbers of unmarried women. In the rural areas, with rapid diminishing employment opportunities in the second half of the century, women moved into the urban areas in proportionately larger numbers than men. It was, as migration always is, selective, and it was inevitably to the areas of female employment that the greatest volumes of migrants moved. They moved to Nottingham rather than to Sheffield; away from the mining areas, to cities where the demand for domestic service was always high – to London, for example. And while the female surplus was not the cause, it inevitably made its impact both upon the sexual division of labour and, above all, on the attitudes of men to women. Among both middle class and working class communities, sexual sub-ordination was built into social structures. But for working class women it is difficult to estimate precisely the effects of the widely argued inferiority of women that was so commonly expressed in middle class circles. In the latter, there was a good deal of dogmatic rationalization concerning the intellectual inferiority of women to men. Right down to the First World War, well-known publicists such as Sir Almroth Wright were loudly proclaiming the dependence of women upon men as the result of inescapable physical and mental differences; and pronouncements such as these, by distinguished idiots of various professions, were widely popularized. A well-known compendium entitled *Enquire Within upon Everything*, published in several editions in the decades before 1914 would have informed you that the average weight of a man's brain was three pounds and that of a woman's was only two pounds and eleven ounces – the implication being that the one was superior to the other.

To what extent these middle class fallacies worked their way down the income scale in not easy to evaluate. In spite of a strong patriarchal family life, poverty and class oppression often brought the members of working class families together. The biographies of working men in the nineteenth century constantly refer to the ways in which the mother of the household kept the family in a supportive framework. The women developed their own defensive social mechanisms, their own support groups among their neighbours, and above all within their own family network. We know from the survey of

Rowntree in York in 1902, and from other sources, that the mother regarded it as her obligation and duty to keep the wage earner or earners in work, which meant that on many occasions she went without food herself. We know also of the affection and tenderness that mothers showed to their children, often in the most wretched domestic situations. And in industrial disputes the women were staunchly loyal and supportive.

It is necessary to appreciate the full implications of the central importance of the women in nineteenth century families, as well as the appalling lives that so many of them led. It is also clear that some, at least, of the sexual and social disabilities working class women suffered were not historically inevitable, although many were; but the variation in life styles within the same occupation and within the same communities is truly remarkable. The ideology of sexism that was so firmly embedded in Victorian society must, therefore, always be reckoned with and never discounted – from it flowed the deep pools of misery and unhappiness that were an inescapable part of working class existence.[21] I end with what I have always thought to be the most moving, the most pathetic, and in some respects the most bitter story to come out of the nineteenth century – one that encapsulates the psychological burdens imposed by the pervasive idea of male superiority. It was told by Helen Taylor, the step-daughter of John Stuart Mill, and the date must have been the late 1860s or early 1870s. The story is of a crofter's wife mourning the death of her little baby boy. Helen Taylor was trying to comfort her, but she was inconsolable. 'What worries me', she said, 'is that they be all men up there, and they won't know how to do for him.'

Notes

1 Ireland has been excluded partly because of my own lack of knowledge of Irish history, partly because its social structure was different from that of mainland Britain.

2 The official title of the enquiry was *Return of Owners of Land*, British Parliamentary Papers, 1874, LXII. The most useful re-working of the statistics was in John Bateman, *The Great Landowners of Great Britain and Ireland*, 1st ed. 1876 and, the most useful, the 4th ed. of 1883. The enquiry was popularly known as 'The New Domesday Book'.

3 Clapham, J.H., 1939, *An economic history of modern Britain. The early railway age, 1820–1850*, Cambridge University Press, Cambridge, p. 536ff.

4 Mitchell, B.R. and Deane, P., 1962, *Abstract of British historical statistics*, Cambridge University Press, Cambridge, p. 366.

5 The female surplus was much debated by the Victorians. For a modern discussion, Saville, J., 1957, *Rural depopulation in England and Wales, 1851–1951*, Routledge and Kegan Paul, London, Chs I and III.

6 John, A., 1984, *By the sweat of their brow: women workers at Victorian coal mines*, Cambridge University Press, Cambridge.

7 The literature on women's work is now considerable. For a brief general comment on the importance of the non-mechanized sector of the Victorian economy, the editorial in *History Workshop*, 3 (Spring 1979): 1–4 and Samuel, Raphael, 'Workshop of the world: steam, power and hand technology in mid-Victorian Britain, in ibid.: 6–72.

8 The figures in the text are from Meacham, S., 1977, *A life apart. The English working class, 1890–1914*, Thames and Hudson, London, p. 100.
9 The writings of Elizabeth Roberts are the main sources for women's lives and work in North-East Lancashire: beginning with her doctoral thesis 'The Working Class Family in Barrow and Lancaster, 1890–1930' (University of Lancaster, 1978) and subsequent publications including Roberts, E., 1984, *A Woman's place: an oral history of the working-class women, 1890–1940*, 1984, Blackwell, Oxford. Lewis, J., 1984, *Women in England, 1870–1950: sexual divisions and social change*, Harvester, Brighton.
10 Seccombe, W., 1986, 'Patriarchy stabilized: the construction of the male bread-winner wage norm in nineteenth century Britain', *Social History*, 11 (1): 53–76.
11 Webb, S., 1921, *The story of the Durham miners*, Fabian Publishing Co., London.
12 On the relationships between men and women, Stearns, P.N., 'Working class women in Britain, 1890–1914', in Vicinus, M., 1972, *Suffer and be still*, University of Indiana Press, Bloomington, pp. 100–120; Meacham, S., 1977, *A Life Apart*; Tomes, N., 1978, 'A "torrent of abuse": crimes of violence between working class men and women, 1840–1875', *Journal of Social History*, 11 (3): 328–45; Fox-Genovese, E., 1982, 'Placing women's history in history', *New Left Review*, 133; 5–29, with an excellent bibliography.
13 Roberts, E., *A Woman's place*.
14 The classic study of birth control in history is Himes, N.E., 1936 and 1963, *Medical history of contraception*, Gamut Press, New York. For the story of the struggle for commonsense in Britain, see Leathard, A., 1980, *The fight for family planning. The development of family planning services in Britain 1921–74*, London, Macmillan.
15 Langer, W.L., 1974, 'Infanticide: an historical survey', *History of Childhood Quarterly*, 1, (3): 353–65.
16 Among the many Victorian writers on the subject, see Ryan, Dr. W.B., 1862, *Infanticide: its law, prevalence, prevention and history*, Churchill, London.
17 *Report of the Select Committee on Patent Medicines . . . Minutes of Evidence* (414), IX, 1914: Qs 6431 ff.
18 Bulmer, M., (ed.), 1978, *Mining and social change. Durham Country in the twentieth century*, Croom Helm, London, Chs 1–5. The story of the leek competition is in Ch. 5.
19 The mining districts are probably better documented than any other region save London. See, for example, Chaplin, S., 1950, 1965, *The thin seam*, Phoenix House, London; Dennis, N. Henriques, F., and Slaughter, C., 1956, *Coal is our life*, Eyre and Spottiswoode, London; Colls, R.M., 1977, *The collier's rant: song and culture in the industrial village*, Croom Helm, London; Chaplin, S., 1978, 'Durham mining villages, in Bulmer, M., *Mining and social change*, 59–82.
20 For general surveys, the works of Meacham, S., *A life apart* and Lewis, J., *Women in England*.
21 The methodological problems of women in capitalist societies have not been discussed in this paper. A useful introduction is Himmelweit, S. and Mohun, S., 1977, 'Domestic labour and capital;, *Cambridge Journal of Economics*, 1 (1): 15–31; Stacey, M., and Price, M., 1981, 'Women in the fishing: the roots of power between the sexes', *Comparative Studies in Society and History*, 27 (1): 3–32.

10 Variety and volatility: Some aspects of the labour market in Britain, 1880—1913

C.H. Feinstein
All Souls College, Oxford

Sidney Pollard has made many notable contributions to economic history, and among these, studies of wages and working conditions have been a prominent theme of his work over many years. A notable example was the fine chapter on 'Labour in Great Britain' which he wrote for volume VII of the *Cambridge Economic History of Europe*. This displayed his characteristic ability to combine original research, basic economic theory, and a wealth of learning, and produced a valuable historical analysis of the labour market's operation over a span of some two hundred years. I had contributed a companion chapter on 'Capital in Great Britain' to the same volume, and we subsequently co-operated on a study of capital formation in Britain from 1750 to 1920. It might thus seem appropriate that my paper for this *Festschrift* should be devoted to some aspect of capital accumulation. However, labour has always been closer to Sidney Pollard's heart than capital, and for this essay I should like to look at some features of the labour market in late Victorian and Edwardian Britain.

In his chapter for the *Cambridge Economic History* Pollard commented in relation to the period 1750–1850:

> It was well known that there was nothing like a single national labour market at the beginning of the period, nor was such a market operating very smoothly even at the end, though its creation is one of the chief features of the hundred years of change. Even the most general and common wages – those of agricultural and general labourers – were widely different as between regions, and they moved in different ways.[1]

The main theme I want to examine in relation to the subsequent period is the extent to which such diversity in the pattern of change in earnings over time remained a feature of the labour market. I shall do so, however, in relation to a comparison of wage variation by industrial sector rather than by region.[2] In much – if not all – of the work of the economically and econometrically-minded historians with whom Sidney so frequently crossed swords, it is common to model the behaviour of the labour market in terms of an aggregate function. For example, a single equation may be specified in which movements

in average wages are 'explained' by movements in unemployment and consumer prices.[3] Is this aggregation a convenient simplification which does rough
justice to actual conditions, or a distortion which fails to capture a principal
feature of Victorian and Edwardian labour markets?

The first aspect of this issue which will be considered is the difference
between sectors in the frequency with which earnings changed during these
years and, following from this, in the comparative volatility or stability in the
year-to-year movement of earnings. The second section is devoted to a detailed
consideration of the sectoral variations in the rate of growth of earnings
between 1880 and 1913. This leads finally into a discussion of the dispersion of
relative earnings and of changes over the period in the ranking of different
sectors.

The estimates underlying this discussion of the pattern and pace of changes
in earnings are a revision and extension of the famous series constructed many
years ago by Bowley and Wood. The basic sources and methods used to
compile the present estimates are set out elsewhere.[4] Three aspects of the
definition should be noted. The most important is that the series are designed
to measure *earnings*, not wage-rates, and so attempt to allow both for the effect
of changes in the composition of the labour force in each sector by age, sex,
skill, and area; and also for the variations resulting from use of piece rates and
other systems of payment by result. Where relevant, the value of board and
lodging and other payments in kind is included. Secondly, the estimates relate
to *weekly*, not hourly, earnings and so do not reflect any rise in hourly rates
where this was paid to offset a reduction in standard hours worked. Thirdly,
they attempt to measure earnings for a worker in *full-time* employment, and so
are not adjusted for time lost as a result of unemployment, short-time working
or illness. For the original series there was also no deduction for the
irregularity of employment of casual labour. However, in order to make a
comparison of absolute levels of earnings in the final section of the present
study, the earnings of dock workers, seamen, carriers and carters, and general
unskilled labourers were reduced to allow for this factor.[5]

The use of a single, consistent definition – weekly full-employment earnings
– for all sectors is obviously desirable where the objective is to make
comparisons across sectors. The present estimates are thus an improvement on
those previously available.[6] However, if these trends are to be correctly
interpreted it is important to keep in mind that, with this particular definition,
movements over time can occur as a result of a variety of different factors. For
example, the estimates for printing reflect both changes in the earnings of
specific groups of workers in that sector, such as those of adult males who were
skilled hand-compositors; and also changes in the balance of skilled, semi-
skilled and unskilled workers, in the relative numbers of men and women, and
in the area composition of the labour force in printing. Similarly, a rise in the
average age of female domestic servants was responsible for a substantial part
of the increase in their average earnings between 1891 and 1913.[7]

The new indices cover 35 separate groups of workers, classified in most cases
on the basis of the industry in which they were employed, but in a few cases – in
particular, carters, carriers and other road haulage workers – on the basis of an
occupation common to several industries. There are 20 separate estimates for

Table 10.1 Indices of average annual full-time wage earnings for selected years, 1881–1913 (1911 = 100)

	1881	1886	1891	1896	1901	1906	1913
Agriculture – England & Wales	89.7	87.6	88.6	90.3	97.6	98.9	109.2
Agriculture – Ireland	76.5	80.5	82.9	86.5	90.1	94.2	108.6
Agriculture – Scotland	85.7	86.7	89.7	90.6	96.3	97.4	107.8
Army	67.0	65.4	78.1	79.1	80.0	98.7	101.2
Building	87.0	87.0	90.4	94.8	100.0	100.0	103.5
Central government messengers	96.9	97.3	98.9	100.3	98.6	100.8	100.1
Clothing – females	100.0	100.0	100.0	100.0	100.0	100.0	100.0
Clothing – males	72.6	76.6	80.8	85.2	89.9	94.8	102.2
Coal mining	59.0	57.2	86.8	76.2	104.0	90.4	110.2
Cotton	75.9	75.5	84.7	86.3	91.3	97.6	103.2
Docks	83.0	83.0	93.8	95.4	96.9	98.5	118.0
Domestic service – females	83.9	81.6	83.2	82.8	89.2	93.3	103.5
Domestic service – males	80.1	80.6	83.5	85.0	91.2	95.3	104.9
Engineering	76.5	75.8	84.7	88.3	93.9	95.5	104.1
Footwear	95.9	86.4	91.0	94.9	96.1	97.1	103.3
Furniture	92.2	91.0	94.0	95.1	100.2	100.0	100.5
Gas	81.5	81.5	90.0	90.9	94.7	95.6	100.7
General labour	83.9	84.3	89.1	91.2	95.3	97.9	106.7
Glass	83.4	82.9	96.6	86.8	107.5	94.4	104.2
Iron and steel manufacture	67.0	63.9	81.6	74.6	100.5	97.4	123.9
Iron ore mining	73.1	67.5	85.6	86.7	105.3	102.5	115.8
Jute	74.5	67.1	87.2	85.2	91.3	95.3	114.8
Linen, hosiery, and silk	96.8	87.2	92.4	96.0	97.0	96.6	106.6
Local authorities	81.9	82.9	84.5	88.5	94.7	97.1	105.0
Navy	78.5	78.0	85.8	81.7	85.4	91.1	100.9
Pig iron	85.7	77.1	90.3	84.4	102.5	101.3	112.7
Police	79.3	81.1	88.9	93.5	96.5	98.6	102.0
Post office	84.3	96.6	97.9	84.7	87.2	91.9	102.7
Printing	85.4	86.5	90.9	92.9	95.7	96.9	101.3
Railways	83.2	84.6	86.5	90.0	93.7	95.2	104.7
Road transport	87.0	87.0	87.0	92.3	96.4	97.2	102.2
Shipbuilding	82.0	78.2	89.7	89.1	96.1	95.5	104.1
Shipping	81.4	76.0	90.0	81.8	90.1	90.4	114.4
Shop assistants	82.0	83.8	85.7	87.5	90.8	95.3	101.9
Wool and worsted	86.2	82.2	82.9	84.9	88.7	93.7	102.5
ALL SECTORS*	82.2	81.3	87.5	88.0	94.8	96.2	104.8

*Fixed (1881) weights
Source: Feinstein, 'New estimates', pp. 608–12.

manufacturing industries, and 15 for other industries and services. The only regional classification is in agriculture, for which separate estimates were made for England and Wales, Scotland, and Ireland. The 35 individual indices (with 1911 = 100) are given for selected years in Table 10.1.

10.1 Stability and volatility

Perhaps the most immediately striking feature of the individual earnings series is the differences in the frequency and extent of year-to-year changes. At one extreme were the sectors where earnings were related to product prices, either by a formal sliding scale, or by conciliation or arbitration procedures which produced basically similar results.[8] Earnings in these industries were subject to frequent and often quite violent fluctuations, and in periods of rapid price movements it was not unusual for earnings to be adjusted as often as four times within a year. At the other extreme were industries where employers resolutely refused to have any dealings with workers' organizations, no regular procedure for wage negotiation – either formal or informal – was ever established, and nominal wage rates remained stationary for years, even decades, at a time. Workers in these industries did not normally suffer the periodic reductions in nominal wages which were such a marked and unwanted feature of sliding scale or equivalent agreements, but neither did they have the industrial strength to win improvements in their pay or conditions during cyclical upswings. Shifts in the composition of the labour force or in systems of remuneration could, however, generate slight movements in earnings. Between these extremes were industries where some institutional procedures existed through which changes could be negotiated between groups of employers and workers, but with adjustments which were relatively limited in frequency and scope.

In Figure 10.1, nine series have been selected to indicate these widely differing patterns of change. The cases of exceptional volatility are represented in panels A and B of the chart by coal mining and manufactured iron and steel. An intermediate group of industries, in which earnings were subject to appreciable cyclical fluctuation but with adjustments confined to much narrower limits, is illustrated in panel C by the earnings of wage earners in cotton and engineering. The contrast between their experience and that of workers in mining or iron and steel stands out very clearly. Other industries within this intermediate category of moderate negotiated changes (though not necessarily for all wage earners or the whole of the period) include shipbuilding, Birmingham metal-working trades, some of the smaller textile industries such as hosiery, linen, and jute, many of the building trades, pottery and glass bottle manufacture, and the boot and shoe trades.[9]

Industries such as coal, cotton, and engineering figured prominently in previous wage indices, and this may have led to some overstatement of the sensitivity of earnings to cyclical conditions.[10] In fact, many other industries showed prolonged periods with little or no change in earnings. The series for dock labour and for the furniture trades in panel A, and for compositors (one component of the estimate for printing) in panel B, all display this remarkable pattern of long-run stability interrupted only by an occasional upward correction. Even the slight incline in the compositors' earnings was partly the result of regional changes; many individual towns showed greater constancy. In London, for example, compositors' weekly wage rates were changed only twice in the entire period: in 1890 when they moved up two shillings from the level fixed in 1866 (36 shillings), and in 1904 when there was a further advance of one shilling. Changes in the compositors' piece-rate scale were equally rare.[11] Similarly, standard wage rates for London cabinet makers were initially unchanged at 40s 6d per week from 1877 to 1895 and then remained at 43s 9d from 1900 to 1912.[12] The graphs for road haulage in panel B and for building in

Figure 10.1 Indices of annual full-time earnings 1880–1913 (1911 = 100)

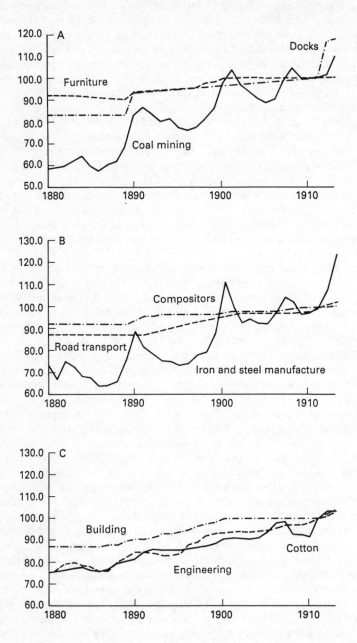

panel C are further examples of industries in which wages were stationary for many consecutive years, though in both these industries it was possible for wage earners to achieve a progressive improvement during the boom of the 1890s.[13]

How can we account for this diversity? In the case of coal, or iron and steel, the potential for bitter disputes between workers and employers in industries subject to large cyclical fluctuations in demand made the introduction of sliding scales desirable; the production of basically homogeneous products with an easily measurable price made it possible. Sliding scales came to be deeply resented by many miners after their experience with falling prices in the 1880s and early 1890s, but even where they were replaced by schemes which provided for less rigid linking of wages to prices, the results were effectively little different. Porter's apt comment applies equally to both types of arrangement:

> The formation of the boards appears to have taken place when the unions had sufficient strength to convince the employers that conciliation and arbitration were necessary, but insufficient power to make an openly militant policy more attractive for themselves.[14]

Similar factors encouraged the process of negotiated agreement in other industries where industrial bargaining was well organized, such as engineering and cotton. However, as was shown by Figure 10.1, fluctuations in earnings in these sectors were more limited. In cotton spinning, for example, the Brooklands Agreement of 1893 specifically provided that general adjustments should be restricted to five per cent in either direction, and should not be made more than once a year.[15] The explanation for this limitation is partly that demand and prices for cotton were considerably less volatile than those for coal or steel, partly because it was customary to meet trade depressions by working short-time rather than by attempting to reduce the cost of production by steep reductions in wage rates.[16] In engineering and shipbuilding similar adjustments were made by sharp variations in unemployment. The same strategy would not have been feasible in the capital-intensive iron and steel industry, where the costs of a temporary shut-down of the plant were very heavy.

The contrasting stability in the docks, in other sectors of the transport industry such as road haulage and shipping, and among unskilled workers generally, reflected the poor organization and very weak bargaining position of such workers in a situation where: 'there appears to be always and everywhere an inexhaustible excess in the supply of labour over the demand'.[17] Even when demand expanded, employers saw no need to offer higher wages, and could easily adjust to changing economic conditions by varying employment rather than wage rates. Thus, wage earners in these industries could normally raise their nominal earnings only when large numbers were goaded into taking strike action. This was not likely to occur until resentment arising from such factors as technical change, inadequate real wages, or excessive hours had accumulated over many years to reach explosive levels, as finally happened with dockers, railwaymen, seamen, and carters in 1911 and 1912.

Where more organized groups of workers, such as the printers or engineers, accepted unchanged wage rates for long periods it may be that they preferred to concentrate their efforts on other objects, such as protecting their existing wage level and employment from the challenge of less skilled operatives during a period of technical change. Alternatively, it may be – as Wood suggests in the case of the piece lists operated by the Spanish morocco leather finishers – that the Unions' basic strategy was to keep their standard list unchanged, knowing that, if they were successful in this, their position would be improved with each increase in productivity.[18] The phrase 'Look after the lists and the wages will look after themselves', cited by Rowe in connection with spinners and other operatives in the cotton industry, suggests a similar policy.[19]

10.2 Variation in the growth of earnings

Individual industries not only showed varied patterns of change from year to year, they also experienced widely different rates of growth over the period as a whole. The basic data are set out in Table 10.2. The first three columns show the levels of average annual full-time earnings for each of the 35 sectors, and for the whole economy, at three dates: 1881, 1896 and 1913. The next three show the percentage increases in the two sub-periods 1881–96 and 1896–1913, and over the full period. The series are listed in the rank order given by column (6), the percentage increase from 1881 to 1913.

The two sub-periods are of roughly equal length, but show very different movements in nominal wages. In the first, earnings in many sectors were badly affected by the deep trade depression of the 1880s, and many sectors made little progress. For the economy as a whole the increase in average earnings was only seven per cent, and only six sectors achieved a rise in money wages of more than 15 per cent. In the second sub-period the rate of advance improved considerably in almost all sectors, and the overall pace of change accelerated to 19 per cent. The result for the full period was thus that average earnings for all wage earners increased by approximately 27 per cent (0.8 per cent per annum) between 1881 and 1913. This is an average of the figures for individual sectors, weighted by their share in total employment in 1881, and so does not allow for any effect of movement between sectors. Over the same period there was a shift in the composition of employment towards sectors with higher average earnings. This added roughly ten per cent more to the overall average, taking the total rise for the economy as a whole, though not for the typical wage earner, to 40 per cent.[20]

These differences between the two sub-periods should be set in the context of the corresponding movements in prices. By 1881 the cost of living had already dropped sharply from its 1873 peak, and in the period to 1896 it fell by a further 13 per cent.[21] Thus even though money wages rose by only seven per cent, this was associated with an increase in real consumption of almost a quarter. In the subsequent period, however, the cost of living rose by 18 per cent, eroding almost the entire advance in average money earnings. Since earnings for many wage earners advanced by less than the average, and many others did not achieve any significant increase until after the industrial unrest

Table 10.2 Average annual full-time wage earnings, 1881, 1896 and 1913 (Ranked by percentage increase, 1881-1913)

	Annual earnings (£s)			Percentage increase (%)		
	1881 (1)	1896 (2)	1913 (3)	1881 -1896 (4)	1896 -1913 (5)	1881 -1913 (6)
Clothing – females	29.3	29.3	29.3	0.0	0.0	0.0
Central government messengers	66.2	68.5	68.4	3.5	-0.2	3.3
Footwear	52.4	51.8	56.4	-1.1	8.9	7.7
Furniture	61.0	63.0	66.5	3.2	5.6	9.0
Linen, hosiery, and silk	36.3	36.0	40.0	-0.8	11.0	10.1
Road transport	46.9	49.7	55.1	6.1	10.8	17.5
Printing	54.8	59.6	65.0	8.7	9.1	18.6
Wool and worsted	38.3	37.7	45.5	-1.5	20.7	18.9
Building	62.4	68.0	74.2	9.0	9.1	19.0
Agriculture – England & Wales	39.6	39.8	48.2	0.6	21.0	21.7
Post office	55.3	55.6	67.4	0.5	21.2	21.8
Domestic service – females	37.6	37.1	46.4	-1.3	25.0	23.4
Gas	65.2	72.7	80.6	11.5	10.8	23.6
Shop assistants	55.4	59.1	68.8	6.8	16.4	24.3
Glass	58.5	60.8	73.0	4.0	20.1	24.9
Agriculture – Scotland	40.5	42.9	51.0	5.8	18.9	25.8
Railways	56.2	60.8	70.7	8.3	16.2	25.8
Shipbuilding	69.0	74.9	87.5	8.6	16.9	27.0
General labour	34.0	37.0	43.3	8.6	17.1	27.2
Local authorities	52.8	57.1	67.7	8.1	18.6	28.2
Navy	60.3	62.7	77.5	4.0	23.6	28.5
Police	76.1	89.8	97.9	18.0	9.0	28.6
Domestic service – males	59.5	63.2	77.9	6.2	23.3	31.0
Pig iron	68.6	67.6	90.3	-1.5	33.5	31.5
Cotton	38.1	43.3	51.8	13.6	19.6	36.0
Engineering	56.5	65.3	76.9	15.5	17.8	36.1
Shipping	45.9	46.1	64.5	0.4	39.9	40.5
Clothing – males	53.4	62.7	75.2	17.3	20.0	40.8
Agriculture – Ireland	21.6	24.5	30.7	13.2	25.4	42.0
Docks	53.0	61.0	75.4	14.9	23.7	42.2
Army	41.0	48.4	61.9	18.0	28.0	51.0
Jute	29.3	33.5	45.1	14.4	34.7	54.1
Iron ore mining	55.5	65.8	87.9	18.6	33.6	58.4
Iron and steel manufacture	63.1	70.3	116.7	11.4	66.0	84.9
Coal mining	50.5	65.2	94.3	29.1	44.7	86.8
All sectors*	48.2	51.6	61.4	7.1	19.0	27.5
Standard deviation	12.4	14.2	18.8	7.2	12.7	18.9
Mean (unweighted)	51.6	55.8	67.3	8.1	20.6	30.6
Coefficient of variation (%)	24.0	25.4	27.9	89.6	61.8	61.7

*Calculated with fixed (1880) weights.
Source: Feinstein, 'New estimates', pp. 603-12.

of 1910-13, the common experience in many working class households was of declining real standards for most of the Edwardian period.

As can be seen from Table 10.2, the experience of individual sectors showed a wide dispersion around the average for 1881–1913, with a range from zero growth for women employed in the clothing industry to an increase of 87 per cent (2.0 per cent per annum) for coal miners. The standard deviation of the percentage increases in average earnings was 18.9 and the coefficient of variation thus 61.7 per cent. To judge how wide a spread this represents, it needs to be set in some perspective by comparison with similar calculations for later periods. Since any measure of dispersion will be strongly influenced by the underlying degree of disaggregation, it is essential to classify the estimates of earnings for later periods on a basis as close as possible to that in Table 10.2. Fortunately, it has proved possible to make estimates for 1911 and 1935 matching 34 of the 35 sectors from Table 10.2, and the result also gives an accurate measure of the overall change between the two dates.[22]

Since these were years which covered the divergent impact of World War I on different industries, the economic upheaval of the post-war boom and slump, and the great depression of 1929–32, it might be expected that the fortunes of different sectors would vary quite widely, so that the spread in the growth of earnings would be greater than was shown by the data for the more stable pre-war years in Table 10.2. In fact, it was considerably narrower:

	1881–1913	1911–1935
Unweighted mean increase (%)	30.6	96.4
Standard deviation	18.9	31.0
Coefficient of variation (%)	61.7	32.1

Thus, the coefficient of variation for the later period was only 32.1 per cent, roughly half that for the years before 1913.[23]

10.2.1 Industries in which earnings increased least

To get some indication of the factors responsible for this very varied pattern of change over the period, we can look more closely at particular sectors in each of the two extremes of the distribution. At the bottom end, those wage earners who made the least progress over the three pre-1913 decades include those in clothing (female workers); boots and shoes; furniture and upholstery; linen, hosiery and silk; horse-drawn road transport (carters, carriers and van drivers); printing; the wool and worsted industries and building.

Direct evidence is seldom available to account for the relative deterioration in the earnings of workers in these industries, and far more investigation of the question is necessary before it will be possible to compile a thorough explanation for what occurred. For the present, we can offer only a preliminary exploration based on circumstantial reasoning. Probably the most significant factor, and the one which most differentiates this period from later years, was the introduction of steam-powered machinery in industries which until then had remained largely a preserve of hand work, or of machines operated without power. In the glare of the industrial revolution it is easy to overlook the many industries in which such rudimentary production methods survived until late in the nineteenth century; the process which started on a dramatic scale with the collapse of the handloom weavers in mid-century was effectively not completed until the 1890s. When power-driven machinery was finally introduced into each major industry it overturned accepted wage patterns and undermined the status and remuneration of skilled craftsmen. In subsequent periods, there was no longer the scope for such dramatic shifts in the technical basis of established industries. New industries were created and old ones languished or died, but for various reasons, mainly institutional, this no longer had the same impact on inter-industry wage levels and changes.

In the clothing industry, the first sewing machines crossed the Atlantic in the 1850s, and machinery which could cut many thicknesses of cloth simultaneously was invented in Leeds at the end of that decade.[24] In the closing decades of the century large factories, using power-driven machinery for cutting, sewing, and other operations, expanded rapidly – especially in northern centres like Leeds and Manchester. This mass-production of ready-made clothing put great pressure on the earnings of vast numbers of female workers in the small-scale outwork and homework branches of the industry. As a writer from the Women's Industrial Council noted in 1903, following an enquiry into the work of women in the London tailoring trade, what seemed to be happening was 'a cheapening of the better factory product, which therefore tends to drive out the inferior home-made article'.[25] Over 600,000 women and girls still persisted in the attempt to maintain either an independent living or a contribution to family incomes from employment as dressmakers, milliners, tailors and seamstresses, but they found their money earnings falling increasingly behind those in other occupations. The available information does not permit an accurate estimate for these wage earners, but the general impression derived from a wide range of evidence is that their average money earnings were at best stable, and may even have declined slightly.[26]

The depressing effect of modern machinery and factory production on the earnings of women and girls working at home or in small workshops was reinforced, particularly for the large numbers concentrated in the East End of London, by a further factor – an inexhaustible supply of cheap labour. This was ceaselessly renewed both by the large numbers of women and girls for whom sewing was an obvious occupation and, from the 1880s, by the great influx of foreign immigrants – principally Jews from Russia and Poland. Both groups were desperately anxious to obtain a source of income, however meagre, and with the extreme specialization and subcontracting characteristic of this trade, those not already competent at such tasks as stitching cloth and making button-holes could rapidly acquire the necessary ability. This was, in Clapham's memorable phrase, 'the terrible ease of sewing'.[27]

The impact of mechanization in the closing decades of the nineteenth century can again be seen in the footwear, printing, furniture and hosiery industries. In printing, composition was done entirely by hand until the introduction of the first machines from the United States in the late 1860s. A moderately skilled operator of the early typesetting machines could produce at least three times the output of a really fast hand-compositor. In the provinces, the Typographical Association accepted that the best they could achieve would be to ensure that the actual composing was undertaken by skilled journeymen or legal apprentices, thus allowing the unskilled work of distributing the type (after it had been used) to be done more cheaply by youths or females. As a result, machine composition spread quickly to many provincial towns. It was especially prominent in newspaper printing, which was expanding rapidly following the repeal of the newspaper stamp duty and other 'taxes on knowledge', the extension of mass education, and the rise of popular journalism from the 1880s.

By contrast, in the capital, where a disproportionately high share of the printing trade was located, the well-organized members of the London Society of Compositors were able to prohibit the use of cheaper labour in the distribution of the type, and on this basis the first generation of typesetting machines was not economical. However, from 1889 the more advanced Linotype machines were introduced in Britain. With these, the use of a keyboard was combined with type-casting and line justification to give greatly increased speed and efficiency. Since the line of type was a solid 'slug' of metal, the problem of distribution was also eliminated. As these machines were adopted, the process of displacement of the hand compositors accelerated in both London and the provinces. The leverage which the new machines could exercise was demonstrated very clearly in the 1890s when the Typographical Association attempted to exact too high a price in relation to the training of the Linotype operators. The supplier of the machines responded vigorously by opening 'schools' in London and Manchester offering newcomers to the trade the opportunity to acquire the necessary training in a few weeks.

At the turn of the century there was further technical progress with the introduction of Monotype machines.These immediately put yet more pressure on wages, and mechanical composition also began to spread from newspaper offices to the book and jobbing printers. The hand compositors had originally been among the élite of the labour force, but as machine operation replaced manual skills in the closing decades of the nineteenth century, their successors struggled to defend their claim to operate the new machinery. They succeeded in this, but at a price – they were able to maintain, but not significantly to increase, their money earnings.[28] The actual printing process was also affected by technological change, notably the use of the reel-fed rotary presses from the 1860s onwards, with a comparable effect on earnings.

In furniture the historical sequence is very similar.[29] Until late in the nineteenth century the situation in the ready-made branch of the trade was rather like that in clothing, with a wholesale system based on large numbers of small workshops. The craftsmen worked by hand, with timber which had previously been sawn and planed in the large steam-powered sawmills. At the end of the century, the introduction of machinery lowered costs by reducing both the degree of skill and the amount of labour required per item. This undermined the position of the artisans, and their differential reward for skill was driven down. From the 1870s some machinery started to appear in joiners' shops, but it was not until the 1890s that the trade was transformed by mass production in large factories, based on the application of new machines to a wide range of processes. Early in the decade *The Furniture Gazette* commented:

Machinery . . . has so far changed conditions that in the planing mill, the furniture factory, the cabinet shop, and in all other kinds of woodworking plant, the differences between the old methods and the new are little less than revolutionary.[30]

Electrification played an increasing role in extending this process after the turn of the century. The impact of the change on the growth of earnings was very severe and, as Table 10.2 shows, wage earners in the furniture trades were able to raise their incomes by only six per cent between 1896 and 1913, pushing them close to the bottom of the league.

The situation in the boot and shoe industry was little better over this period, with an increase in earnings of only nine per cent. The introduction of machinery began in the 1860s, but here too it was only in the 1890s that the production process was revolutionized by the installation of a series of new machines using steam power.[31] Growing tension between workers and employers over the accelerating mechanization of the industry came to a head in 1895 with the 'boot war', a six-week lock-out which ended with victory for the employers, giving them the right to introduce and operate machinery, and arrange wage payments, on their terms. The settlement was strongly influenced by the rapidly mounting threat of competition from factory-made exports from the United States; a problem by no means unique to footwear, but one not applicable to printing or furniture.

The textile industries are represented at the bottom end of the range in Table 10.2 by two estimates, one covering linen, hosiery and silk, and the other for wool and worsted. In the former, earnings in linen manufacture increased at about the average rate for all industries; but those in the silk and hosiery trades fared particularly badly and, at the end of the period, were actually one or two per cent lower than in 1880. In hosiery there was a rapid expansion of automatic knitting machines worked by power from the 1890s, and 'the claims of cheapness and rapidity of production, not to mention other points such as uniformity' proved too great for the workers of hand-driven knitting frames to sustain their position.[32] This not only put pressure on earnings but also led to a change in the composition of the labour force – employment was 56 per cent higher in 1911 than in 1881, but the number of men was 19 per cent lower.[33] The use of women and girls to operate the new machines markedly reduced average earnings in the trade.

'Made by protection and undone by free trade' was Clapham's verdict on the decline of the silk industry. The inflow of French silks – following the removal of the 15 per cent protective duty under the Cobden Treaty of 1860 – had a devastating effect, particularly on the thrown silk branch of the trade. Subsequent decades saw fierce competition as silk production expanded behind tariff walls in the United States and Europe. The spun silk section survived and prospered on the basis of the extension of power-loom weaving, but this provided employment for fewer workers and paid lower wages.[34]

In the woollen and worsted industries the story is rather different from those we have so far considered. In other industries mechanization made its adverse impact on earnings in the 1890s, and the widening of the gap is most evident in the second half of the period (see column (5) of Table 10.2). For woollen and worsted manufactures, by contrast, the gap was opened in the first half of the period (Column (4)), and the subsequent advance is broadly in line with the average for all industries. The critical factor which depressed wages and profits in the 1880s and 1890s was not technical change – mechanization of combing, spinning and weaving had effectively been completed much earlier – but foreign competition. The United States, France, Germany, and other European countries adopted high tariffs, and with this protection they developed their domestic capacity to the point where they could exclude UK producers from their home markets and compete successfully in Britain's own market. No other industry lost as much from the United States tariffs as wool and worsted. The recovery in wages occurred after the turn of the century, when many sections of the woollen and worsted trade responded strongly to this challenge by winning new markets in the Empire, especially Canada, and in South America.[35]

The final industry to be considered among those showing relatively little improvement between 1880 and 1913 is road haulage. This covers the drivers of horse-drawn carts, vans, and wagons, and, in a technically-static industry, illustrates a different process serving to weaken the bargaining position of a particular group of workers. Driving horse-drawn vehicles was a source of employment for large numbers of workers who were unskilled – at least in terms of formal, institutionalized notions of skill – so that entry to the trade was easy and the supply of labour typically exceeded the demand – leaving the labour force in a very vulnerable position. Attempts at union organization and strike activity were generally unsuccessful, and there was little improvement in earnings until the massive wave of strikes in 1910–13 finally forced the employers to concede increases. In Glasgow, for example, carters had struck in 1889 demanding an increase of two shillings on their weekly wage of 24 shillings, but only some had achieved this. In 1913 the average wage for Glasgow's general contractors' carters was still only 25 shillings, and they went on strike for an increase of three shillings.[36]

The main conclusion to emerge from this survey of the trend in the earnings of those who did least well over the period 1880–1913 is that by far the most important explanation for their plight was the impact of steam-powered machinery and large-scale factory organization. This technical revolution in industries which had continued to rely on traditional methods until very late in the nineteenth century helped to raise productivity and increase employment, but it generally weakened the position of the skilled handicraft workers, both by direct competition and by facilitating increased employment of semi-skilled males and of women and girls. Where the craftsmen were well organized, as in the printing industry, they were better able to protect their rights to work the new machines, but even they were not able to prevent a decline in their relative earnings.

The adverse impact on relative earnings of steam power, mechanization, and modern factory production was supplemented by two other factors. The first, and most damaging, was that many unskilled and casual workers were the constant victims of an abundant supply of cheap unskilled labour. As Beveridge noted, if an occupation was unskilled as well as casual, it was: 'subject to a constant and practically unlimited pressure of competition downwards'.[37] Secondly, certain industries were subject to intense pressure from foreign competitors, emerging from behind tariff barriers to undercut the prices charged by British producers. In later periods, well-organized workers might resist such pressures and defend wages at the long-run expense of their jobs; in the more flexible labour markets of the Victorian and Edwardian period, it was more often wages which adjusted to preserve employment.

10.2.2 Industries in which earnings increased most

We now turn to the other extreme of the distribution and select for detailed consideration five groups whose earnings are shown in Table 10.2 to have increased by more than 50 per cent. The wage earners in this fortunate position were those in the army, the jute industry, iron ore mining, iron and steel manufacture, and – at the head of the list – coal mining. All of these were genuine increases for specific occupations, not the outcome of changes in the composition of the labour force. One general characteristic of all these industries is also worth noting – none of them experienced significant technical changes in their scale or methods of production. The importance of technical change as a source of reduced earnings in many of the sectors whose earnings showed the lowest increases over this period is thus underlined by its absence in those which improved most.

The large rise in army pay in the twentieth century was the result of a succession of complicated adjustments, including an increase in service pay, and an additional kit allowance (both of 2d per day) awarded – though not immediately implemented – under an Order of 1902. These presumably reflected difficulties in recruiting and retaining the necessary manpower, enhanced by such trends as the decline in the agricultural labour force – the traditional source of recruits for the armed forces – and competition for men from the mining industry. The relationship between army pay (including certain allowances and payments in kind) and that of general unskilled labour as shown by the present estimates was (£'s):

	1881	1891	1901	1911
Army	41	47	49	61
General labour	42	45	48	51

If these figures are accurate, it suggests that the army found it necessary to widen the gap in the early twentieth century. Some indication of this is evident in the following comment in 1906: 'The pay has been so largely increased of recent years that there is no doubt that it compares favourably with that of the unskilled labourer in civil life'.[38] The increase may also reflect the rising cost of food and other provisions after the turn of the century.

Wages for both piece and time workers in the Dundee jute industry were adjusted on the basis of agreed piece price lists, similar to those in cotton. After a number of reductions in the mid-1880s, the subsequent period saw 11 upward adjustments, generally of five per cent, and only one downward correction. Actual earnings for the jute spinners and weavers rose even more than this, as higher productivity was achieved with increases in the speed of the machinery and advances in the skill of the operatives.[39] The position of the jute industry near the top of the list may seem somewhat surprising, but is essentially the result of two factors. First, it was a relatively new industry, its expansion dating effectively from the 1860s, and since power-looms were introduced at an early stage it was not subject in later decades to significant technical change or to substitution of female for male labour. Secondly, the industry was successful, enjoying first a phase of exceptionally rapid growth when it was recognized that jute was a very cheap fibre for the manufacture of bags, sacking, and other packing materials; and then switching to higher value products such as floorcloths and mattings.[40]

The dominant factor responsible for the long-term increase in earnings of coal miners was the great strength, and low elasticity, of demand for coal from the iron and steel industry and other domestic manufacturing, railways and gasworks, household consumption, shipping, and export markets. This pressure of demand in the late Victorian and Edwardian period is reflected in the movement of coal prices, which fell much less than those of all other products between 1880 and the mid-1890s, and increased very much more sharply in the upswing to 1913. As a result, the price of coal at the pit-head was 92 per cent higher in 1913 than in 1881, whereas the average of all wholesale prices was eight per cent lower. For 1896–1913 the corresponding figures are 73 per cent and 32 per cent.[41]

Since miners' wages were effectively tied to product prices either by formal sliding scales or under the broadly equivalent arbitration and conciliation arrangements, a large part of the increase in earnings can be directly attributed to this demand for coal and thus, indirectly, for labour to produce it. This recurrent need to expand the labour supply for the mines was reinforced from the late 1880s by a downward trend in output per man and, after the Eight Hours Act of 1908, by a reduction in hours worked. In addition to these market forces, the increased size and influence of the miners' trades unions after the 1880s may have slightly accelerated the increase in wages at the beginning of each cyclical upturn in demand, and strong pressure from miners for a 'bottom' to their earnings in the downturn may have slightly moderated the subsequent fall in wages.[42]

The experience of workers in the iron and steel industry (and in iron ore mining) was very similar; and they too were beneficiaries of strong demand reflected in a secular rise in prices which was swiftly and peacefully translated into increased earnings by means of sliding scales. However, as Table 10.2 shows, the main surge in prices and wages in the manufactured iron and steel trade was concentrated in the upswing from 1896 to 1913. These years are notorious as the time when Britain fell significantly behind its foreign rivals in terms of market shares at home and abroad, but they were also a period in which the world's consumption of steel rose more than threefold, and, despite their relative inefficiencies, British producers enjoyed a sharp expansion in output and prices. The impact on wages can be illustrated by the scale for puddlers in the Midlands, an index widely used to determine the movements in wages in other areas and branches of the iron and steel trade. In 1881 the standard rate per ton for puddling was 7/3, and after some fluctuation in the intervening years it was again at that same level for most of 1896. By 1913 it had climbed to 11/-, a rise of over 50 per cent, with the main advance coming in the hectic boom years of 1912 and 1913. Moreover, steelworkers also benefited from the effect of productivity improvements on the basic rates to which the sliding scale related. For all wage earners in iron and steel manufacture, this additional element accounts for most of the small increase in earnings between 1881 and 1896, and for approximately one-quarter of the 66 per cent rise from 1896 to 1913.[43]

10.3 The ranking of sectors

Given this degree of dispersion in the changes over the period, it is natural to enquire next to what extent this in turn led to significant changes in the ranking of sectors. In columns (1) and (2) of Table 10.3 the estimated annual earnings in each of the 35 sectors are given for 1881 and 1913, listed in ascending order of the level of earnings in the earlier year. The corresponding rank orders in both years are given in columns (3) and (4). A few sectors did move sharply up or down. Coal mining was by far the most striking example, moving up 19 places from 14th to 33rd. Wage earners in iron ore mining, iron and steel manufacture, the docks, and clothing (male workers) also made appreciable advances. The two sectors which lost most ground were central government, (down 13 places) and furniture (down 12 places).

However, the broad picture is one of relative stability. There was, for example, no tendency for low-paid sectors to gain disproportionate rises, as happened to a considerable extent during the abnormal inflation of the First World War. All of the ten sectors at the lower end of the rank in 1881 were still at the bottom of the list in 1913. There was slightly more movement at the top of the rank, and three sectors which had occupied places in the top ten in 1881 were no longer in that elevated position in 1913. Wage earners in furniture, building and central government gave way to those in coal mining, iron ore mining and engineering. The overall stability is shown by a value for Spearman's rank correlation coefficient of 0.85 (where no change in rank would give a value of 1.0).[44]

A small number of extremely durable differentials explain most of the differences in levels of earnings evident in Table 10.3. These are, in particular, the differential between urban and rural workers, between skilled and un-skilled, and between male and female. As is widely recognized, these margins have proved remarkably resistant to change over very long periods.[45] The stability of the rankings thus arises because most industries did not, or could not, make significant changes in the composition of their workforce which would offset the stabilizing effect of these differentials. Thus if we look at the bottom twelve series in 1881 we see evidence of the rural factor in the inclusion of all three series for agriculture. The gender factor is represented by the inclusion of two series – for clothing and domestic service – relating exclusively to women, and of four series – for textile industries – in which women accounted for 60 per cent or more of the labour force. The skill factor is reflected in the presence of three industries consisting essentially of unskilled

Table 10.3 Rank order of average annual full-time earnings, 1881 and 1913

	Earnings in 1881 (£s) (1)	Earnings in 1913 (£s) (2)	Rank in 1881 (3)	Rank in 1913 (4)
Agriculture – Ireland	21.6	30.7	1	2
Jute	29.3	45.1	2	5
Clothing – females	29.3	29.3	3	1
General labour	34.0	43.3	4	4
Linen, hosiery and silk	36.3	40.0	5	3
Domestic service – females	37.6	46.4	6	7
Cotton	38.1	51.8	7	10
Wool and worsted	38.3	45.5	8	6
Agriculture – England & Wales	39.6	48.2	9	8
Agriculture – Scotland	40.5	51.0	10	9
Army	41.0	61.9	11	13
Shipping	45.9	64.5	12	14
Road transport	46.9	55.1	13	11
Coal mining	50.5	94.3	14	33
Footwear	52.4	56.4	15	12
Local authorities	52.8	67.7	16	18
Docks	53.0	75.4	17	25
Clothing – males	53.4	75.2	18	24
Printing	54.8	65.0	19	15
Post office	55.3	67.4	20	17
Shop assistants	55.4	68.8	21	20
Iron ore mining	55.5	87.9	22	31
Railways	56.2	70.7	23	21
Engineering	56.5	76.9	24	26
Glass	58.5	73.0	25	22
Domestic service – males	59.5	77.9	26	28
Navy	60.3	77.5	27	27
Furniture	61.0	66.5	28	16
Building	62.4	74.2	29	23
Iron and steel manufacture	63.1	116.7	30	35
Gas	65.2	80.6	31	29
Central government messengers	66.2	68.4	32	19
Pig iron	68.6	90.3	33	32
Shipbuilding	69.0	87.5	34	30
Police	76.1	97.9	35	34

Source: See Tables 10.1 and 10.2.

labourers. Among the ten industries with the highest level of earnings, the principal factor appears to be the very large or exclusive employment of males; with a premium for loyalty adding an additional element in the case of the police.

Three main conclusions thus emerge from this preliminary exploration of the new earnings data available for 1880–1913. First, the pattern of short-run movement in individual industries varied very greatly indeed, with highly volatile fluctuations at one end of the range and remarkable stationariness at the other. Secondly, there was an exceptionally wide spread in respect of the long-run rate of growth of earnings over the period as a whole. Certain factors

– in particular, the introduction of steam-powered mechanization, heavy foreign competition, and the relentless competitive pressure for work in unskilled and casual occupations – held down the growth of earnings in some sectors. Probably the most powerful of these factors, and also the most distinctive feature of these years, as compared to subsequent periods, was the final extension of mechanization in the 1890s. By contrast, those sectors in which earnings increased most rapidly in this period were characterized by an absence of revolutionary technological change. Apart from this negative but important point, the primary source of their rapid advance was typically buoyant demand for the goods they produced, swiftly translated into higher earnings by sliding scales. In a few cases, difficulty in recruiting labour was also a factor leading to higher pay.

Thirdly, and despite this variance in the growth of earnings, the ranking of industries by level of average earnings was extremely stable. These levels were largely determined by the composition of the labour force in each sector with respect to skill, gender or location, and the differentials associated with these factors did not change appreciably over the period. Even where industries with low average levels enjoyed above average increases between 1881 and 1913, this was not sufficient to raise their ranking by more than one or two places. This is vividly apparent in the experience of Irish agricultural labourers, female spinners and weavers in the Dundee jute industry, and unskilled recruits to the army. Conversely, however, male-dominated industries which experienced either a prolonged depression (as with the house-building trades in the long downswing of the building cycle after the turn of the century), or a change in the composition of their labour force to include a higher proportion of females (as with furniture), could slide to a lower position in the rank order.

There was certainly a labour market in late Victorian and Edwardian Britain, in the sense that wages within each industry were sensitive to supply and demand, and to customary ideas with respect to skill and other differentials, and earnings were adjusted accordingly. However, each sector was relatively self-contained, and could remain secluded for several decades from the impact of any changes in other sectors. The existence of sliding scales, and of institutional arrangements for conciliation and arbitration, provided mechanisms for regular wage changes for some workers. Other wage earners worked in industries conspicuous by a total absence of any such procedures. Union organization was not sufficiently strong or widespread to create a general ability to obtain broadly uniform increases ('the going rate'). In these circumstances it seems inappropriate to think of the movements in earnings in aggregate terms. Any overall trends in average wages must thus be understood and interpreted as the outcome of wide divergences in the pattern and pace of change in individual sectors.

Notes

1 Pollard, S., 'Labour in Great Britain' in Mathias, P., and Postan, M.M. (Eds), 1978, *The Cambridge economic history of Europe*, VII, part I, Cambridge University Press, Cambridge, p. 103.

172   C.H. Feinstein

2 For excellent studies of regional wage variation see Hunt, E.H., 1973, *Regional wage variations in Britain, 1850–1914*, Oxford University Press, Oxford, and idem, 'Industrialization and regional inequality: wages in Britain, 1760–1914', *Journal of Economic History*, 46, 1986: 935–66.

3 For an illustration of a more elaborate model of wage formation based on aggregate data see Hatton, T.J., 1988, 'Institutional change and wage rigidity in the UK, 1880–1985', *Oxford Review of Economic Policy*, 4: 81. Moreover, the famous Phillips curve, postulating a relationship between the rate of change of money wages and the proportionate excess demand for labour, was tested on an aggregate wage index, part of which covered this period; see Phillips, A.W., 1958, 'The relation between unemployment and the rate of change of money wage rates in the United Kingdom, 1861–1957', *Economica*, 25: 283–99.

4 Feinstein, C.H., 1990, 'New estimates of average earnings in the United Kingdom, 1880–1913', *Economic History Review*, 43: 595–632.

5 A constant 25 per cent was deducted from the estimated full-employment earnings of dock labourers to allow for the much-discussed prevalence of casual labour in this sector. The corresponding deduction for general unskilled labourers was 20 per cent, and for seamen and road transport workers 15 per cent. More research is necessary to establish whether or not the extent of casual labour varied over time. See further Beveridge, W.H., 1930, *Unemployment, a problem of industry*, Longman, London, 2nd ed., pp. 68–110; Dearle, N.B., 1908, *Problems of unemployment in the London building trade*, J.M. Dent, London; Stedman Jones, G., 1971, *Outcast London*, Oxford University Press, Oxford, pp. 19–126; Phillips, G. and Whiteside, N., 1985, *Casual labour, the unemployment question in the port transport industry 1880–1970*, Oxford University Press, Oxford, pp. 12–111.

6 See, for example, the comments on lack of comparability of Rowe, J.W.F., 1928, *Wages in theory and practice*, Routledge, London, pp. 1–14; and Gourvish, T.R., 'The standard of living, 1890–1914' in O'Day, A. (ed.), 1979, *The Edwardian age: conflict and stability, 1900–1914*, Macmillan, London, pp. 24–5.

7 See further Feinstein, 'New estimates', pp. 627–8.

8 Treble, J.G., 1987, 'Sliding scales and conciliation boards: risk sharing in the late 19th century British coal industry', *Oxford Economic Papers*, 39: 679–98; Mitchell, B.R., 1984, *Economic development of the British coal industry 1800–1914*, Cambridge University Press, Cambridge pp. 186–7.

9 See further Clegg, H.A., Fox, A., and Thompson, A.F., 1964, *A history of British trade unions since 1889, I, 1889–1910*, Oxford University Press, Oxford, pp. 184–202; and Hicks, J.R., 1930 'The early history of industrial conciliation in England, *Economica*, 10: 25–39.

10 Cf. Phelps Brown, E.H. and Browne, M.H., 1968, *A century of pay*, Macmillan, London, pp. 72–85.

11 Howe, E., 1947, *The London compositor*, Oxford University Press, London, pp. 59–60.

12 Board of Trade, 1908, *Rates of wages and hours of labour of various industries in the United Kingdom for a series of years*, unpublished, pp. 220–5 and 1912, *15th Abstract of labour statistics*, p. 59.

13 See Wood, G.H., 1901, 'Stationary wage-rates', *Economic Journal*, 11: 151–6 for a previous discussion of this phenomenon. He compiled 55 examples of wage-rates which were unchanged for 20 years or more.

14 Porter, J.H., 1970, 'Wage bargaining under conciliation agreements, 1860–1914', *Economic History Review*, 23: 461. See also Smart, W., 1895, 'The sliding scale' in *Studies in economics*, Macmillan, London, pp. 63–104; Ashley, W.J., 1903, *The*

adjustment of wages, Longman, London, pp. 45–86 and 142–51; and Clegg, Fox and Thompson, *History of British trade unions*, I, 202–12.
15 Chapman, S.J., 1904, *The Lancashire cotton industry, a study in economic development*, Manchester University Press, Manchester, p. 252.
16 Rowe, *Wages in theory and practice*, p. 165.
17 Beveridge, *Unemployment*, pp. 69–70.
18 Wood, 'Stationary wage-rates', p. 155.
19 Rowe, *Wages in theory and practice*, p. 166.
20 See also Feinstein, 'New estimates', pp. 606–7.
21 Feinstein, C.H., 'A new look at the cost of living' in J. Foreman-Peck (ed.), 1991, *Reinterpreting the Victorian economy: essays in quantitative economic history*, Cambridge University Press, Cambridge, pp. 151–79.
22 The main source for the 1935 estimate was the official earnings enquiry, *Ministry of Labour Gazette*, 45, 1937, pp. 46–7, 88–9, 133–5, 174–6 and 257–8; supplemented by Chapman, A.L., 1953, *Wages and salaries in the United Kingdom 1920–1938*, Cambridge University Press, Cambridge, and Routh, G., 1965, *Occupation and pay in Great Britain 1906–60*, Cambridge University Press, Cambridge, pp. 92–9. A weighted average for 1935 was compiled using the numbers of wage earners given in Chapman, op. cit.; this shows an increase of 100 per cent over the corresponding figure for 1911, compared to the rise of 97 per cent given by the index of average weekly wage earnings in Feinstein, C.H., 1972, *National income, expenditure and output of the United Kingdom 1855-1965*, Cambridge University Press, Cambridge, p. T140.
23 The proposition that the inter-sectoral increase in earnings was more varied between 1880 and 1913 than subsequently is also supported by other evidence, though with some reservations because of differences in classification. Salter, W.E.G., 1960, *Productivity and technical change*, Cambridge University Press, Cambridge, p. 108 gives data for the increase in earnings per operative in 28 manufacturing industries from 1924 to 1950 which show a coefficient of variation of only 10.9 per cent. See also the evidence on the narrowing of inter-industrial earnings, differentials between 1924 and 1955 reported in Haddy, P. and Currell, M.E., 1958, 'British inter-industry industrial earnings differentials, 1924–1955', *Economic Journal*, 68: 104–11.
24 Thomas, J., 1955, *A history of the Leeds clothing industry*, (Yorkshire Bulletin of Economic and Social Research, Occasional Paper, No. 1), pp. 9–10.
25 Black, C., 1904, 'London's tailoresses', *Economic Journal*, 14: 564.
26 Feinstein, 'New estimates', pp. 620–1.
27 See further, Hall, P.G., 1962, *The industries of London since 1861*, Hutchinson University Library, London, pp. 52–66; Blythell, D., 1978, *The sweated trades, outwork in nineteenth century Britain*, Batsford, London, 65–80; Schmiechen, J.A., 1984, *Sweated industries and sweated labour: the London clothing trade, 1860-1914*, Croom Helm, London, pp. 24–79; Clapham, J.H., 1938, *An economic history of modern Britain*, 3, Cambridge University Press, Cambridge, p. 184.
28 See Howe, *The London compositor*, pp. 58–68 and 438–509; and Musson, A.E., 1954, *The typographical association*, Oxford University Press, Oxford, pp. 189–227. Musson notes (p. 163) that the rise in wages achieved by the Typographical Association from 1849 to 1914 was 'considerably less than the average for all trades'.
29 See Jones, G.T., 1933, *Increasing return*, Cambridge University Press, Cambridge, pp. 94–5; Hall, *Industries of London*, pp. 85–93; and Musson, A.E., 1978, *The growth of British industry*, Batsford, London, p. 238.
30 *The Furniture Gazette*, 15 September, 1893, p. 410. I am indebted to Andrew Hildreth (and another research project) for this reference.
31 See Fox, A., 1958, *A history of the national union of boot and shoe operatives*

1874–1957, Basil Blackwell, Oxford, pp. 10–28 and 201–321; Church, R.A., 1968, 'The effect of the American export invasion on the British boot and shoe industry, 1885–1914', *Journal of Economic History*, 28: 227–40; and Head, P., 'Boots and shoes' in Aldcroft, D.H. (ed.), 1968, *The development of British industry and foreign competition, 1875–1914*, Allen and Unwin, London, pp. 158–85.

32 Porter, G.R., and Hirst, F.W., 1912, *The progress of the nation*, Methuen, London, p. 392 quoting an article by a Hawick manufacturer, T. Henderson, in *The Scottish Banker's Magazine*, 1910.

33 Clapham, *Economic history*, 3, p. 179.

34 Porter and Hirst, *Progress of the nation*, pp. 349–50 and Coleman, D.C., Courtaulds, I., 1969, *The nineteenth century, silk and crape*, Oxford University Press, Oxford, pp. 158–66.

35 Jenkins, D.T. and Ponting, K.G., 1982, *The British wool textile industry, 1770–1914*, Heinemann, London, pp. 206 and 219–95; and Saul, S.B., 1960, *Studies in British overseas trade, 1870–1914*, Liverpool University Press, Liverpool, pp. 151–7.

36 Tuckett, A., 1967, *The Scottish carter: the history of the Scottish horse and motormen's association 1898–1964*, Allen and Unwin, London, p. 117.

37 Beveridge, *Unemployment*, p. 107.

38 *General Annual Report on the British Army for the year ended September 1905*, PP. 1906 LXVII, p. 35.

39 Board of Trade, 1915, *17th Abstract of Labour Statistics*, p. 69. See also Wood, G.H., 'The course of women's wages during the nineteenth century' in Hutchins, B.L. and Harrison, A., 1903, *A history of factory legislation*, P.S. King, London, pp. 272–7.

40 Clapham, *Economic history*, 2, pp. 84–5 and 3, p. 128.

41 For pithead coal prices see Church, R.A., 1986, *The history of the British coal industry*, 3, *Victorian pre-eminence*, Oxford University Press, Oxford, p. 54. The comparison is made with the Board of Trade wholesale price index, *17th Abstract of Labour Statistics*, 1915, p. 88.

42 The preceding paragraphs draw heavily on the excellent analysis of the trends in money wages in Mitchell, *Economic development of the British coal industry*, pp. 192–249. See also Church, *British coal industry*, pp. 694–757.

43 See further Feinstein, 'New estimates', pp. 618–9 and the sources quoted there.

44 T. Hatton has kindly drawn my attention to a similar excercise covering the changes in ranking of industries between 1906 and 1938; see Norris, K., 1979, 'The industrial wage structure in Britain', *Economic Journal*, 89: 370–6. However, these calculations cover only male employees in manufacturing, and because of the exclusion of farm workers and of females are thus not properly comparable with the present results.

45 For a recent discussion see Phelps Brown, H., 1988, *Egalitarianism and the generation of inequality*, Oxford University Press, Oxford, pp. 394–409.

11 Cities, modernization and architecture: Before and after the Paris building code of 1902

Anthony Sutcliffe,
University of Leicester

11.1 Cities, building control, and the economic historian

Industrialization tends to increase the proportion of the population living in towns and cities. Europe's transformation from a predominantly rural to a largely urban society took place in the nineteenth century and the first half of the twentieth. Economic historians have shown great interest in this rapid urbanization. Towns and, still more, the great cities, have been supremely visible and have appeared to embody all the features, both creative and destructive, of industrial society.

During the last two decades, however, the attention of the historian has moved somewhat from the city as a social organism to the city as a physical phenomenon. Major difficulties were encountered in distinguishing the specifically *urban* character of economic and social phenomena. Regions, rather than towns, have been increasingly identified as the most meaningful spatial units of economic activity. From the early 1970s, the growth of planning history helped to focus attention on the creation of the physical structure of towns, and the institutions and ideology associated with it.

This essay is intended to relate the history of architecture to the aspects of urban development more readily perceived by economic historians. It deals with a city which, by the end of the nineteenth century, combined a distinctive physical form and aesthetic character with an economic role which, in Europe, was second only to London's. Like other large cities, it combined high average per capita incomes with serious problems generated mainly by external diseconomies and congestion costs. As by far the largest city in France and the home of its legislature and central executive, it tended to stimulate the formulation of public policies which were diffused throughout the whole country. As the national centre of activity in the professions, it provided a rich source of expertise for technical debates. Finally, as a world communications centre and the residence of many distinguished and capable foreigners, it was open to outside influence, except when a strong sense of French tradition and achievement discouraged the adoption of international practice.

Building regulations have not been widely studied by historians[1] This neglect does not reflect their importance. It is widely acknowledged that a stringent building code prevented a repetition of the Great Fire of London. Health-related building regulations contributed to the modernization of British cities from the 1840s, and produced a classic industrial housing form in the second half of the century, the bye-law terrace set in the bye-law street[2] More questionable is the contribution of the regulations to architectural design, and this relationship has never been carefully examined. There can be no doubt, however, that the evolution of building regulations can shed light on the history of professionalization and ultimately of modernization, because of the interplay of interests and professional expertise which it involved.

Building regulations bear principally on residential construction, partly because this accounts for some four-fifths of all urban building and partly because public welfare considerations make them more stringent than those applied to commercial, industrial and public building. Notwithstanding the neglect of building regulations, there has been a growth of interest in the history of residential design in recent years.[3] This has produced an important convergence of housing history and architectural history. Architecture has traditionally been seen as the creation of individual artists, free from social constraints and even from the wishes of their clients. The study of residential design tends to identify continuity and even conservatism, the insertion of each house in a broad urban aesthetic, emulation, the influence of class distinctions and societal values, and a general quest for reassurance, as influences on the architect. The typical client is no longer a rich noble, the Church, or the State, but an owner or speculator of limited means, depending heavily on credit, and eager above all to secure a ready and profitable sale for his building, or a steady rental return over a lengthy period. Residential design thus tends to provide a valuable corrective to studies of architectural history which emphasize change and invention by focusing on public buildings and other large, ostentatious projects.[4] In housing, design relates closely to mass demand and popular taste, albeit of a middle class minority.

11.2 The Parisian context

The new Paris building regulations of 1902 were introduced at a time of considerable architectural debate and experiment in Paris. Ever since the seventeenth century, Paris had enjoyed a world reputation for architectural creativity, taste, and high standards of execution. This reputation had survived, or had even been enhanced by, the massive reconstruction and extension of the Second Empire, which epitomized the impact of industrialization on the cities of France. By the close of the century it was being affected by the new building materials produced or cheapened by the industrial system, such as glass, iron and steel. New building techniques influenced by engineering precedents were beginning to make their appearance. So were stylistic forms derived from innovative artistic movements, the most influential being the Art Nouveau wave which sprang from the Arts-and-Crafts tendency of the 1880s. Although these new developments largely originated outside France, they were strongly expressed in the work of French architects and designers at the universal expositions held in Paris in 1889 and 1900. Here was no architectural backwater, for all the respect for classical tradition which prevailed over, or tempered, the new currents.

The strongest architectural continuity was to be found, nevertheless, in the residential sector. Beginning in the 1880s, Parisian architects, both individually and through their organizations, had begun to call for a fuller expression of new techniques and styles in the apartment buildings which made up the bulk of new building in the city. They were instrumental in securing new building regulations in 1882 and 1884, in the hope that a greater latitude of design would result. In this they were largely disappointed, and pressure built up in the 1890s for a new reform of the building code. The incoming Prefect of the Seine accepted this case in 1896 when he set up a committee to revise the regulations. Introduced in 1902, the new building code generated more praise than criticism, but within a few years it was being attacked as an unprecedented assault on the traditional aesthetic of Paris. This outcry led to an angry debate in the Chamber of Deputies in 1909, measures to protect historic areas, and a new review of the building regulations which was to begin in earnest after the First World War. More fully documented than previous reforms of the building regulations, the creation and impact of the 1902 code offer a unique perspective on architecture and building in Europe's second-largest city at the great turning-point of design history, during industrialization. It also provides a valuable perspective on the French modernization process.

11.3 Building regulation in Paris: tradition and innovation

Building regulation in Paris had begun well before industrialization.[5] The main components were the establishment of building lines (*alignements*) from 1607, and the control of heights from 1783. Both reflected the growing congestion of a huge city governed directly by the Crown.

The height restrictions of 1783/4 were built around the principle that the facades of new houses should not exceed a height of sixty feet, even in the widest streets and squares. It was accepted that the roof would rise above this height and that it could include a further floor lit by dormers or skylights, the construction of mansard roofs being a long-established practice, especially in inner Paris. The limit of sixty feet was probably chosen because it permitted the construction of six storeys, which had become the norm for the new apartment houses which had multiplied since mid-century in the fashionable districts of the central city.[6] These regulations were to be of great importance for Parisian archiecture and building not only under the *Ancien régime* but into the industrialization period. Careful enforcement prevented abusive heights, but at the same time most owners built up to the full height allowed, in a precocious recognition of the value of air rights. With construction at the *alignement* (building line) also the norm, Paris acquired a growing number of standard-height apartment houses forming continuous lines along the streets. The authorities meanwhile developed the view that what had been legally authorized, and acted upon by individual owners, could not rightfully be taken away – not, at any rate, without compensation. The result was that developments of the building regulations during the industrialization period, in response to newly-perceived needs such as public health, did not threaten the six-storey house with a mansard roof, fronting directly onto the thoroughfare. This result also conformed to the classical Parisian street aesthetic adopted from the early seventeenth century for prestige schemes like the Rue Royale.

This process of consolidation reached its apogee under the Second Empire (1852–70) when the imperial reconstruction programme prompted a massive building boom. Napoleon III's Prefect of the Seine, Georges Haussmann, detected the need for a modernization of the building regulations and an amended code was introduced in 1859. With public health a major issue since the 1830s, the new regulations had a sanitary dimension which distinguished them from the pre-industrial building codes. However, in design terms the new buildings differed little from their predecessors. The model building type which had emerged in the later eighteenth century was thus confirmed as the authorized housing form in the capital of industrializing France. Efficient and sanitary, it was a valued component of the numerous new streets planned by Haussmann to modernize the city, which clung to the traditional aesthetic. Encouraged by the *architectes-voyers*, the municipal architects who granted the building permits, private architects were normally happy to accept a supporting and even anonymous role for their buildings. The result was a degree of architectural conformity without parallel, even in the history of Parisian architecture.

So extensive was the design conformity achieved under the Second Empire that the subsequent reaction should not cause surprise. After 1870, during a Third Republic which rejected some of the values and practices of the Second Empire, a general sentiment grew up that greater freedom should be permitted to the architect. In 1882 and 1884, the 1859 regulations were relaxed in two areas – projections (*saillies*), and heights, these latter applying principally to roofs. The most visible change resulting from this cautious reform was the proliferation of 'bow-windows', enclosed window bays rising normally through two or more storeys. They had to be built on a metal frame rather than on a masonry structure in order to satisfy the authorities, who were reluctant to authorize structural additions to the facade beyond those approved in 1823. But they and other changes marked a willingness to reconsider the principles of the 1823 decree, which had been largely inspired by fear that tall vehicles might collide with projections in narrow streets.[7] The height changes were also limited, but they included the important principle that the roof profile might rise to a height greater than one storey. This was achieved by replacing the modest 1859 roof profile by a quadrant rising in the wider streets to a maximum of 8.5 metres. In many cases two attic floors could be constructed and the volume of the attics was almost always increased.

The result was an opportunity for a greater volume of decoration and projecting accommodation on the facade, and a larger roof with a greater potential for architectural treatment. Both the architects and the authorities nevertheless took the view within a few years that the changes were too restricted to have much effect on the design of new buildings. In its essence, therefore, the established Parisian apartment house continued to be built into the 1890s.

11.4 The building code inquiry

During the late 1880s and the 1890s there built up a general sense of dissatisfaction with Parisian domestic architecture. The main source of the *malaise* was the architects themselves, including those who worked for the city authorities as *architects-voyers* and in the more senior posts. The origins of this new thinking were complex. To some extent it reflected an awareness of developments in urban architecture abroad, especially in England and Belgium, and a movement of opinion within Parisian architectural circles that the city's architecture was failing to participate in the new international design currents. Instead, it was clinging through inertia to a Parisian or national tradition which no longer occupied, as it once undoubtedly had, the centre of the world stage. An important domestic influence was the growth of interest in historic buildings and townscapes which had begun in the 1880s.[8] Less tangible, but probably most influential of all, was the feeling that the somewhat severe and spartan style of the Second Empire, which now dominated Paris, was out of date. More varied, decorative and even pictur-esque designs were seen as appropriate to the more prosperous and leisured age which has come to be known as the *belle époque*.

Although it was by no means universally agreed that the building regulations were responsible for the lack of innovation in design, the main reformist pressure focused on them. The installation of a new Prefect of the Seine, Justin de Selves, in 1896 was seen as a key opportunity. Edmond Huet, who had replaced the Haussmannic stalwart, Jean Alphand, as director of works in 1891, wrote to the new Prefect calling for more generous regulations for projections.[9] Although Huet had been associated with a new mood of innovation in the post-Alphand years, he would not subsequently be concerned personally with the building regulations and it is likely that his letter was prompted, and even drafted by, the senior members of his architectural department. These would have been closely associated, in their turn, with the private architects of Paris.

The most important personality at this stage was almost certainly the Prefect himself. Justin de Selves was soon to be closely associated with a number of initiatives designed, in the broadest sense, to modernize the city and to bring it into closer touch with practice in foreign capitals. His creative reputation appears to have preceded him, Huet's letter for instance being dated several days in advance of his arrival at the Hôtel de Ville. De Selves would relate later, when the revised regulations were under heavy attack, that in the first month of his administration he had had discussions with the director of his architectural department, M. Bouvard, about the beauty of Paris and ways in which new buildings could be made attractive. Both men agreed that a powerful committee was needed, like the *Commission des artistes* which had replanned parts of Paris after the Revolution.[10] In this and other respects de Selves brought the Haussmannic era implicitly to an end, creating unprecedented scope for the reform of a century's tradition of building regulations.

De Selves, however, had no professional expertise to contribute to the elaboration of specific reforms, and the agenda was essentially set by the architects. The initial problem was to justify the review of building regulations which had undergone major revisions only fourteen years before. During the long debate over the reforms and their results, two main arguments were used. Huet, in his initial letter, made a largely utilitarian case. The existing regulations, he claimed, were – at any rate in certain respects – '. . . no longer in step . . . with advances in building and the needs of Parisian business.' He also blamed 'the constant rise in the price of building land' for the failure of owners to build back from the building line in order to include projections which would not intrude on the street. Underlying this argument, however, was a purely aesthetic aspiration, with Huet expressing implicit support for '. . . more pronounced and lively (mouvementés) projections which would give a less banal appearance to the houses and would contribute in this way to the embellishment of the city.'[11]

This aesthetic factor was developed by de Selves into a second major argument for reform. From his arrival in Paris, he evinced a lively and informed interest in the general question of the beauty of the city, which had begun to preoccupy Parisian artists and intellectuals in the late 1880s. This was also an International movement, with the work of Charles Buls in Brussels, and the 'public art' movement in general, being known in Paris by the mid-1890s. Less well known but equally representative of the international trend, were the writings of Camillo Sitte in Vienna, and the burgeoning City Beautiful movement in the United States. Paris, universally recognized as a paradigm of urban beauty, was more an example than a follower, but even a vague awareness that efforts were being made elsewhere to enhance urban beauty was enough to sharpen the Parisian debate. De Selves drew constantly on this climate of opinion in an effort to arouse enthusiasm for aesthetic affairs in general. As a consequence, he saw the reform of the building regulations as a major contributor to the beauty of Paris, rather than technical adjustment to current building practice.

11.5 The committee of inquiry

Prefect de Selves lost no time in setting up a committee to review the building regulations, on 13 June 1896. He restricted its remit to projections, much as Huet's letter had foreshadowed. There was, however, more in projections than met the eye. It was here that architects had put most pressure on the authorities to relax the regulations in specific cases.[12] Projections, moreover, were widely viewed by architects, and by de Selves, as the key element of a building for the creation of the desired new aesthetic, because they would break up the continuous, flat façades and roof lines of Haussmannic Paris. Practicality and the broad view could thus be readily reconciled in the projection question. The committee was a large body which met only at the beginning and the end of the

inquiry, and then on a mainly formal basis. The detailed work was done by two sub-committees, staffed from the general committee. The committee, and consequently the sub-committees, were composed almost entirely of architects. Of the grand total of 17 architects, 15 were employed by the Prefecture of the Seine. The remaining two were Parisian architects nominated by the *Société centrale des architectes*, the principal national association of practising architects.[13]

This composition was striking in two respects. On the one hand, this was the first time that the Parisian community of architects had been allowed to draw up new regulations *ab initio*, previous regulations having been administrative creations.[14] On the other hand, representatives of builders, owners, tenants, and public health experts were entirely absent from the committee. This bias towards architecture was justified by the architects themselves on the grounds that the previous reform procedure of 1880–4 had been dominated by public health considerations, and that the new inquiry was intended to make good its glaring aesthetic deficiencies.[15]

What reconciled, perhaps, these two contradictory characteristics was that most of the architects on the committee were municipal employees, exercising a broad range of functions – most of them highly practical and not biased towards aesthetics. In numerical terms, the predominant member was the *architecte-voyer*, a distinctive official whose origins dated back to the *Ancien régime*. The fundamental role of these officials in Parisian building has been so neglected that it requires a word of explanation here. Each of the 20 *arrondissements* of Paris had at least one *architecte-voyer*. His main duty was to inspect building plans and to liaise with the architect when modifications were required. Often in touch with a design from its earliest stages, he exercised a more or less subtle influence on a large number of projects and could set his mark on an entire *arrondissement*. What made this system tolerable to the mass of private architects was that the *architects-voyers* were themselves fully qualified, and usually very capable, architects who normally carried on a private practice in addition to their municipal duties. The post of *architecte-voyer* had its attractions for these people, principally because it was less onerous than an independent career and offered an involvement in a wider range of architectural activity. They thus acquired a wider range of experience than most independent architects and were widely regarded as authorities on both the theory and the practicalities of Parisian architecture. In fact, the most influential figure in the whole inquiry was to be an *architecte-voyer*, Louis Bonnier. Bonnier was an experienced and respected figure who used his position of *architecte-voyer* of the thirteenth *arrondissement* over a number of years to establish himself as an authority on precisely the issue which concerned the inquiry, the relationship between architectural creativity and the necessary regulation of building in a congested city.[16] Not initially appointed to the inquiry, Bonnier was one of two *architectes-voyers* who secured their own appointments after the nominations were announced.[17] Although Bonnier was to claim later that there had been some opposition to his appointment within the Prefecture, the addition of two further *architectes-voyers* to a committee that was already loaded with them implied that the authorities expected this unique group to be the main source of the revisions.

11.6 The new architectural vision

A brief meeting of the main committee in July 1896 inaugurated the review proceedings. Speeches by Huet and Bouvard made clear that the main objective of the inquiry was an aesthetic one.[18] Indeed, Bouvard would later be even more explicit: 'The very essence of the planned decree is to facilitate the decoration of buildings.'[19] In practice, however, other considerations would loom large.

The administrative sub-committee was the first to start work, under the chairmanship of the distinguished architect and painter, Paul Sédille. His appointment reflected the official desire to carry through as radical a review as possible. Sédille was one of the two nominees of the *Société centrale*. He had a reputation as a modern architect thanks partly to his reconstruction of the Printemps department store, an exercise in glass and iron. He had designed numerous apartment houses, in contrast to most of the leading architects of the day. Finally, he had an unusual English connection. He was probably unrivalled in France in his admiration of the picturesque tradition in English architecture, and particularly its recent manifestations. He was an honorary corresponding member of the RIBA. In 1890 he had published a book, *L'architecture moderne en Angleterre*, mainly featuring the Gothic revival, in which fulsome praise spilled over into an extreme version of the *anglomanie* which affected the other arts in the period, but which was much less prominent in architecture.[20] Unfortunately, Sédille proved to be subject to bouts of illness which prevented his attending a number of meetings and probably contributed to the relaxed chairmanship which prolonged its work. In fact, Sédille died in 1900, shortly after the sub-committee disbanded and he did nothing to impose personal solutions on his colleagues.[21]

The early meetings of the sub-committee revealed a great enthusiasm for a greater toleration of projections. Proposals were put forward from a number of sources but as time passed, one man, Louis Bonnier, came to the fore, as the chairman of the working group responsible for the drafting of precise revisions to the regulations. He combined a sense of the practical and a considerable expertise with a design philosophy incorporating and amplifying the goals expressed by de Selves and Bouvard. Bonnier's ideal was 'the picturesque', which he contrasted with 'the deplorable, infinite perspective of the streets of modern Paris'.[22] Like Huet, he referred to a rapid change in Parisian life since 1882, both in its appearance and in its style of life (*moeurs*).[23] The main novelty, however, was Bonnier's concept of beauty (*l'esthétique*) as a public right which should shape the new regulations just as their predecessors had been determined by hygiene – which itself had been conceived as public property. More than once he repeated the dictum: '. . . aesthetics is not a luxury for a people, but a need and a right just as hygiene is.'[24] Bonnier was less precise in his presentation of the likely product of the new aesthetics, but he clearly favoured breaking up the facades with setbacks and greenery, incorporating decorative elements into the structure, applying colour both to the buildings and the pavement, and encouraging an eclectic mixture of building styles. These would include styles drawn from the past – he once referred approvingly to the recent development of the fashionable Avenue de Villiers

district as using 'all the fantasies of the architecture of the past'[25] All this amounted to a major challenge to the traditional Paris design aesthetic. There was, however, not a hint of 'modern' architecture or its associated rhetoric.

11.7 Looking upwards: skylines and roofs

Very early in its discussions, the sub-committee agreed that to encourage larger, more ambitious projections required them to consider roofs. The technical justification was that the new projections would often need to terminate above the top of the facade in the form of turrets, finials, loggias, or incorporated dormer windows. However, there is a wealth of circumstantial evidence to suggest that the prefectoral administration had intended from the start that the inquiry should include roofs. Its main motive was the further pursuit of the picturesque, but it may have been aware that only in the roof could the authorities permit the creation of extra floor space without challenging the historic principles underlying the Paris building code. There is no evidence to support this inference. However, the association of projections and roofs was present in the proposed new regulations submitted at the very start of the inquiry by the *Société centrale*. The committee which drew up these proposals had Louis Bonnier as its secretary, while its chairman, an honorary *architecte-voyer*, was also a member of the Sédille sub-committee.

In June 1897 the technical sub-committee started work.[26] There was some overlap in membership, but independent architectural expertise was more prominent. The chairman was Charles Garnier, architect of the neo-baroque opera house (1861) and by now acknowledged as the leading authority on Parisian architecture and aesthetics. Among his many interests was the conservation of historic buildings in Paris, so his judgement spanned both the past and the future in a way which won him the respect of both the authorities and the whole of the architectural profession.

Partly owing to the change in membership, the new sub-committee was more in favour of drawing on foreign experience than the Sédille committee had been. The appointment of Emile Trélat, the leading public health expert – not to say enthusiast – among the Parisian architects, meant that aesthetics could no longer be considered in isolation (though Trélat's ideal of a city of wide streets and low buildings, with minimal projections in order to maximize natural lighting, was out of tune with the general sentiments of the sub-committee). Ironically, Trélat's rooted objection to projections led him to espouse the Second Empire aesthetic as the only one appropriate to the 'city of Haussmann'. He found himself completely isolated on this point as well as on the hygienic issue, and his frequent and lengthy interventions, ironically, tended to reinforce the dominant consensus.

Most of Trélat's interventions on public health were made in the context of the building heights issue, which arose in the new sub-committee even before much work had been done on projections. Garnier was sympathetic to this extension of his remit, referring to the Prefect's general objective of allowing architects to 'make Paris more beautiful'.[27] On 8 July 1897 he allowed his sub-committee to discuss heights, pending his request for prefectoral approval.

Opinions were mixed, but there was a strong argument for allowing greater heights in wide streets of more than twenty metres[28] This was more a commercial than an aesthetic case, and from this point onwards the whole character of the inquiry would begin to change.

11.8 Building heights as the main issue

Before Garnier could make much use of his new remit, there intervened one of those long summer breaks which typify French official life. When activities began again, in October 1897, de Selves set up a completely separate committee to study building heights. The official reason for this step was that the projections inquiry could study only those aspects of heights that related to projections. However, the sequence of events suggested that the administration already wanted to review the height regulations and had used Garnier's approach as a pretext. In practice, however, there was no brutal digression. The membership of the new committee was much the same as the old, with Louis Bonnier in particular retaining his influential role, as *rapporteur* of the sub-committee which carried out all the detailed study.

When the heights committee held its inaugural meeting on 23 November 1897, Bouvard's introduction again stressed aesthetics and called for great care in dealing with heights:

> It is my personal opinion, gentlemen, that if there is good reason to allow bigger projections on the facades, we ought to be more careful about heights, for an increase here would do nothing to improve the appearance of Paris. . . . Speaking personally, I think that the only extensions should be in matters of detail.[29]

No doubt subdued by this official caution, the administrative sub-committee on heights generated less excitement than the projections discussions. Instead, it became involved in both minor matters and issues of principle which were so broad that they became sterile. However, the proceedings marked a significant shift of interest from aesthetic issues to the relationship between the regulations and building economics. Under Sédille's chairmanship, the administrative sub-committee on heights made a start similar to that of the administrative sub-committee on projections. Bonnier introduced a draft heights code submitted by the *Société centrale des architectes* – and no doubt prepared, for the most part, by himself. The *Société* did not recommend an increase in heights, even in the widest streets, concentrating instead on a more precise relation of heights to street widths. To help compensate owners for the absence of a more generous concession, no increase in the minimum ceiling height was proposed above the existing 2.6 metres, notwithstanding its advocacy in public health circles.[30] However, the code did include one radical proposal which in later forms would be of great influence on the building history of Paris.

This idea involved departing from the idea of a maximum vertical facade height, related to street width. Change was possible without serious disruption of building practice because of the existing principle according to which facades should not break a line drawn at a 45° angle from the opposite side of

the street. As this line continued to rise above its point of intersection with the top of the facade, it created further space, much of it normally occupied by the roof, but built according to the special regulations relating to roofs which produced a much smaller volume. To create rectangular storeys in this way, rather than cramped attics, would go some way towards meeting the demands of owners who, thanks to the diffusion of passenger lifts in the richer parts of the city, were already planning luxurious accommodation on the upper floors of new buildings.[31]

Later developments would show that the proposal was linked to an even more radical innovation involving setting back the whole of the facade from the street, and allowing greater height in compensation. This proposal may have been linked to the influential municipal engineer, Eugène Hénard, whom Marrey has identified as Bonnier's associate in the preparation of the draft regulations.[32] It took an even more radical form in the scheme advocated in the sub-committee with some force by Eugène-Georges Debrie, *architecte-voyer* of the thirteenth *arrondissement*. Debrie, aware of the new building techniques and electric lifts, began from the principle that owners had the right to build up to any height, provided that the interests of third parties were not threatened.[33] These heights should be related to open spaces on all sides of the building, and not just to street width, producing 'un système de pyramide capable', a pyramidal volume receding at an angle of 45° and permitting many buildings to rise in ziggurat form above traditional heights, without damaging recognized lighting standards. Debrie envisaged Parisian buildings rising overall to heights of up to fifty metres, roughly twice the current maximum.[34]

All in all, these ideas had great potential for achieving extra height and floorspace, in line with the inclinations of the owners and technical developments, without undermining established principles of hygiene. As such, they appear to have had the support of the administration, no doubt from the moment of their formulation by Bonnier. However, it would eventually emerge that they, together with related changes in the roof regulations, would be seen as threatening the traditional Parisian aesthetic.

Initially, however, the sub-committee's discussions on the height proposals became bogged down in questions of owners' rights versus tenants' rights. When Sédille, as chairman, tried to change tack by asking Bonnier to bring forward his report on height regulations in foreign cities, a lengthy bout of reading aloud again resulted. After two sessions had been occupied in this way, the Paris debate resumed without significant reference to foreign example. Instead, the discussion centred on greater building heights versus greater ceiling heights. The hygienists were represented on both sides, and various trade-off formulae were proposed. Sédille wanted the sub-committee to retain existing heights, but he secured no consensus. Bonnier, on the other hand, allied himself with the view of a number of members that an increase in heights could be justified if the minimum ceiling height were increased.[35] This issue of compensation was all the more important because the administration had put the question of courts and airshafts on the agenda, after they had secured inadequate attention in previous regulations. If their minimum area were to increase, only greater heights could compensate the owners. Although the debate on the regulations affecting the interior of sites is too lengthy and technical to be discussed in detail here, it contributed towards a movement towards greater heights related to more open space around the structure.

This step towards the planning concepts of twentieth century modernism was, however, only one of the ideas considered – in no visible order of preference – by the sub-committee. With one exception, the members were generally sympathetic to the idea of greater heights. There was general agreement that owners could not be deprived of rights embodied in previous legislation. This meant that tougher regulations on courts and airshafts, linked to growing concern over the Paris tuberculosis problem, were seen as requiring compensation in the form of greater heights[36] Unfortunately, Sédille's lax chairmanship prevented the sub-committee from agreeing clear proposals. The discussion rambled on until October 1898 when Bouvard made a formal visit, asking the sub-committee on behalf of the Prefect to complete its work as soon as possible.[37]

The work of the committee was now transformed. Meeting were held once a week instead of once a fortnight, and Bonnier, who had been a minor participant in the multiple discussion of principles, now came more to the fore as the source of many essential working documents. By December, Sédille could announce that the work of the sub-committee was at an end, leaving Bonnier to prepare the sub-committee's report.

These two months of practical study had removed some of the more grandiose reform concepts generated by the sub-committee during its more expansive phase. Bonnier's report stressed the minor nature of the changes proposed.[38] He implied that the study of foreign examples had tended to confirm the validity of Parisian practice. A fascinating passage revealed, for the first time in the whole inquiry, that he at least was aware that the most striking examples of tall building lay outside Europe altogether. However, these had not been examined because '. . . the *"buildings"* [towers, skyscrapers] of America still seemed a long way off to us.'[39] Instead, Bonnier maintained that the sub-committee had finished where it began, by emphasizing at all points the principle of proportionality – as, for instance, in the proportionality between the height of the facade and the width of the street. That proportionality was, he went on, '. . . basically just one of the forms of equity.'[40]

This philosophical distillation is so little present in the minutes that it seems to be part of Bonnier's efforts to create a coherent image. However, it clearly reflected the Parisian building and design tradition dating back to the Renaissance. It showed, moreover, that major departures from the existing controls were not to be expected. At the same time, it allowed Bonnier to present the proposed reforms as a single formula, with new restrictions being counterbalanced by concessions. Maximum heights were reduced on the narrower streets, but a new formula for roof sections allowed greater roof heights, especially in wide streets and on deep sites. However, there would be no increase in facade heights even on very wide streets, even though during its more imaginative phase the sub-committee had shown much interest in an increase up to a maximum of 22 metres. Balancing these concessions were more stringent standards designed to achieve better lighting in courts and airshafts.[41]

11.9 From inquiry to implementation

Lengthy and sometimes diffuse as the discussions had been, they had produced a collection of reforms capable of resisting major changes in the numerous examinations which they still had to undergo. The sub-commission of the technical committee on heights, meeting between May and June 1899, worked fast and, thanks partly to overlapping personnel, endorsed the Bonnier proposals.[42] The agreement of the full committee on heights was purely formal and on 20 October 1899 the Prefect sent the new regulations, incorporating the regulations approved by the projections committee, to the City Council. Two months later the Council approved them by acclaim.[43] The vice-chairman of the third committee (thoroughfares), who brought the regulations before the Council, based his case on the need to maintain the beauty and distinction of Paris without imposing restrictions on architects which would force them either to break the rules or to perform beneath their potential, as had been the case in recent years.[44] This measured report, which was read out to the Council *in extenso*, may well have helped to secure the Council's approval without a word of debate. However, it suggested that educated Parisians saw the changes as aesthetic in character rather than related to public health and building. There were to be less happy reflections of this perspective in later years.

The regulations then had to go to the Ministry of the Interior, where they were studied by an expert body, the *Conseil général des bâtiments civils.*[45] A number of amendments, mainly affecting courtyards, were sent to the Prefect and the revised regulations were approved by the City Council on 12 July 1901.[46] After a minor detour through the Ministry of the Interior, they subsequently went to the *Conseil d'Etat*, in November 1901.[47]

One of the main tasks of the *Conseil d'Etat* was to restrain over-ambitious local authorities, especially where the interests of private property were affected, but it was sympathetic to the new regulations. A valuable link with the city authorites was maintained, notably by the inclusion of Bonnier in the discussions. Like the *Counseil général des bâtiments civils*, it expressed especial interest in the new courtyard and interior space regulations, which infringed on private property to an extent for which it was difficult to compensate. After lengthy debates in June 1902, the *Conseil d'Etat* gave its approval, the only amendments being those confirmed by Bonnier on behalf of the city authorities.[48] With this important hurdle cleared, the regulations were embodied in a decree signed by the President of the Republic on 13 August 1902.[49]

11.10 The aftermath

The official presentation of the new regulations as a modest measure was not questioned at the time of their adoption, and there was no visible popular reaction. The whole review, which had lasted for six years at the hands of a number of expert bodies, might therefore be regarded as a triumph of tradition, leading to a prolongation of the established Paris building forms with which this discussion began. Ironically, however, within a few years the application of the new building code had produced an unprecedented popular outcry. This public ire was directed not at the survival of traditional forms, but, on the contrary, at the desecration of the townscape and the creation of disturbing architectural designs. Such a reaction marked a further step away from modernism.

The new regulations came into effect during a period of gradual decline in Paris building, which lasted from 1897 to 1909. Global trends do not suggest that they were in themselves a stimulus to building but, within a few years, numerous large apartment houses had been built – especially in the wealthy west of the city. A building upturn from 1910 included many more such houses. The main additional latitude accorded to owners was in the projections on the facade, and in the roof space above the facade. Just as the existing permitted volume of the building had for some time past been completely filled by the owner in order to maximize rentable space, the new regulations were used in the same way. This is not the place to discuss the resulting design changes. They did not however normally generate the imaginative turrets, spires, loggias and other picturesque features for which De Selves and his inquiry had hoped. As for the larger volumes permitted in many roof spaces, these normally produced an additional floor – or even two floors – fully occupying the bulbous section conceded by the new regulations. These massive roofs resembled a completely capsized ship-of-the-line. Since 1898 the City of Paris had held an annual contest for the best new facades, but the post-1902 results were held to be, for the most part, conventional and unimaginative by the jury members.

This continuity would not normally have disturbed Parisian opinion, which was not closely in touch with the ideas of the more advanced architects. What aroused general concern was the impact of a small number of large, new buildings on historic monuments and treasured views. Critics maintained that the new regulations had been abused in some cases to produce excessive heights, for instance at the Etoile and the Champ-de-Mars. Bonnier eventually admitted that distortions had occurred, and the regulations were modified from 1908 to prevent the worst abuses.[50] However, it proved possible to restrict the height and bulk of new buildings in protected zones around listed buildings and historic sites, and the essentials of the new building code survived this difficult passage.

No further reform of the building regulations took place until a completely new code was introduced in 1967,[51] In 1909 the study of Paris building regulations had been brought under the control of a State body, the Commission on Monumental Perspectives. This prolonged the life of the 1902 decree because procedures for preparing its replacement were so complicated, and because a greater importance was given to the protection of the townscape. Thus, the 1902 regulations linked the 1850s and the 1960s, when radical changes were at last made in belated homage to modern architecture and France's new wave of industrialization.

11.11 The building code inquiry and French modernization

Economic and social historians usually regard France as one of the slower European industrializers.[52] Although there is no necessary link between a poor

economic performance and societal backwardness, some historians have detected in France a widespread amalgam of prejudice, privilege, and general slackness and muddle.[53] The building code inquiry permits an examination of French institutions in an area – architecture – in which the country enjoyed an acknowledged primacy. Were the same defects visible?

The outstanding feature of the whole procedure was that it was conducted almost exclusively by architects. Within the architect group the most influential participants were the Paris *architectes-voyers*, one of whom, Louis Bonnier, gradually emerged as the unofficial author of the reforms. Indeed, his close association with the strategic objectives of the administration, which seems not to have wanted major changes, may well explain why he was not nominated to the inquiry in the first instance. However, as one follows the records of the inquiry, Bonnier emerges as that classic figure in French administrative reform – the gifted enthusiast – who conceives and carries through a major policy change either single-handed or with the help of a group of friends and associates, most of them in non-official positions. In a country like nineteenth century France, where the bulk of domestic reform legislation was carried through the legislature in the form of private members' Bills, individual authorship of municipal reforms should cause no surprise.[54] Bonnier clearly carried out his task very well, helping to attach architectural credibility to minor changes. However, other features of the inquiry cannot be justified so easily.

These features relate to the field of expert evidence, and the representation of legitimate interests. The absence of submissions from the building and property industry is perhaps the most striking gap. No owners or builders, and no representatives of their associations, were called before the prefectoral inquiry. Nor were they invited to submit written evidence. The rare references to the property interests were made by architect members of the committees, who clearly felt that they were in touch with this field of business endeavour. Admittedly, it should be made clear that *no* witnesses were brought before the prefectoral inquiry, and that the only outside evidence sought related to building regulations in other cities (which was virtually ignored). There was perhaps a tacit assumption that the administration would bring forward most of the necessary evidence, but the record gives no sign that information was provided, other than in relation to the existing condition of the building regulations.

One should expect neither the *Conseil d'Etat* nor the *Conseil général des bâtiments civils* to make up this deficit as they were purely administrative and technical bodies, expected solely to identify weaknesses and contradictions in local proposals. The records of the *Conseil d'Etat* confirm that no outside evidence was brought in. The unfortunate gap in the records of the *Conseil général* leaves a trace of uncertainty, but the indirect evidence suggests that its review was staffed mainly by architects, whose combined competence was deemed adequate. It is, of course, difficult to estimate the potential contribution of experts who were not called. Engineers might have spoken of the development of building techniques and lift technology. The official response here would no doubt have been that some of the architect members of the inquiry had engineering qualifications. More important, in view of the

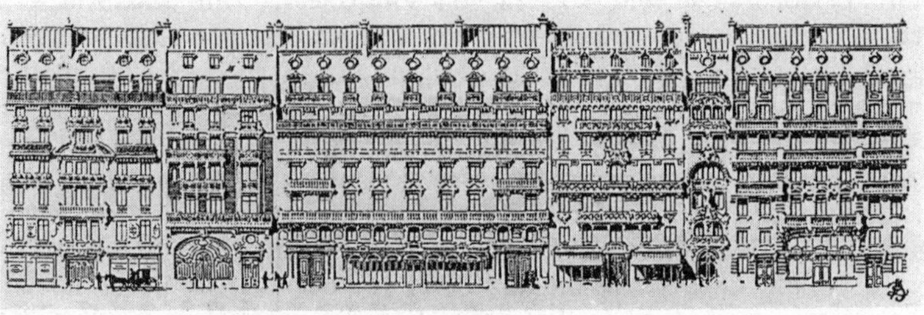

Figure 11.1 One of the elevations drawn by Louis Bonnier to demonstrate the likely impact of the 1902 building code. This is a hypothetical street of twenty metres developed under the 1882 regulations at maximum intensity.

Figure 11.2 A hypothetical street of thirty metres developed under the 1902 regulations. Although such a result was entirely conceivable, Bonnier was clearly at pains to emphasize the potential contrast, especially in terms of verticality, variety, relief, and picturesque effects.

constant reference to hygiene, was the absence of evidence from public health experts. Trélat and one or two others spoke at length on public health, but as architects they lacked precision, objectivity, and up-to-date knowledge in a field that was developing very rapidly. It might of course be said that the length of Trélat's interventions made up for the absence of other health experts, but the real weakness of his contribution lay in his relentless and repetitive advocacy of hygienic standards which would have turned Paris into a garden suburb. Not until the very end of the proceedings, on 27 July 1899, did a medically qualified person contribute to the discussion, when Dr A.J. Martin asked some questions as a member of the technical sub-committee.[55] Significantly, his public health goals were much less ambitious than those of Trélat, though this was perhaps due to his association with the administration.

Ironically, it was in the field of architecture and aesthetics that the strongest signs of modernization were visible. Although the debates in the sub-

Figure 11.3 Perspective view of thirty-metre street. Note the effect of the projections, particularly where they are incorporated into the taller roofs. Each building is more of an individual statement, and the perspective effect of the continuous facades is reduced. The result stresses individualism both on the part of the architect and the building owner.

committees were broad, diffuse, and often confusing, a strong impression was given that the traditional Parisian aesthetic scheme, dating back to the Renaissance, no longer generated confidence. Instead, the broad concept of 'the picturesque', the origins of which in Paris dated back to the 1880s, was taken up with much enthusiasm. The sub-commissions, nevertheless, made no effort to discuss examples of picturesque architecture in foreign cities such as Vienna and Brussels. Camillo Sitte, Europe's main anti-classical theorist, was never mentioned. Bonnier alone seemed willing to refer systematically to foreign example, with his dossier of foreign building regulations and the impressive elevations and perspectives, with their Belgian and German aura, which he drew to show the desired effects of the new regulations. (See Figures 11.1–11.5) On the other hand, the participants all knew that since the mid-1890s the administration had been permitting experimental exceptions to the regulations, particularly in relation to projections, and the resulting examples of 'the picturesque' must have been well known to the *architectes-voyers*.[56] However, individual examples and case histories of these experiments were never discussed. As far as the record shows, no sub-committee ever made a site visit. Not a single photograph, lantern slide, drawing or print was ever displayed. Not one model was ever made, still less the kind of adjustable model which could demonstrate the impact of different courtyard regulations. All

Figure 11.4 Bonnier's version of the narrow street. This perspective of a six-metre street indicates the maximum development possible under the 1884 regulations.

was, as it is said, *dans la tête*. However, here we may have encountered, not an absence of modern procedures, but a national professional demeanour – which still survives today in a fully modernized France. Powerful professions can sustain change even if their work and philosophy stress continuity.

A similar foundation for change was the stony structure of the city of Paris. As a massive accumulation of capital, with a distribution of land values evolving on predictable lines, it was the main conservative influence on the building regulation review. It gradually emerged from the debates that the administration would permit neither a major increase nor a major reduction in the building rights of the owners, which were regarded as a legally established freedom closely linked to the structure of property. No changes could be allowed which, for instance, would distort the existing land value structure.[57] This economic and political reality meant that there was no scope for a revolution in Parisian architecture, for all the talk of the picturesque. The reforms did what was to be expected in the circumstances. They allowed peripheral accretions to be added to the frontages, and they inflated the roofs. 'Decoration' was indeed the appropriate term, though a minor increase in floorspace was permitted to compensate for the increase in the area of interior spaces which, in such a cramped city, made no contribution to the townscape and rarely offered scope for architectural excellence.

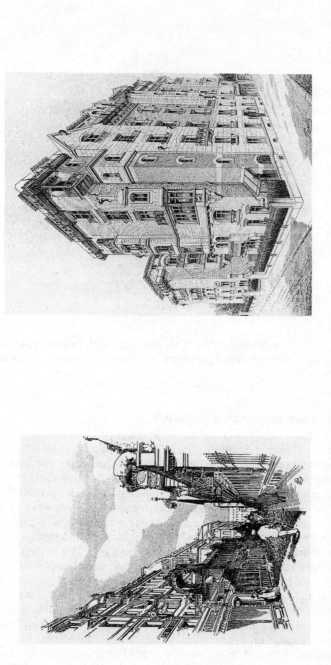

Figure 11.5 Under the 1902 regulations, setbacks are encouraged to gain extra height, but the vibrant atmosphere of the street is preserved by a low row of commercial premises. The committee was aware of the London example, where many front gardens on main roads in the inner suburbs had been filled with single-storey shops. Very little of this development was undertaken after 1902 in Paris, as owners believed that their economic advantage still lay in building to full height at the frontage.

Figure 11.6 Castel Béranger, by Hector Guimard. Built in 1898 under special building regulations anticipating the forthcoming reforms, this is the best known of the radical apartment house designs associated with the new building code of 1902. It won fourth prize in the Paris facades competition of 1898.

Figure 11.7 This house in the Boulevard de la Villette won sixth prize in 1898. It may well have benefited from relaxed regulations but the style does not mark a sharp break with the past.

11.12 Modernization and continuity: a postscript

Even a discussion highlighting continuity within modernization must have some limits, and there can be no room here to do full justice to the ironic developments of the 1970s and the 1980s. The new building regulations of 1967, which had been unofficially in force since 1961, were a spectacular departure from tradition – permitting much greater heights and volumes, and breaking up the intimate, enclosed streetscape in deference to modern planning concepts. This new approach sprang from the revolutionary modernization philosophy of the Fifth Republic. However, by the early 1970s Parisian opinion had turned strongly against many of the non-traditional results of the new regulations and, in 1974, a new code was introduced. With their related planning policy, the 1974 regulations marked a return to tradition – limiting heights and requiring building at the *alignement*. Much new building since 1974 has been of a modest, conformist character, but even more striking has been the movement of capital into the refurbishment of older buildings. In this recent episode the links between modernization, tradition and professional expertise still have to be examined in detail. It echoes, nevertheless, some of the features of the 1902 debate and, through that episode, echoes some of the issues of the 1780s, which were themselves defined by an older Paris. Cities

Figure 11.8 This house on the Quai d'Orsay was premiated in the facades competition of 1910. Built for a rich clientele, it represented the best of architectural practice for the period. The importance of projections is clear, but even more striking is the pyramidal roof which the open site made possible. The style, however, is clearly linked to pre-1902 traditions, with swags, vases set in niches, and a giant order of pilasters rising through three storeys. Buildings of this type, rather than the Castel Béranger, set the tone for Parisian domestic architecture until the First World War.

may rightly be regarded as the vortex of change during industrialization, but as a locus for continuity they may play a bigger role than has previously been acknowledged.

Notes

1 But see Evenson, Norma, 1979, *Paris: a century of change, 1878–1978*, Yale University Press, New Haven. Rebecca Neeves, a University of Leicester Ph.D. student, is about to submit a thesis on building regulation in Sheffield before 1914.

2 See e.g. Muthesius, Stefan, 1982, *The English terraced house*, Yale University Press, New Haven.

3 See e.g. Muthesius, *The English terraced house;* Olsen, Donald J., 1986, *The city as a work of art*, Yale University Press, New Haven; Loyer, François, 1987, *Paris XIXe siècle: l'immeuble et la rue*, Fernand Hazan, Paris.

4   A classic example is Chemetov, Paul and Marrey, Bernard, 1980, *Architectures: Paris, 1848–1914*, Dunod, Paris.
5   The best survey of the history of Paris building regulation is to be found in 'L'évolution des formes au travers des règlements', *Paris-Projet*, 13/14, n.d. [1975], pp. 24–36. For the texts of the regulations, see Jourdan, M.G., 1887, *Recueil de règlements concernant le service des alignements et les logements insalubres dans la Ville de Paris*, Imprimerie Chaix, Paris.
6   See Loyer, *Paris XIX siècle*, pp. 48–49.
7   See Bonnier, Lous, 1903, *Les règlements de voirie*, Charles Schmid, Paris, p. 6.
8   The only full account is still Sutcliffe, Anthony, 1970, *The autumn of central Paris: the defeat of town planning, 1850–1970*, Edward Arnold, London, pp. 179–212.
9   Bouvard, M. and Jourdan, M.C., 1900, *Documents relatifs à la révision des décrets: (1) du 22 juillet sur les saillies permises dans la Ville de Paris; (2) du 23 juillet 1884 sur la hauteur des maisons, les combles et les lucarnes dans la Ville de Paris*, Chaix, Paris, p. 2.
10   Conseil municipal de Paris, *Procès-verbaux*, 9 June 1909, pp. 902–5. De Selves was Prefect of the Seine from 1896 to 1911. His legal career had led him to four previous prefectures and the director-generalship of the Post Office. In 1910 his aesthetic preoccupations won him an independent membership of the *Académie des Beaux-arts*. He was later to hold two senior ministerial portfolios and he served for three years as President of the Senate. This outstanding record requires no comment other than that his qualities were quite visibly recognized and appreciated on all sides throughout his Parisian administration. See Casselle, P., 1977, *Les préfets de la Seine et les préfets de Paris, 1800–1977*, Préfecture de Paris, Bibliothèque Administrative, Paris.
11   Bouvard and Jourdan, *Documents*, p. 2.
12   Bonnier, *Règlements de voirie*, p. 8.
13   Bouvard and Jourdan, *Documents*, pp. 2–5.
14   Anon., 1882, *Examen du projet de décret sur la hauteur des bâtiments . . .*, Ducher et Cie, Paris, p. 16.
15   See Préfecture du Départmement de la Seine, 1881, *Documents relatifs à la révision des règlements sur les constructions et à la salubrité intérieure des bâtiments dans Paris*, Préfecture de la Seine, Paris.
16   Bonnier's standing has recently been confirmed by Marrey, Bernard, 1988, *Louis Bonnier 1856–1946*, Pierre Mardaga, Liège.
17   Bonnier, *Règlements de voirie*, p. 9.
18   Bouvard and Jourdan, *Documents*, pp. 77–8.
19   *Ibid.*, p. 86.
20   See his biography in *Revue encyclopédique, 1900*, Larousse, Paris, 1900. pp. 273–4.
21   The author is grateful to Bernard Marrey for his perception of Sédille's capacities towards the end of his life.
22   Bouvard and Jourdan, *Documents*, pp. 33, 57. Loyer traces the origins of the Parisian picturesque movement back to the early 1880s. See *Paris XIXe siècle*, pp. 402–6.
23   *Ibid.*, p. 55.
24   *Ibid.*, p. 58.
25   *Ibid.*, pp. 57–8.
26   *Ibid.*, pp. 105ff.
27   *Ibid.*, pp. 111–2.
28   *Ibid.*, p. 113
29   *Ibid.*, p. 412.
30   *Ibid.*, pp. 234–5.

31 Examples of this new, top-heavy, type of apartment block are to be found in *Le parisien chez lui au XIXe siècle, 1814-1914* (exhibition catalogue), 1976, Archives Nationales, Paris.

32 See Marrey, *Louis Bonnier*. For the later development of Hénard's ideas on setbacks, see his, 1903-9, *Etudes sur les transformations de Paris*, Librairies-imprimeries réunies, Paris.

33 Bouvard and Jourdan, *Documents*, pp. 357-8.

34 The first use of the term 'système de pyramide capable', to be taken up by Bonnier in his subsequent review of the 1902 regulations, is to be found at *ibid.*, pp. 239-40.

35 *Ibid.*, p. 244.

36 The special character of the Paris tuberculosis problem, which tended to impregnate all public health issues from the later 1880s to the 1930s, is discussed in Sutcliffe, *Autumn*, pp. 108-14.

37 Bouvard and Jourdan, *Documents*, p. 273.

38 The text of Bonnier's report is in *ibid.*, pp. 297-347.

39 *Ibid.*, p. 299.

40 *Ibid.*, p. 300.

41 *Ibid.*, p. 300-4.

42 *Ibid.*, pp. 465-72.

43 Conseil municipal de Paris, *Procès-verbaux*, 28 December 1899, p. 1321.

44 Conseil municipal de Paris, *Rapports et documents*, 1899, p. 511.

45 See Magny, Charles, 1911, *Des moyens juridiques de sauvegarder les aspects esthétiques de la ville de Paris*, Bernard Tignol, Paris, p. 70. The relevant records of the *Conseil général des bâtiments civils* fall within a lengthy period for which the *Archives Nationales* have no deposits. As it was the normal practice of the *Conseil* to make such deposits, it is unlikely that these papers remain in a government office.

46 Conseil municipal de Paris, *Procès-verbaux*, 12 July 1901, pp. 410-11.

47 See Rapport à Monsieur le Ministre de l'Intérieur [by Direction de l'Administration Départementale et Communale], 4 November 1901 (Archives du Conseil d'Etat, Intérieur 129,674).

48 For the key discussions, see Conseil d'Etat, Procès-verbaux, Annexes, 1902, pp. 767-887. On this occasion at any rate, the *Conseil d'Etat* was far from reflecting the atrocious reputation for obfuscation and obstructionism which it acquired during the nineteenth century and still retains.

49 *Journal Officiel*, 22 August 1902, pp 5781—5.

50 Commission des Perspectives Monumentales, 1938, *Révision du décret du 13 août 1902 portant règlement sur les hauteurs et sur les saillies des bâtiments dans la Ville de Paris* Ministère de l'Education Nationale, Paris, pp. 2, 4.

51 See *Paris-projet*, nos. 13/14, n.d. [1975], p. 36.

52 See e.g. Kemp, T., 1972, *The French economy, 1913-39: the history of a decline*, Longman: London.

53 The best essay on these lines is Zeldin, Theodore, 1973-9, *France, 1848-1945* (3 vols.), Clarendon Press, Oxford.

54 The drafting of major legislation by gifted amateurs is discussed at greater length in Sutcliffe, *Towards the planned city*, pp. 150-4.

55 Bouvard and Jourdan, *Documents*, p. 496.

56 *Ibid.*, p. 164.

57 See e.g. *ibid.*, p. 466.

Sidney Pollard's publications

Books

1 *Three Centuries of Sheffield Steel*, (Sheffield: Marsh Brothers, 1954) pp. 82.
2 W.M. Thomas (ed.), *A Survey of English Economic History*, (London: Blackie, 1957), pp. 568 2nd ed. 1960, 3rd, enlarged ed. 1967 (Co-authors: D.C. Coleman and K.G.T. McDonnell).
3 *Sheffield Trades Council 1858–1958*, (Sheffield, 1958), pp. 105.
4 *A History of Labour in Sheffield, 1850–1939*, (Liverpool: Liverpool University Press, 1959), pp. 372.
5 *Shirley Aldred & Co. Ltd. 1796–1958*, (Worksop, 1958), pp. 41.
6 *The Development of the British Economy, 1914–1950*. (London: Arnold, 1962), pp. 422 reprinted 1963, 1967. New edition, including new chapter, covering 1950–1967 (1969), pp. 517 Paperback ed.
7 *The Idea of Progress: History and Society* (London: C.A. Watts, 1968) 215 pp. Hardcover edition published by Basic Books Inc. of New York, 1968, pp. xii + 220. Paperback edition published by Penguin, in Great Britain and in the U.S.A. 1971.
8 *The Genesis of Modern Management: A Study of the Industrial Revolution in Great Britain* (London: Arnold, Cambridge: Harvard U.P. 1965) 358 pp. (Penguin ed. 1968) 391 pp. Awarded the prize of the American Newcomen Society as the best book on Business History for the years 1964–1966.
9 with D.W. Crossley, *The Wealth of Britain, 1085–1966* (London: Batsford, 1968), 303 pp. Braille ed. 1972. Paperback ed. 1972.
10. with C. Holmes, *Documents of European Economic History*, Vol. I: *The Process of Industrialization, 1750–1870* (London: Arnold, 1968) pp 574. Vol. II: *Industrial Power and National Rivalry, 1870–1914* (London: Arnold, 1972), pp. 509 Vol. III: *The End of the Old Europe 1914–1939* (London: Arnold, 1973), pp. 623.
11 *The Gold Standard and Employment Policies Between the Wars* (London: Methuen, 1970), pp. 164. (Edited with introduction).
12 with J.P.P. Higgins *Aspects of Capital Investment in Great Britain 1750–1850* (London: Methuen, 1971), pp. 200 (Edited with introduction).
13 with John Salt, *Robert Owen, Prophet of the Poor. Essays in Honour of the Bicentary of His Birth* (London: MacMillan, N.Y.; Buckness University Press, 1971), pp. 309 (Edited, with introduction).
14 *The Sheffield Outrages* (Bath: Adams & Dart, 1971), pp. xviii + xvi + 452. (Edited, with introduction).

15 *European Economic Integration, 1815-1970* (London: Thames and Hudson, 1974), pp. 180.
16 with C. Holmes *Essays in the Economic and Social History of South Yorkshire* (Barnsley: S.Y.C.C.), 1977, pp. 309 (Edited, with introduction).
17 with Paul L. Robertson, *The British Shipbuilding Industry 1870-1914* (Harvard: Harvard University Press 1979), pp. 368.
18 *Region und Industrialisierung* (Göttingen: Vandenhoeck und Ruprecht, 1980), pp. 297 (Edited, with Introduction).
19 *Peaceful Conquest. The Industrialization of Europe 1760-1970* (Oxford: O.U.P., 1981), pp. 449. Recorded for the Royal Inst. for the Blind as a 'Talking Book', 1984. Italian version: *La Conquista Pacifica* (Il Mulino, 1984), pp. 633, in paperback (ibid. 1989, pp. 595).
20 *The Integration of the European Economy Since 1815* (London: Allen & Unwin, 1981), pp. 109.
21 *The Wasting of the British Economy* (London: Croom Helm, 1982), pp. 197. Second enlarged edition (1985), pp. 199.
22 *The Development of the British Economy 1914-1980* (London: Arnold, 1983), completely revised edition pp. 440.
23 with Charles H. Feinstein, *Studies in Capital Formation in the United Kingdom 1750-1920* (Oxford: Clarendon Press 1988), pp. 476.
24 *Britains's Prime and Britain's Decline. The British Economy 1870-1914* (London: Arnold 1988), pp. 334.
25 with Peter Mathias (ed.) *The Cambridge Economic History of Europe, VIII. The Industrial Economies: The Development of Economic and Social Policies* (Cambridge: Cambridge University Press, 1989), pp. 1243.
26 *Typology of Industrialization Process in the Nineteenth Century* London: Harwood, 1990), pp. 107.
27 *Europa im Zeitalter der Industrialisierung. Eine Wirtschaftsgeschichte Europas 1750-1980* (to appear with Göttingen: Vandenhoeck & Ruprecht) c. pp. 200.

Articles

1 'The Decline of Shipbuilding on the Thames', *Economic History Review*, III/1 1950, 72-89.
2 'Laissez-faire and Shipbuilding', *Economic History Review*, V/1, 1952, 98-115.
3 'The Ethics of the Sheffield Outrages', *Hunter Arch. Soc. Trans.* VII/3, 1954, 118-139, 154.
4 'North-west coast railway politics in the eighteen-sixties', *Trans, Cumberland and Westmorland Antiqu. and Arch. Soc.*, LII, New Ser., 160-177, 1953.
5 'Wages and Earnings in the Sheffield Trades, 1851-1914', *Yorkshire Bulletin*, VI/1, 1954, 49-64.
6 with J.D. Marshall, 'The Furness Railway and the growth of Barrow', *J. Transport Hist.*, 1/2, 1953, 109-206.
7 'Town Planning in the Nineteenth Century: the Origins of Barrow in Furness', *Lancs. and Chesh. Antiq. Soc. Trans.*, LXIII, 1954, 87-116.
8 with J.D. Hughes, 'Costs in Retail Distribution', *Oxford Economic Papers*, VII/1, 1955, 71-93.
9 'Mr. Bowden's Wool Prices', *Yorkshire Bulletin*, VII/2, 1955, 159-161.
10 'Barrow and the 7th Duke of Devonshire', *Economic History Review*, VIII/2, 1955, 213-221.
11 with J.D. Hughes, 'Retailing Costs: a reply', *Oxford Economic Papers*, VII/3, 1955, 327-328.

12 Three chapters in D.L. Linton (ed.), *Sheffield and its Region*, (Sheffield, 1956) prepared for the British Association: 'The Trade Unions'; 'The Development of Banking'; 'The Growth of Population' (with A.J. Hunt), (pp. 168–80, 190–195).

13 'Real Earnings in the Sheffield Trades, 1851–1914', *Yorkshire Bulletin*, IX/1, 1957, 54–62.

14 with J.D. Hughes, 'A Note on Managerial Incomes in Retail Distribution', *Manchester School*, 1956, 68–76.

15 with J.D. Hughes, 'Labour in British Retail Trade', *Yorkshire Bulletin*, VIII/2, 1957, 54–62.

16 with J.D. Hughes, 'Gross Margins in Retail Distribution', *Oxford Economic Papers*, IX/1, 1957, 75–87. Reprinted in *Explorations in Retailing*, (Michigan: Michigan State University Press, 1959), pp. 96–102, and in K.A. Tucker and B.S. Yamey, *Economics of Retailing* (Harmondsworth: Penguin, 1973), pp. 258–271.

17 'British and World Shipbuilding, 1890–1914', *Journal of Economic History*, 1957, 426–444.

18 'Investment, Consumption and the Industrial Revolution', *Economic History Review*, 2nd Ser., XI/2, Nov. 1958, 215–226.

19 'Der Bericht der englischen unabhängigen Kommission über das Genossenschaftswesen', *Zeitschr.f.d.ges. Genossenschaftswesen*, IX/1, 1959, 1–19.

20 'Dr. William King: A Co-operative Pioneer', *Co-operative College Papers*, No. 6, April 1959, 17–33.

21 'Nineteenth Century Co-operation: From Community Building to Shopkeeping', one of the *Essays in Labour History* (eds Asa Briggs and John Saville), (London: Macmillan, 1960), pp. 74–112.

22 with J.D. Hughes, 'Costs in Retail Distribution in Great Britain, 1950–57', *Oxford Economic Papers*, June 1961, pp. 166–183.

23 'Capital Accounting in the Industrial Revolution', *Yorks. Bull, Econ. Soc. Res.*, XV, 2 (Dec. 1963), 254–271. Reprinted in F. Crouzet (ed.), *Capital Formation in the Industrial Revolution* (London: Methuen, 1972), pp. 119–144, and in Richard P. Brief (ed.), *Accounting Thought and Practice Through the Years* (N.Y. and London: Garland, 1986), pp. 125–141.

24 'Factory Discipline in the Industrial Revolution', *Economic History Review*, 16, No. 2, 1963, 254–271. Reprinted in W. Fischer and G. Bajos (eds) *Die Soziale Frage* (Stuttgart: Köhler, 1967), pp. 159–185, in K.A. Tucker (ed.), *Readings in Business History* (London: Frank Cass, 1977), pp. 126–147, in Mary Robischon, Bruce C. Levine and Martin Glaberman (eds), *Work and Society* (Detroit, Mich.: Wayne State U., 1977), pp. 33–47, and in Michael Cheniavsky, Arthur Slavin and Stuart Ewen (eds), *Social Textures of Western Civilization: The Lower Depths*, II (Waltham, Mass: Xerox College Publishing, 1972), pp. 70–81 and in Richard Golden, *Social History in Western Civilization* (N.Y.: St. Martins' Press, 1988), II, pp. 127–40. Also (part) reprinted in Werner Braatz (ed.), *Reading in European History since 1500* (Berkeley: McCutchan, 1971).

25 'The Factory Village in the Industrial Revolution', *English His. Rev.*, LXXIX, 312 (July 1964), 513–531.

26 'Fixed Capital in the Industrial Revolution in Britain', *J.Econ.Hist.* 24 (1964), 299–314. Reprinted in F. Crouzet (ed.), *Capital Formation in the Industrial Revolution* (London: Methuen, 1972), pp. 145–161.

27 *The Co-operatives at the Crossroads* (London: Fabian Soc., 1965), 44 pp.

28 'The Genesis of the managerial profession: the experience of the industrial revolution in Great Britain', *Stud. Romanticism*, IV (1965), 57–80.

29 'Economic History – a Science of Society?', *Past and Present*, 30 (1965), 1–22. Reprinted in Japanese in *Methods in Economic History* (Tokyo: Kabundo

Shin-Sha, 1969), and in N. Harte (ed.), *The Study of Economic History* (London: Frank Cass & Co., 1971), 289–312.
30 'Trade Unions and the labour market, 1870–1914', *Yorks. Bull. Econ. Soc. Res.*, 17 (1965), 98–112.
31 'Die Aufgaben der Britischen Genossenschaften in einer Wachstumswirtschaft', *Zschr.f.d. ges. Genossenschaftswesen*, XVI, 3 (1966), 253–266.
32 'Die Ausbildung der Industriellen Klassen Britanniens im 18. Jahrundhert', *Jahrb. f. Wirtschaftsgeschichte*, IV (1966), 11–29. Reprinted in *Gesellschaft in der Industriellen Revolution* (eds R. Braun, W. Fischer, H. Groszkreutz and H. Volkmann) (Cologne: Kiepenheuer & Witsch, 1973), pp. 127–146.
33 'Materials for the study of industrial history', in *The industrial past and the industrial present*, ed. K. Hudson (Bath: Bath Univ. Press, 1967), 53–75.
34 'Co-operative principles in the modern world', in *Essays in memory of Arnold Bonner* (Manchester: Co-operative Union, 1967), 71–80.
35 'The Growth and Distribution of Capital in Great Britain, c.1770–1870', in *Third International Conference of Economic History*, Munich, 1965, Report (Paris: Mouton, 1969) 335–365.
36 'Trade Union Reaction to the Economic Crisis', *J. of Contemporary History* 4/4 (Oct. 1969), 101–116. Reprinted in *The Gold Standard and Employment Policies* (see above).
37 'La Grande Bretagne au Lendemain de la Guerre,' *Revue d'histoire moderne et contemporaine*, XVI, Janvier-Mars 1969, 161–6.
38 'The Present State of the British Economy and its Background' (in Japanese), *Asian Affairs Research Council* Lecture Series No. 26, Tokyo, June, 1969, pp. 50–72.
39 'The Foundation of the Co-operative Party', *Essays on Labour History, 1886–1923*, pp. 185–210, edited by Asa Briggs and John Saville, (London: Macmillan, 1971).
40 'Robert Owen as an Economist', in *Robert Owen and his Relevance to our times* (Co-operative College Papers No. 14, Sept. 1971), pp. 23–36.
41 'History, Economic and Social', in B. Cox and A. Dyson (eds) *The Twentieth Century Mind, Vol. III, 1945–1965*, (Oxford: O.U.P., 1972), 29–57.
42 'Industrialization and the European Economy', *Econ.Hist.Rev.* 2nd Ser. XXVI/4, Nov. 1973 636–648. Reprinted in Italian as 'Processo d'industrializzazione ed economie europea: Georgio Mori, *L'industrializzazione in Italia* (1861–1900) (Bologna: Il Mulino, 1977), pp. 41–56; and in Joel Mokyr (ed.) *The Economics of the Industrial Revolution* (Totowa, N.J.: Rowman & Allan Leid, 1985), pp. 165–176.
43 'Trade Unions and the Depression of 1929–1933', in Mommsen, Petzina, Weisbrod (eds), *Industrielles System und politische Entwicklung in der Weimar Republik* (Düsseldorf: Droste, 1974), pp. 237–248.
44 'Wirtschaftliche Entwicklung und Politik in der modernen Gesellschaft', *Geschichte und Gesellschaft*, II/3, (1976), 58–85.
45 With Robert Turner, 'Profit-Sharing and Autocracy – The Case of J.T. and J. Taylor of Batley, Woollen Manufacturers, 1892–1966', *Business History* 18/1 (1976), 4–34.
46 *The British Economic Miracle* (Economics Association, 1976), pp. 19.
47 'Industrialization and Integration of the European Economy', in Büsch, Fischer, and Herzfeld (eds), *Industrialiserung und die europäische Wirtschaft im 19. Jahrundert* (Berlin: Gruyter, 1976) 3–16, 58–62.
48 'Labour in the United Kingdom', in *Cambridge Economic History of Europe*, vol. 7 (Cambridge: Cambridge University Press, 1978), pp. 97–179, 649–664.
49 'The Rise of the Service Industries and White-Collar Employment', *The Post-Industrial Society*, Bo Gustafsson (ed.), (London: Croom Helm, 1979), pp. 17–47.

50 'Sheffield during the Industrial Revolution', in G. Brucker (ed.), *Western Civilization* Vol. 2 (Homewood, Illinois: Dorsey, 1979) pp. 117–158.
51 'The Nationalisation of the Banks: the Chequered History of a Socialist Proposal', in *Ideology and the Labour Movement*, eds, David Rubinstein and David Martin, (London: Croom Helm, 1979), pp. 167–190.
52 'Merchandise Trade and Exploitation', *Journal of European Economic History* 6 (1977), 745–749.
53 'Englische Arbeitkerkultur im Zeitalter der Industrialisierung: Forschungsergebnisse und Forschungsprobleme', *Geschichte und Gesellschaft*, V/1 (1979), pp. 150–166.
54 'Co-operative Study and Research', *Bulletin for Co-operative Studies* 36 (1979), 21–7.
55 'The Co-operative Ideal, Then and Now', (Co-operative College, 1980), pp. 16.
56 'A New Estimate of British Coal Production, 1750–1850', *Economic History Review*, 33/2 (1980), 212–235.
57 'Management and Labour in Britain in the Period of Industrialization', in Keiichiro Nakagawa (ed.), *Labour and Management* (Tokyo University Press, 1979), 45–73.
58 'Engineers and Technologists', in Alan Bullock (ed.), *The Faces of Europe* (Oxford: Phaidon, 1980), 302–336.
59 'Soziale Ungleichheit und Klassenstruktur in England: Mittel- und Oberklasse', in H.-U. Wehler (ed.), *Klasse in der europäischen Sozialgeschichte* (Göttingen: Vandenhoeck & Ruprecht, 1979), 33–52.
60 'Industrialisierung als europäische Erscheinung', in Karl-Ernst Jeismanr und Rainer Riemenschneider (ed.), *Geschichte Europas für den Unterricht der Europäer* (Georg-Eckert Institut, Braunschweig, 1980), 112–7.
61 'The New Economic History Re-assessed: Railroads and Slavery', *Interdisciplinary Science Review*, VI/3 (1981), 229–238.
62 'Sheffield and Sweet Auburn – Amenities and Living Standards in the British Industrial Revolution', *Journal of Economic History*, 41/4 (1981), 902–4.
63 'The Industrialisation of Europe' *Eighth International Economic History Congress* (Budapest, 1982), B1 Themes, pp. 5–16.
64 'More of the Same Medicine: Comments on Economic Policy in Britain, Past and Present', *Journal of General Management*, 8/1 (1982). 43–57; Reprinted in Gustav Schmidt, Karl Rohe, Wolf D. Guner (eds), *Arbeitskreis deutscher Englandforschung*, I, *Krise in Großbritannien?* (Bochum 1987), pp. 134–156.
65 'Capitalism and Rationality: A Study of Measurements in British Coalmining, c. 1750–1850', *Explorations in Economic History*, 20 (1983), 110–129.
66 'Region und Industrialisierung im Vergleich – Minden-Ravensberg und die englischen Industriegebiete', *Vortragsreihe der Gesellschaft für westfälische Wirtschaftsgeschichte* 25 (1983), 43–61.
67 'Wirtschaftswachstum: Theorie und Erfahrung aus historischer Sicht', *Wirtschaft ohne Wachstum*, Loccum Protokolle, 15/1982, 2–18.
68 'England: Der unrevolutionäre Pionier', in Jürgen Kocka (ed.) *Europäische Arbeiterbewegung im 19, Jahrhundert* (Göttingen: Vandenhoeck & Ruprecht, 1983), 21–38.
69 'Keynesianismus und Wirtschaftspolitik seit der Großen Depression'. *Geschichte und Gesellschaft* 10/2 (1984) 185–210.
70 'Wege aus der Arbeitslosigkeit-Großbritannien und Schweden', Deutsches Institut für Wirtschaftsforschung, *Vierteljahreshefte zur Wirtschaftsforschung*, Heft 1 (1984), 48–61.
71 'Region und Markt. Zur Entwicklung der Paumordung der Wirtschaft im Industrialisierungsprozeß des 18. und 19. Jahrhunderts', in: Schweizerische Ges. für

Wirtschafts- und Sozialgeschichte, Heft 2/2, *Raumordnung der Wirtschaft*, (Lausanne, 1983), 8-20.

72 *The Neglect of Industry: A Critique of British Economic Policy since 1870*, Centrum voor Maatschappijgeschiedenis, Vol II, (Rotterdam, 1984), 27 pp.

73 'Wirtschaftliche Hintergründe des *New Unionism*', in: Wolfgang J. Mommsen und Hans-Gerald Husung (eds) *Auf dem Wege zur Massengewerkschaft. Die Entwicklung der Gewerkschaften in Deutschland und Großbritannien 1880-1914* (Stuttgart: Klett-Cotta, 1984), S. 46-75. English ed., *The Development of Trade Unionism in Great Britain and Germany 1880-1914* (London: Allen & Unwin, 1985), pp. 32-52.

74 'Probleme der europäischen Integration im 19. und 20. Jahrhundert', in: Helmut Berding (ed.), *Wirtschaftliche und politische Integration in Europa im 19. und 20. Jahrhundert* (Göttingen: Vandenhoeck & Ruprecht, 1984), pp. 9-33.

75 'Die europäische Industrialisierung', in: Ottfried Dascher (ed.), *'Mein Feld ist die Welt'. Musterbücher und Kataloge 1784-1914*, (Dortmund: Westf. Wirtshafts-archiv, 1984), pp. 17-22.

76 'Current German Economic and Social History: attitudes to hermeneutics and objectivity', *South African Historical Journal* 16 (Nov. 1984), 6-25.

77 'Capital Exports, 1870-1914 - Harmful or Beneficial', *Economic History Review*, 38/4. November 1985, 489-514.

78 'Economic Management 1974-1984, an Overview', *Catalyst* 1 (Spring 1985), 1-10.

79 'The Industrialization of Europe', in J. Kocka and G. Ranki (eds) *Economic Theory and History* (Budapest: Akademiai Kiado, 1986), pp. 47-67.

80 'Robert Owen and the Reduction in Working Hours: Some Considerations in the Light of Recent Research', *Annual Bulletin of Business Research, Chuo University* 8 (1987), pp. 189-203.

81 'Betrachtungen zur Dynamik britischer Industrieregionen', *Vierteljahrschrift für Sozial- und Wirtschaftsgeschichte* (2, 1987), 305-322.

82 'Stagflation, Fiscal Deficits and Balance of Payments - Great Britain and Germany', *Hitotsubashi Journal of Economics* (27, Special Issue 1986), 39-53.

83 'Robert Owen's Contribution to Economics', in C. Tsuzuki (ed.), *British Socialism Considered. The Pursuit of the Alternative* (Tokyo: Sanseido, 1986), pp. 11-32, (Japanese).

84 'Made in Germany - die Angst vor der deutschen Konkurrenz im spätviktorianis-chen England', *Technikgeschichte* 54/3 (1987), 183-195.

85 'Die Übernahme der Technik der britischen industriellen Revolution in den Ländern des europäischen Kontinents', in Theo Pirker a.o. (ed.), *Technik und industrielle Revolution* (Opladen, Westd. V. 1987), 159-167.

86 'The Co-operative Party - Reflections on a Reconsideration' *International Review of Social History* 32 (1987), pp. 168-73.

87 'Die Gesellschaft' in Wolfram Fischer a.o. (eds), *Handbuch der europäischen Wirtschafts-und Sozialgeschichte* (Stuttgart, Klett-Cotta 1987), pp. 308-335.

88 'Die Logik der Grundschulen für die ärmere Klasse im viktorianischen England', *Victorian Values: Arm und Reich im viktorianischen England* (ed. B. Weisbrod), Bochum: Brockmeier (1988), pp. 149-176.

89 'Die deutsch-britischen Wirtschaftsbeziehungen, Geschichte, Gegenwart, Zukunfts-perspektiven', (Dietmar Storch ed., *Deutschland-England: Geschichte einer pro-duktiven Nachbarschaft*. Niedersächsische Landeszentrale für politische Bildung). Hannover 1988, pp. 28-46.

90 'Le regioni comme unita fundamentali de processo di industrializzazone', Franco Andreucci and Alessandra Pescarollo (eds), *Gli spazi di potere* (Florenz: Usher, 1989), pp. 107-112.

91 'Die Herausforderung des Wirtschaftsliberalismus', in Adolf M. Birke and Günther Heydemann (eds,), *Die Herausforderung des europäischen Staatensystems* (Göttingen: Vandenhoeck & Ruprecht, 1989), pp. 76–95.

92 'Wirtschaftsbeziehungen Deutsches Reich – Großbritannien in den Jahren 1870–1914: Rivalität oder Komplementaritat', in Dietmar Petzina and Jürgen Reulecke (eds), *Bevölkerung, Wirtschaft, Gesellschaft seit der Industrialisierung. Festschift für Wolfgang Köllmann zum 65 Geburtstag* (Dortmund: Ges. f. Westfälische Wirtschaftsgeschichte, 1990), pp. 181–192.

93 'Economic Policies and Traditions', in Andrew Graham with Anthony Seldon (eds), *Government and economies in the postwar world* (London and New York: Routledge, 1990), pp. 292–302.

94 'Reflections on Enterpreneurship and Culture in European Societies' *Transactions of the Royal Historical Society*, 5th Series, 40 (1990), pp. 153–173.

95 'German Trade Union Policy 1929–1933 in the Light of the British Experience', in Jürgen Baron von Krudener (ed.), *Economic Crisis and Political Collapse: The Weimar Republic 1924–1933* (New York, Oxford, Munich, 1990), pp. 21–44.

96 'Regional Markets and National Economic Development', in Maxine Berg and John Davis (eds), *Markets and Manufactures in Early Industrial Europe* (London: Methuen, 1990), pp. 29–56.

97 'Old and New Industrial Areas in Britain during the Revolutionary and Napoleonic Wars', in Erik Aerts and François Crouzet (eds), *Economic Effects of the French Revolutionary and Napoleonic Wars* (Leuven: Univ. Press, 1990), pp. 95–103.

98 'The Dynamism of the British Economy in the Decades to 1914 – Change of Direction or Failure of Nerve?', in Fred Halliday, Michael Mann (eds), *The Rise and Decline of Nation States* (Oxford: Blackwell, 1990), pp. 47–70.

99 'Dr August Oetker (1862–1918)' in J. Kocka and R. Vogelsang (eds), *Rheinisch-Westfälische Wirtschaftsbiographien* (Münster: Aschendorff, 1990).

Index

Townsend, H., xxiv
Trélat, E., 183, 190
Trevithick railway engineering family, 34
Trippett, H., xvii
Truman, President, 106
Turkey, 105
Turner, B., xxiv
Typographical Association, 163

Ullastres, A., 111
Ulster, 75
Unilever, 96
United Kingdom
  Census on Religious Observance
    (1851), 149
  Department of Scientific and
    Industrial Research, 68
  Enquiry into the State of Large Towns
    and Populous Districts (1844), 150
  Treasury, 92
United Nations, 103, 110, 111
United States of America, 51
  Congress, 106
  Defense Support Programme, 107, 109
  economic development, 119–21
    and staple theory, 11
  economic influence in C. and E.
    Europe after 1918, 87
  isolationism after 1918, 45
  tariffs, 166
Unwin, G., xviii

Varela, M., 111
Venezuela, 12
Versailles Peace Conference, 44–5
  Treaties, 87–8, 96
Vienna, ix, x, xvii, 93, 131, 180, 191
Vitkovicke Mining and Foundry Works,
  94–5
Vulcan Foundry, 37

WEA, 149
wages
  aggregate movements in UK (1881–
    1913), 160–1
  armed forces (1880–1913), 167–8

building trades (1880–1913), 156–9
clothing industry (1881–1913), 163
coalmining (1880–1913), 156–9, 168
dockwork (1881–1913), 156–9
engineering (1881–1913), 156–9
furniture trades (1881–1913), 156–9,
  164–5
iron and steel (1881–1913), 156–9, 168–
  9
printworkers (1881–1913), 156–9, 163–
  4
road haulage (1881–1913), 156–9, 166
shipbuilding, (1881–1913), 156–9
textiles (1881–1913), 156–9, 165–6
Walker, J., 105, 106
Wall Street crash, 72
Walschaerts valvegear, 30
Webb, F.W., 29–30, 34, 35
Webb, S., 144
Westphalia, 129
Whittinghame School, xi
Wigan, 148
Women's Industrial Council, 163
Wood, G.H., 155, 160
World Bank, 7
world economic development (1850–
  1987), 116–21
  productivity movements of the various
    sectors, 119–21
  role of tertiary sector in, 116–21
world wars
  first, 85, 86
  second, 10, 19, 44, 51, 67, 78, 89
Worsdell, W., 30, 33
  Worsdell railway engineering family,
    34
Wright, Sir A., 151
Wrigley, E.A., xxii

York, 151–2
York Street Flax Spinning Company, 67,
  69
Yorkshire, 75, 143, 144, 147
Yugoslavia, 88–90, 107

Zollverein, 15
Zurich, 126